Fat Shame

Fat Shame

Stigma and the Fat Body
in American Culture

Amy Erdman Farrell

NEW YORK UNIVERSITY PRESS
New York and London

NEW YORK UNIVERSITY PRESS
New York and London
www.nyupress.org

References to Internet websites (URLs) were accurate at the time of writing.
Neither the author nor New York University Press is responsible for URLs
that may have expired or changed since the manuscript was prepared.

Library of Congress Cataloging-in-Publication Data

Farrell, Amy Erdman.
Fat shame : stigma and the fat body in American culture /
Amy Erdman Farrell.
p. cm.
Includes bibliographical references and index.
ISBN 978-0-8147-2768-3 (cl : alk. paper) — ISBN 978-0-8147-2769-0
(pb : alk. paper) — ISBN 978-0-8147-2834-5 (ebook)
1. Body image. 2. Stigma (Social psychology) 3. Discrimination against
overweight persons. 4. Physical-appearance-based bias. I. Title.
BF697.5.B63F37   2011
306.4'613—dc22   2010047480

New York University Press books are printed on acid-free paper,
and their binding materials are chosen for strength and durability.
We strive to use environmentally responsible suppliers and materials
to the greatest extent possible in publishing our books.

Manufactured in the United States of America
c   10 9 8 7 6 5 4 3 2 1
p   10 9 8 7 6 5 4 3 2 1

Contents

Acknowledgments

I began thinking about this book in 1999, while I was living in England and teaching at the University of East Anglia. My husband and I were visiting instructors there, on leave from our home institutions; we had swapped homes (and jobs) with another couple from Norwich. Our daughter, Catherine, was just three years old, a curly haired towhead who changed into a princess dress each day she came home from the UEA Nursery, experiencing our travels in her "push chair," with lots of stickers and cellophane tape to keep her occupied. Our eight-year-old son, Nick, buried himself in the first Harry Potter books as we navigated through the countryside, on our way to explore castles, dungeons, and Roman ruins, compensation for the shock of being transplanted into the British school system.

During that year I would make frequent trips to the British Library, and later to the Fawcett Library of Women's History (now known as the Women's Library), to begin my project on the history of dieting. Trying to identify the first dieting tracts, I soon found myself more interested in what the authors had to say about *fat* than I was about their various plans for making readers *thin*. That transformation in interest, from *thin* to *fat*, was the beginning of the decade-long journey of researching and writing *Fat Shame*. So, as I reflect on the many debts I have incurred during this project, I must begin with thanks to those who allowed this exchange to take place, thus providing the context in which the idea for this vast, interdisciplinary project could take root: my own family, of course; the Norwich-based Fear-Segals; and the University of East Anglia and Dickinson College, both of which were supportive, detail oriented, and flexible in their encouragement of this scholarly adventure.

Throughout the last decade, many institutions, colleagues, and friends have helped me with this project, from its earliest stages through its various shapes and permutations to the final form that is this book. To all of them I owe thanks. The librarians at the British Library, the Fawcett Library, the New York Public Library, the Library of Congress, and the Columbia University Library were models of professionalism, who helped me gain access to fascinating material, both when I wasn't sure exactly what I was looking for and when I had identified some hard-to-find document. Closer to home, the librarians at Dickinson, particularly Chris Bombara, Malinda Triller, and Jim Gerencser, all at various times helped me to locate important material. Archivists at the College of Physicians of Philadelphia, the University of Texas Medical Center, and the American Medical Association all helped me to understand their collections and to find the material for which I was searching. When I was doing research for my previous book, *Yours in Sisterhood: Ms. Magazine and the Promise of Popular Feminism*, I had found the archivists at both the Schlesinger Library and the Sophia Smith Archives to be especially astute and helpful; and for *Fat Shame* I found them equally wonderful. And, finally, I want to give a particular thanks to Martha Sachs at the Alice Marshall Women's History Collection at the Pennsylvania State University Harrisburg Library. With her assistance (and also thanks to the assiduous collecting of Alice Marshall, who gathered the material in the first place), I found the Fat Women Postcards Collection, which transformed the direction of my research and confirmed some of my earliest suspicions about gender and fatness.

While I was writing this book, the national and international outcry about the "obesity epidemic" promoted the funding of research projects on methods of weight loss and the perils of fatness. Thus I am particularly grateful to those who funded this project on *fat stigma*, despite the fact that it fit very uncomfortably within the larger paradigm about the "dangers of obesity." The Wood Institute provided me a short-term fellowship for research at the College of Physicians Library and Mutter Museum. Smith College provided a travel-to-collections grant for research at the Sophia Smith Collection. Dickinson College provided me with extensive support, including a Dickinson Summer Grant, a Sabbatical Supplement Grant, travel-to-collections grants, and funding for a Dana Research intern. Gretchen Mielke, a Dickinson American studies major, did extensive research on statistics and stigma as my Dana intern during the early days of my project.

Throughout the long course of this project, many friends and colleagues have commented on my work, shared citations, and listened while I thought through yet another key point about fat stigma. I would like to thank Deb Fulham-Winston, Marie Helweg-Larsen, Jim Hoeffler, Wendy Kozol, Stephanie Larson, Rennie Mapp, Pat McDermott, Sharon O'Brien, Jerry Philogene, Kim Rogers, Susan Rose, Cotten Seiler, Regina Sweeney, Bob Winston, and Julie Winterich. Vickie Kuhn, Elaine Mellen, and, in particular, Denise McCauley both shared relevant news articles and helped me with the details of manuscript formatting. Bonnie Berk, the Unitarian Universalists of Cumberland Valley, and the Ferry Beach crowd inspired me to think about how I might share my research in a more popular format, by offering "radical body acceptance" workshops. The Schlesinger Library's Summer Seminar on Gender History, "Sequels to the 1960s," came at a crucial time in my writing. I wish to thank Nancy Cott for organizing the seminar, Nancy Hewitt for her comments on my essay and for leading our workshop, and various participants who both challenged and encouraged my thinking, especially Martha Arguello, Tamar Carroll, Ruth Feldstein, Emily Hobson, Ian Lekus, Betty Luther, Natalia Mehlman-Petrzela, Claire Potter, and Jessica Weiss.

In writing this book, I have benefited tremendously from the comments of a number of anonymous reviewers, all of whom I would like to thank. I am especially grateful to Anne Enke, one of the outside reviewers provided by NYU Press, whose extensive and thoughtful comments were crucial in the development of this project. Eric Zinner, Despina Papazoglou Gimbel, and Ciara McLaughlin, my editors at NYU Press, have stuck with the project even as it changed shape dramatically. Eric deserves particular kudos for distracting me with conversation about the Midwest and the culture of New York as I waited to be interviewed on the *Colbert Report*.

This book would have been impossible without the encouragement and wisdom of so many people whom I've met in the fat activist movement and the burgeoning field of fat studies, whose work both challenges and inspires me. I particularly want to thank Carrie Hemenway, Deborah Harper, and Lynn McAfee for agreeing to share their lives with me through their oral histories, Susan Stinson for the beauty of her writing and her friendship, Kathleen LeBesco for sharing ideas over dinner one night, and Esther Rothblum and Sondra Solovay for their long-standing work in the field and the spectacular feat of pulling together the *Fat Studies Reader*. Marilyn Wann is due particular thanks, for introducing me to the world of fat activism, for being so generous with her ideas and time, and for visiting my campus, bringing her wit and her YAY! Scale with her.

Over the years I have had many wonderful students whose interest and faith in this project has been essential to my life as a scholar and a writer. I wish to thank them all—from the first students who heard of these ideas in the American studies and women's studies senior seminars, to my most recent students who were brave and curious enough to sign up for one of the first fat studies courses in the United States. So many good friends have also bolstered me over the years, sharing good times and bad: Laurie Santilli, Cindy Nicely, Kathleen Dillon, Gina Bertoglio, and Barry and Johanna Tesman.

Finally, I must turn my attention to my family, that extended bunch which continues to grow, with new in-laws to be added by the time this book sees print. I first want to thank my niece Allison Thumma, who introduced me to fat activism back when she was in fifth grade, telling me about a brave schoolmate who promised to "ban all fat jokes" if she were elected student council president. She didn't win the election, but her courage started me thinking about body size activism long before I started this project. Everyone in the family has at some point asked me a prodding question, shared a piece of information, or simply provided love, encouragement, and a few laughs: Jim, Kristena, Amy, Patrick, Allison, Eric, Haily, Maddy, Alex, Anna, Sammy, Pat, Kirby, Laura, Jake, Griffin, Anna Rose, Matt, Jenn, and Sylvia. Just as with my first book, Maxine and Sidney have continued to be an important source of news clippings and media updates—thank you. My sister Ann deserves special thanks for her friendship and her willingness to accompany me to the Colbert interview among other adventures. I am especially grateful to my parents, Jim and Lois Farrell, for their love, support, and strength of character.

My immediate family deserves more thanks than I can ever articulate here. That three-year-old and eight-year-old are now in high school and college, having lived much of their growing-up years in the shadow of this book. I am so fortunate to have two children who have shared with me so much love and joy—as well as books, music, friends, ideas, and experiences—that I would never have had without them. My husband, John, is a true partner in composing this life, with his friendship, his delicious meals, and his model of perseverance. All three have talked fat with me for many years, and I suspect they are as happy as I am that the project is complete. I love you very much, John, Nick, and Catherine.

Considering Fat Shame

Toward the end of fall semester in 2006, leaders from the national office of Delta Zeta sorority visited its DePauw University chapter, ostensibly to encourage the sisters in their recruitment efforts. Membership in what one unofficial survey on the campus had called the "socially awkward" Delta Zeta chapter had declined to the point that the national office was considering shutting it down. The national officers met with the thirty-five members individually, discussing each one's specific plans to increase membership. A week before finals, twenty-two of the members received a letter from the national chapter explaining that they had been placed on "alumna status"—in other words, they had been kicked out. By the beginning of the following semester, the letter explained, they had to find other housing.

According to a *New York Times* interview, the ousted members included all the "overweight" women as well as the only Vietnamese and Korean women. (The one African American member never received an expulsion letter, nor did she receive a letter asking her to stay. She presumed she had been kicked out.) The national officers countered that the evictees demonstrated insufficient commitment to the sorority. According to the evicted sisters themselves, it was all about looks and popularity, not about commitment. They pointed out that the national office had purged the sorority of the girls who did not match the stereotypical image of a "sorority girl," one who was attractive and well liked by fraternity brothers. Indeed, the national officers had actually requested that these same "unpopular"—that is, fat or nonwhite—sisters stay upstairs during a recruitment party, instead bringing in slender Delta Zeta sisters from neighboring Indiana University to meet with prospective sorority members.

While many of the rejected sorority sisters described feeling depressed after they received their letters, their sorrow soon turned to activism. Many of those who had been allowed to stay in the sorority quit in solidarity with their sisters. DePauw faculty began a petition objecting to the focus on these women's looks over their academic and service accomplishments. The president of DePauw, Robert Bottoms, wrote a letter of recrimination to the national office of Delta Zeta. By the end of February, the *New York Times* had picked up on the story, followed by stories in *Time*, *Newsweek*, and *Ms.* Public outrage, as well as the anger of alumni and parents, led the president to kick the Delta Zeta chapter off of campus. After refusing any more communication with what it termed a hostile media, the Delta Zeta national office launched a federal lawsuit against DePauw for defamation and breach of contract. In its press release, however, it did acknowledge the "negative impact caused by the stereotypes imposed on college women in general and sorority women in particular."[1]

The story of this Delta Zeta saga may seem of little import—certainly all the rejected young women found housing for the winter term and the fate of Delta Zeta as a whole may not much interest readers other than Delta Zetas themselves. On a larger level, however, it is an interesting story about the creation of social hierarchy in the United States. While the mission statements of U.S. sororities often focus on the role of the organization in philanthropy and in creating a supportive network for its members, the reality is that sororities and fraternities are also deeply about the construction and maintenance of social status, both within the collegial environment and after graduation. Perhaps in a way the national leaders of Delta Zeta were speaking honestly when they said the twenty-two young women they kicked out were inadequately committed to the sorority; that is, if, de facto, to be a sorority member is to be concerned with maintaining and reaching the height of the social scene, and, if, de facto, this meant that one needed to be white, thin, and "American," then, by definition, these twenty-two young women could never "look" committed.

Within this Delta Zeta controversy, what particularly interests me is the way that "fatness" served as a crucial marker of social status, or rather the lack thereof. Interesting as well is the way that fatness intersected so pointedly with issues of ethnicity, class, and gender within this saga of college life in the 21st century. Indeed, the attempt by the Delta Zeta national office to reinstate a hierarchy of "white, thin, and privileged" encapsulates many of the key social issues and struggles that this book addresses: the enduring power of fat stigma; the way fat denigration overlaps with racial, ethnic, and national discrimination; the connections between both of these (fat and ethnic denigration) and class privilege; and, finally, the ways that all these elements (fat denigration, ethnic discrimination, and class privilege) intersect with gender and the construction of what it means to be a "popular girl," a properly constituted gendered subject. What is it about fat that makes it so stigmatized? What are the connections between fat denigration and ethnic, class, and gender discrimination? What does it mean that an institution known for bolstering economic privilege and normative femininity—a college sorority—would kick out the young women who are too "fat," too "ethnic"? Why is body size connected to a "right to belong," a "privilege of membership"? What is it, in particular, about *fat* that makes it such a liability? Why did the rejected sisters experience lingering feelings of shame and depression although they knew they had been victims of discrimination? Despite these powerful negative feelings, what gave them the strength to resist the judgment of the national officers?

Fat Shame: Stigma and the Fat Body in American Culture takes up these questions through a historical exploration of the links between body size and notions of belonging and social status, or, to use a term more common in contemporary studies of culture, to ideas of citizenship. The connections between body size and citizenship are particularly salient today, when the concern about a national "obesity epidemic" garners extraordinary attention and resources, vying for front-page coverage against news of economic collapse, two wars, elections, and environmental disasters. Indeed, popular and scientific literature often argues that Americans' body size puts the United States at more risk than the failing economy, the ongoing wars, or problems of global warming, pollution, or other forms of ecological degradation. We are an extraordinarily "fat-aware" culture, yet little attention is given to the cultural meanings attributed to fatness or the fat person, or how these meanings might shape the experiences of the fat person or the discourse surrounding this "health crisis." This book attempts to address this silence by exploring the roots of our contemporary ideas about fatness, the ways these cultural narratives still percolate today, and the voices and actions of those who have rejected dominant ideas about the rights and identities of the fat person.

Prompted by intense student interest in eating disorders and thin body ideals, I began this project interested in the history of dieting in the United States. I regularly taught Joan Jacobs Brumberg's *Fasting Girls*, an important history of anorexia nervosa in the United States, and I was curious about the industrial and commercial apparatus that supported the cultural mandate for thinness. My research quickly led me to two discoveries. The first is that the date generally understood as the advent of the diet industries and a thin body ideal—1920—was incorrect. Periodicals like *Harper's Weekly* and *Life* included countless ads for diet products and numerous cartoons lampooning fat people throughout the late 19th century. It is more accurate to understand 1920, then, as the moment when the burgeoning advertising and consumer industries could tap into and exacerbate the fat denigration and early reducing industries that were clearly in existence by the second half of the 1800s. The second thing I discovered is that the endless parade of diets from the last decades of the 1800s to the present resemble one another in surprising ways. William Banting's 19th-century high-protein and no-starch diet became today's South Beach and Atkins diets. The milk diets of the early 20th century became today's Slim Fast and NutriSlim liquid diets. The incongruous mixture of whole grain foods and Christianity by Sylvester Graham, Horace Fletcher, and John Harvey Kellogg became today's wheat and fig "Bible Bar" marketed by Tom Ciola, the author of *Moses Wasn't Fat*. One-food fixes for obesity have remained a constant, though the specific item has changed: in the early 20th century it was the banana; in the 1960s, melba toast and cottage cheese; in the 1970s, grapefruit; in the 1990s, cabbage; in the first decade of the 21st century, olive oil. Mechanical "flesh reducers" have long remained popular, from the obesity belts of the 19th century to the French-originating "Bergonie" chairs of the early 20th century, to the recently marketed "Ab Energizers," the electric stimulating abdominal belts. Difficult as it is to mark a clean line between the dieting industries and the medical industries, one must include as well the long history of pharmaceutical products designed to suppress appetite (from arsenic to fen-phen and leptin) or "burn off" fat (from tapeworms to amphetamines to ephedra), as well as the surgical procedures focused on excising fat (the gynecologist Howard Kelly performed the first fat-removal surgeries in the late 1880s) to contemporary liposuction. Even reconfiguring the digestive tract has had a long history, from Kellogg's anal sphincter surgeries to the stomach stapling of the 1960s to the increasingly popular gastric bypass surgery of today.[2]

What began to interest me more than the particular permutations of weight loss methods was the formidable *meaning* attributed to fatness in these dieting tracts. The authors of weight loss tracts and the advertisements for weight loss products articulated anxiety, scorn, even outrage toward the fat they promised to eradicate. It is easy for us to assume today that the cultural stigma associated with fatness emerged simply as a result of our recognition of its apparent health dangers. What is clear from the historical documents, however, is that the connotations of fatness and of the fat person—lazy, gluttonous, greedy, immoral, uncontrolled, stupid, ugly, and lacking in will power—preceded and then were intertwined with explicit concern about health issues. Every diet that has emerged on the scene has come with a larger social agenda and cultural meaning. In all of them, fat is a social as well as physical problem; in most of them, the social stigma of fatness—and the fantasy of freeing oneself from this stigma—coincides with or even takes priority over issues of health.

I began this project interested in the history of dieting in the United States, then, but the sources I discovered transformed my work into an exploration of the *meaning* of fat. As I read political cartoons, advertisements for commercial reducing methods and products, doctors' manuals, and popular articles, I realized that *fat* was neither neutral nor insignificant, but was a central protagonist in the cultural development of what constituted a proper American body. The development of fat stigma, I realized, related both to cultural anxieties that emerged during the modern period over consumer excess *and*, importantly, to prevailing ideas about race, civilization, and evolution. This book argues, then, that fat denigration is intricately related to gender as well as racial hierarchies, in particular the historical development of "whiteness."

In the fall of 2008 the *New York Times* published a poster titled "Measure of a Man" that listed the height and weight of each presidential candidate since the late 1800s to identify whether taller, thinner, shorter, or fatter men are more likely to be elected to the highest office a citizen in the United States can hold.[3] Only in a culture that is fixated on the significance of body size could such a poster—which linked weight and the privileges of citizenship—be imagined, even in a comic way. As I conducted this research over the last ten years, during a time of heightened concern about the fatness of the American public, I have been keenly aware of the interplay between these earlier ideas of fat denigration and the contemporary manifestations of fat stigma, whether they emerged in popular culture portrayals that explicitly mocked fat people or in the language of physicians and government documents that couched fat denigration simply as concern over people's health or well-being. In the late 19th and early 20th centuries, physicians, politicians, and academics used body size as one important marker—along with gender, race, ethnicity, and sexuality—to measure one's suitability for the privileges and power of full citizenship. These ideas about body size continue to have salience, as fat stigma divides people into those who belong and those who don't, those who are praised and those who are mocked, those who merit first-class treatment and those who are expected to accept second-class, inferior status, those who might become president and those who, as the poster suggested, might not.

As I explored the links between body size and citizenship, I also quickly became attentive to the voices and activism of those who have resisted dominant ideas about fat stigma. Cultural denigration of fatness is powerful today, drawing on over a century's development of fat stigma, but it is not monolithic. That is, people have resisted and challenged fat stigma, most explicitly since the late 1960s. Through novels and poems, "big-only" dances and swim clubs, Internet chat rooms, online magazines, and organizations like the

We create such standards by reinforcing norms . . . .

National Association to Advance Fat Acceptance and the International Size Acceptance Association, these activists have worked to "rewrite the fat body" and to claim their full rights as citizens. That is, they challenged the connotations of fat as ugly, as lazy, and as unhealthy. The ousted sisters of Delta Zeta may not have recognized themselves as fat activists, but their vocal rejection and organized reaction to the discrimination they faced as fat women was an important form of fat acceptance work. Just as the sisters of Delta Zeta supported one another, fat activists over the last four decades have challenged both explicit discrimination and more subtle fat denigration. Their work and voices are important to understand both for the light they shed on the manifestations of fat stigma and its limits.

Stigma and Fatness

The May 2010 cover of the *Atlantic* pictures a bloated Statue of Liberty, whose triple chins rest heavily on a distended robe that looks more like fat rolls than draped cloth. "FAT NATION," the headlines read, continuing, "IT'S WORSE THAN YOU THINK. HOW TO BEAT OBESITY." The visual image of this cover story by Marc Ambinder speaks to the shame and anxiety evoked by the contemporary "obesity epidemic," of a nation trying to shed what Erving Goffman called a "discrediting attribute." Published in 1963, Goffman's *Stigma: Notes on the Management of Spoiled Identity* still serves at the classic study of how stigma works.[4] While his study does not focus on fatness, his concepts allow us to understand the implications of fat denigration for both individuals and an entire culture. Clearly, fatness is a *discrediting attribute*, for which people will go to *extraordinary extremes* to eliminate. One has only to think of the tapeworms and arsenic of the early 20th century or the digitalis/amphetamines of the middle 20th century or the debilitating gastric bypass surgery of today to recognize these extreme measures. It is a *physical* stigma, or what Goffman calls an "abomination of the body," one that is clearly *visible*. Fat people cannot hide their stigma, though marketers of bathing suits and clothing certainly attempt to convince consumers that their product will make the person look ten pounds slimmer. Because our culture assigns many meanings to fatness beyond the actual physical trait—that a person is gluttonous, or filling a deeply disturbed psychological need, or irresponsible and unable to control primitive urges—it also has many traits of what Goffman calls a *character* stigma. As the essays of writers like Susan Stinson and Marilyn Wann demonstrate, fat people are often treated as *not quite human*, entities to whom the normal standards of polite and respectful behavior do not seem to apply. They might be accepted in certain circumstances, but, as the fat protagonist in Neil LaBute's 2004 play *Fat Pig* finds out when she begins to date a thin man who consistently hides their relationship and then rejects her because of her weight, that acceptance will only go so far.[5] Often that tolerance is only extended as long as the fat person does not expect too much—an actual romantic relationship or a decent, well-paying job, for instance—and also consistently puts on a self-deprecating mask. The various forms of *discrimination* that fat people experience, in schools, at doctors' offices, in the job market, in housing, and in their social lives, means that, effectively, their *life chances*—for a good education, for fair and excellent health care, for job promotion and security, for pleasant housing, for friends, lovers, and life partners . . . in other words, for a good and safe life—are *effectively reduced*.

Like all other forms of stigma, fat stigma is *relative*, dependent on the historical and cultural context. Perceptions about fat—whether it's considered beautiful or ugly, dangerous or healthy, a sign of wealth or a sign of poverty—differ from place to place and from time to time. Women in the United States today face a far different standard regarding body size than those of other times or other cultures. In 1825, the French writer Jean Anthelme Brillat-Savarin exclaimed that "thinness is a horrible calamity for women." "A scrawny woman," he continued, "no matter how pretty she may look, loses something of her charm with every fastening she undoes."[6] From the perspective of an American woman in the 21st century, it's difficult to imagine a world where being thin would be a calamity. The ways that a fat American colonist would have experienced his body in the 18th century, probably as a sign of prosperity and health, differs greatly from those of a man living in the context of the 21st century, when his body is a sign of our contemporary "obesity epidemic." Even today, however, body size standards in some cultures are far different from those in the United States. Young women in Namibia, for instance, describe themselves in positive terms as "fat and attractive." Among the Arab population in Mauritania, "plumping up" is the goal for marriageable young women.[7] And it was only with the introduction of American television in the 1990s that the Fijians in the South Pacific began to experience eating problems on any significant level. Until then, a plump, rounded body meant the epitome of social approval.[8]

Drawing from Goffman's taxonomy, fat is both a clearly visible *physical* stigma and a *character* stigma insofar as people assume the presence of fat means something negative about the person. Fatness has become a sort of *tribal* stigma for the United States at large, as the *Atlantic* cover indicated. More fundamentally, however, the political cartoons, advertisements, and physicians' writings I explored from the 19th century suggest that fat stigma is deeply rooted in the development of ideas about race, gender, and civilization. Fatness was a motif used to identify "inferior bodies"—those of immigrants, former slaves, and women—and it became a telltale sign of a "superior" person falling from grace. In today's terms, fat, if it had a color, would be black, and if it had a national origin, it would be illegal immigrant, non-U.S., and non-Western.

While a fat person thus faces the formidable consequences of this physical, character, and tribal stigma, this is not to say, of course, that all will suffer to the same extent or in the same way. Indeed, Goffman points out the various forms of *resistance* that a person with a stigmatized identity will enact, and the many ways that other non-stigmatized individuals might serve as their allies.[9] In other words, fat people, just as thin people, will vary in their resilience to threats to their self-esteem. One of the key ways that people cope with adversity is to connect with others who face similar problems. For some, this has meant joining support groups for weight loss, such as Overeaters Anonymous and Weight Watchers. While these groups do allow fat people to meet and commiserate with others, they certainly do not address the fundamental *stigma* of fatness. In contrast, many fat people beginning in the late 1960s began to organize themselves into fat acceptance and fat activist groups such as the National Association to Aid Fat Americans (now known as the National Association to Advance Fat Acceptance). While these groups bolster members' self-esteem through friendships and survival tips, they also challenge fat stigma itself. In their radical acceptance of their fat bodies, these activists become what Ophira Edut has called in a different context, "body outlaws."[10] The kind of dubious media attention these groups have received suggests that mainstream culture is reluctant to provide any but the most circumscribed acceptance of these groups, or what Goffman calls *tolerance* only if the deviant group stays within the *ecological boundaries of their community*. An example of this might be the willingness of hotels to host fat-only swim nights and social events, but the unwillingness of most Americans to support legislation to ensure the fair treatment of fat people in education, work, housing, and health care. Nevertheless, the voices and work of fat activists, mobilizing into a social movement, certainly hold the potential to radically transform fat stigma.

Contextualizing Fat Shame

As I was researching and writing *Fat Shame*, two intertwining developments exacerbated the stigma surrounding fatness: the mainstream anti-obesity movement and food activism. According to the National Institutes of Health, two-thirds of the U.S. population are currently medically defined as "overweight" or "obese," constituting what has become popularly known as an "obesity epidemic." With its connotations of disease, contagion, and proliferation, the choice of the term "epidemic" is deliberately alarmist, suggesting imminent danger and sure catastrophe if not addressed.[11] American journalists, medical practitioners, and educators regularly claim that fatness is our number one public enemy. Journalist Frank Deford's March 2003 commentary, delivered just prior to the United States' declaration of war against Iraq, demonstrates the popular perception of obesity as a national threat. "For the long term," he wrote, "the greatest threat to our society is not al-Qaeda and it is not North Korea and it is not Iraq. It is the way we choose to live. How much we choose to sit, how much we choose to eat."[12] Identifying fat as a threat greater to the United States than any political enemy or terrorist is perhaps uncommon, but the note of alarm is not. Certainly it became commonplace in the 1990s and the first decade of the 21st century to refer to obesity as the principal public health enemy facing the United States, and, increasingly, the global population. Nearly every day some newspaper headline highlights our "obesity epidemic," featuring articles about new diets, weight loss surgery, exercise plans, proposed taxes on junk foods, and lawsuits against fast-food corporations. Distressing booklets like the American Heart Association's 2007 "A NATION AT RISK: Obesity in the United States" lay out statistics about body size and focus on the dangers of too much fat: high blood pressure, heart disease, arthritis, and so on. Worries about children and weight are particularly disturbing, as the headline of one article attested: "Child Obesity Taken Too Lightly, Experts Say."[13] Medical conclusions quoted in the William J. Clinton Foundation's Alliance for a Healthier Generation claim that "if childhood obesity continues to increase, it could cut two to five years from the average lifespan." This would mean, the experts continue, that "for the first time in American history, our current generation of children could live shorter lives than their parents."[14]

Taken as a whole, these kind of troubling, alarming headlines constitute what other scholars, in their work on AIDS and the HIV virus, describe as apocalyptic thinking.[15] Such thinking not only clouds judgment, it also induces a moral panic about the "guilt" of the one who "causes" such a catastrophe, often leading to extraordinary and discriminatory actions on the basis of "health" and "well-being." This kind of apocalyptic thinking has justified our national "war on fat," which began with Surgeon General C. Everett Koop in the 1990s.[16] Unlike earlier campaigns such as President Kennedy's Presidential Council on Physical Fitness and Sports, which, as its name implies, focused on overall issues of fitness, the war on fat zeroes in on bodily fat as the health problem. And just as the term "epidemic" merits attention, so does the military metaphor for the public health campaign designed to halt it. It is difficult—perhaps impossible—to think clearly about fatness and our bodies once we are engaged in a "war against fat," for if we are at war, then fat must be the enemy. And, by definition, we seek to destroy enemies in a war, not to engage in diplomatic missions of understanding or research. Calling for a war presumes we have clear and uncontested evidence of the danger the enemy poses sufficient to justify the tremendous expense and risk that a war entails.

This returns us to the Delta Zeta story, which, considering it is largely a saga of appearance-based snobbery, may seem to have little to do with the national concern over disease and fatness. These situations do seem to differ: the first is about looks and discrimination, the second is about the health of our citizens and future generations. One perspective is abhorrent, the other may be perceived as more justified. One is based on a subjective, aesthetic point of view, the other on supposed objective, factual evidence. Thinking about these two perspectives in tandem, however, one realizes how deeply intertwined they actually are. As many scholars have pointed out, all biological crises are also cultural crises. From the plague in the Middle Ages, to hysteria in the 19th century, to AIDS in the 20th century, biological and medical problems are also cultural sites where social power and ideological meanings are played out, contested, and transformed. The "obesity crisis" is no different. For the most part, however, the journalistic accounts, the public health warnings, and the medical discourse take at face value the biological significance of the "obesity epidemic," ignoring both its cultural implications and the need to interrogate the definition of the "problem" itself.

In her pathbreaking book *Illness as Metaphor*, Susan Sontag describes the harmful meanings our culture has imposed on tuberculosis, cancer, and AIDS. She points out that we often associate certain diseases with specific types of personalities, blaming the victims and shaming them into silence. In a similar vein, I would argue that we have imposed equally dangerous cultural meanings onto fatness.[17] Fatness in the United States "means" excess of desire, of bodily urges not controlled, of immoral, lazy, and sinful habits. Much more than a neutral description of a type of flesh, fatness carries with it such stigma that it propels us to take drastic, extreme measures to remove it.

The same stigma that propels the Delta Zeta officers to single out the fat members for exclusion also infuses medical research, physicians' expert advice, public health policies, commercial weight loss programs, and, of course, the complex ways that individuals understand and experience their own bodies. The cultural stigma surrounding fatness inhibits our ability to think clearly about health issues, so that it is difficult for most people to recognize the difference between our aesthetic and our medical concerns. Heightened national health concerns regarding weight, articulated so clearly and loudly in the headlines that scream "obesity epidemic," can quickly become justification for discrimination against fat people. The war against fat can become, too easily and too rapidly, a war against fat people.

While references to the "obesity epidemic" are themselves pandemic, not all health experts agree on the physical dangers of fatness. As Eric Oliver discusses in *Fat Politics*, it was not until the 1990s that U.S. agencies and medical organizations began to discuss obesity as a "disease," a designation that legitimated tremendous amounts of money spent in research and treatment. Indeed, most reports arguing for the status of "disease," it turns out, were written—or ghostwritten—by those with a large financial stake in research: pharmaceutical and medical firms that focus on eradicating obesity.[18] The definition of obesity as a "disease" has come under debate by many important health researchers, particularly those within the Health at Every Size movement. The HAES movement draws from medical and social research of scholars such as Paul Campos and Glenn Gaesser to offer an alternative paradigm to that of conventional medical and public policy, shifting our perspective from "How do we make fat people thin?" to "How do we make fat people healthy?" Much of the work of HAES points out the connections between discrimination, stigma, and ill health, arguing that one of the main reasons *the life chances of fat people are limited* is because of the unfair treatment they receive in employment, medical care, and social life. HAES advocates challenge the conventional medical understanding of fatness, pointing to studies that suggest fatness is not particularly malleable, and that restrictive dieting causes only short-term weight loss but results in long-term metabolic disturbances. They argue that studies with headlines that tout the "dangers of obesity" usually demonstrate that a sedentary lifestyle and a diet of processed foods result in ill health; and that a diet rich in fruits and vegetables and an active lifestyle will improve health, but it *may or may not* result in weight loss.[19]

The two-year study completed by Linda Bacon and other nutrition researchers at the University of California, Davis, challenges the dominant perspective that dieting for weight loss will improve health. In this study, a group of fat women was divided into two groups, one receiving coaching in restrictive eating (dieting) and exercise, the other being encouraged to eat a healthy diet, to listen to their body's cues, to foster ways to engage in fun exercise, and to take part in a fat acceptance discussion group. Significantly, group 1—the traditional diet/exercise group—initially lost weight, but by the end of the two-year study half had dropped out; most had regained weight; blood pressure, cholesterol, and other metabolic measures had not improved; and self-esteem levels dropped. In contrast, group 2 hadn't lost any weight, but most stayed with the two-year program; their blood pressure, cholesterol, and other metabolic measures had improved dramatically; their self-esteem levels increased substantially; and they exercised regularly. Encouraged to pay attention to their bodies, to stop restricting calories, to fight the discrimination they experienced as fat people, and to *enjoy* their bodies through physical movement and eating well—with more fruits and vegetables and fewer processed foods—the non-dieters showed significant health improvements. But, and this is the key point, they never became thin.[20]

According to HAES advocates, the conventional focus on weight loss, rather than healthy living, fuels a dangerous and profitable diet industry as well as the growing field of weight loss surgery. In 1992, the American Society for Bariatric Surgery (today the American Society for Metabolic and Bariatric Surgery) estimated that physicians performed 16,200 weight loss surgeries. In 2003, the ASBS reported 103,200 weight loss surgeries; that number jumped phenomenally to 140,640 procedures by 2004, 177,600 by 2006, and 220,000 by 2008, with an average cost ranging from $17,000 to $50,000 per procedure. Health at Every Size advocates point out that the rationale for weight loss surgery is as much about "culture" as it is about health. That is, experts acknowledge that modest changes in diet and exercise will improve a patient's health but will not necessarily make the patient *look* healthier—that is, thinner. In a culture permeated by fat stigma, a thinner body provides the illusion of health, despite the fact that the person who has undergone weight loss surgery now has a massively debilitated digestive system and will experience lifelong digestive problems, chronic malnutrition, and uncertainty about how the surgically malformed body will be able to withstand the processes of aging.[21]

HAES advocates, then, focus on challenging discrimination against fat people, on encouraging fat people to exercise in pleasurable ways (and within environments that are conducive to movement and free from harassment), and on supporting a fat person's ability to take pleasure in eating, to listen to his or her own bodily cues, and to eat healthful food. HAES advocates reject and critique the food, diet, and medical industries' focus on "special" diet foods (usually highly processed, expensive items), dieting products, and pharmaceutical and surgical cures for "obesity." They argue that, contrary to their well-funded and publicized advertising campaigns, the diet industries hurt human beings.

But the ideas promoted by HAES advocates regarding the deleterious effects of fat stigma and the complexity of medical research regarding body size and health are rarely addressed. The extent to which the complexities surrounding health and weight get lost within the rhetoric of the "obesity epidemic" and the "war on fat" is often dramatic. Evidence about the dangers of anti-fat measures, from weight loss drugs to bariatric surgery, is often dismissed or discounted. In 1997, when Wyeth-Ayerst Laboratories withdrew their drugs Pondimin (fenfluramine chloride) and Redux (dexfenfluramine hydrocholoride) because of heart valve problems, C. Everett Koop urged Americans "not to give up on the war against obesity because the stakes—in terms of disability and disease—are much too high." The "war on obesity," he said, "must continue unabated."[22] Government literature regularly touts the statistic that obesity causes three hundred thousand deaths a year, despite the fact that the research on which this figure is based suggests a "link," as opposed to a "cause"; and that many reputable scientists challenge the validity of this study. Indeed, the top editors at the *New England Journal of Medicine* called the three-hundred-thousand figure "by no means well established" and "derived from weak or inconclusive data."[23] In May 2005, the Centers for Disease Control and Prevention published a refined study that called into dispute the 300,000 figure, estimating the deaths linked to obesity at a much-lower 112,000 per year and indicating that being moderately overweight actually was linked with improved longevity. Outcry about this study was so great, however, that the CDC backpedaled, not with any data, but with a firm statement that "what we don't want is for this debate to continue to confuse people. We need to be absolutely explicitly clear about one thing: obesity and overweight are critically important health threats in this country." In other words, even when the scientific data looked challenging to the earlier statistics, the CDC was going to stick firmly to its war against obesity.[24]

Certainly the national stigma of fat helps to explain this stubborn unwillingness to listen to the *possibility* that the "war on fat" is misguided. Importantly, there is also significant financial investment at stake in maintaining this war on fat. Just as Dwight D. Eisenhower in his 1961 Farewell Address called on Americans to be wary of the military-industrial complex, we need, I argue, to be just as wary of the diet-industrial complex. Eisenhower coined the phrase to point to the "total influence—economic, political, even spiritual" of a massive military establishment enmeshed with a large arms industry whose point becomes more about maintaining itself than about the ultimate purpose of the government—to maintain peace. Maintaining the giant military-industrial complex actually precludes the push for peace, as it requires that our nation maintain a constant state of war.[25] Our national "war on fat" has created a colossal health and diet industry closely enmeshed with government agencies. Profit motives for our sixty-billion-dollar diet industries and fat stigma have become so entangled that it has become difficult, perhaps impossible, to even entertain the possibility that we are fighting the "wrong war." In a profit-driven, consumer society, diet product manufacturers, pharmaceutical corporations, the advertising industry, and medical practitioners all benefit financially from fat stigma. Through their lobbying efforts, these entities influence our government agencies and public health campaigns; many in the corporate and medical world also serve as consultants or members of government offices and agencies. It is difficult to challenge this arrangement as our powerful fat-denigrating ideology means that it "makes sense" to fight fat. Yet just as the purpose of the military-industrial complex is to maintain itself, not to seek peace, the purpose of the diet-industrial complex is to keep people dieting (or choosing surgery, diet pills, or membership in clubs) rather than to seek health.

Dovetailing with the antiobesity efforts of the last decade, the food activist movement also provided additional fuel to the power of fat stigma. The growth of the Slow Food movement, farmers' markets, Community Supported Agriculture memberships, organic foods available in Wal-Mart as well as Whole Foods, and a host of books and films on the best-seller lists—from *The Omnivore's Dilemma* to the *Skinny Bitch* series—all point to the explosion of a food counterculture. Food activists work to educate the public about the problems of a food-industrial system that are quite complex and largely invisible to most American consumers: the environmental degradation caused by intensive mono-agriculture and genetically modified foods; the animal brutality of concentrated animal feeding operations; the tremendous carbon footprint of conventional agriculture and the global system of distribution; the malnutrition caused by the lack of a varied diet that is too high in processed, pesticide-filled, "empty" food products and too low in fresh fruits and vegetables; and the loss of a food system that sustains local communities both economically and culturally. Finally, of course, what concerns food activists is what links their work to mine: fat.

Indeed, what I have found in my exploration of food activism is that frequently all these more complicated—and often invisible—problems regarding our food system are reduced to the problem of obesity in the United States. To be sure, many of the writers and activists appear sincerely concerned with people's health and well-being, and they argue that our food system has made us fat and thus sick. Unfortunately, though, their unwavering acceptance of the language and medical evidence touted within the discourse of the "obesity epidemic" falls far short of the complexities they evoke in other aspects of their work. Other food activists' use of the catastrophic language of the "obesity epidemic" and the motif of the fat person, however, seems to be less concerned about health and well-being than a means to gain the public's attention and to condense and simplify their more complicated messages regarding the food system.

One of the most glaring uses of fat stigma by food activists is the billboard campaign by PETA (People for the Ethical Treatment of Animals). Like much of PETA's publicity, this "Obese in the U.S.A.? Go Vegetarian" ad is both witty and has shock value. Clearly a takeoff on Bruce Springsteen's "Born in the U.S.A.," this ad shows the backside of a white man against the backdrop of an American flag. Unlike Springsteen's ultra-masculinity, his taut buns encased in skin-skimming jeans, however, we see butt cleavage, fat hanging over a belt, hairy arms, and small hands. The tagline plays to one of PETA's most common themes, that vegetarians are never fat.[26] PETA's "Obese in the U.S.A." ad obviously draws on prevalent fat stigma to arouse interest in its larger cause of animal treatment and vegetarianism. The overall cultural discourse on the "obesity epidemic" supports their advertising campaign, but PETA doesn't deliberately or actively invoke concerns about health; instead, the aesthetic contempt for the fat body is all that is clearly denoted. In this billboard, PETA reduces their larger, and much more complicated, argument about animal ethics to an abhorrence of the fat body. More specifically, this fat, meat-eating man is insufficiently masculine (unlike Springsteen), simultaneously typical of Americans but also an affront to the flag itself.

PETA's reduction of their complicated message regarding the ethical treatment of animals to a mockery of fat people is one of the most obvious examples of how those in the food activist movement use the motif of fatness to simplify, publicize, and garner support for their cause. Other food activist literature also relies on and exacerbates already-existing fat stigma, repeatedly drawing on the motif of the fat person as the symbol of a degraded food system. Morgan Spurlock's 2004 documentary *Super Size Me*, for instance, exposes the dangers of a fast-food diet. Everything in *Super Size Me*, however, reinforces the denigration of fat people, from the title, to the movie poster of him stuffing fries into his mouth, to the cartoons ridiculing fat people, to the camera shots of the fat woman's behind set against Queen's 1978 song "Fat Bottomed Girls." Rory Freedman and Kim Barnouin's *Skinny*

Bitch has remained on the *New York Times* best-seller list for more than a year, and, according to their website, has sold over a million copies. Freedman and Barnouin describe in graphic terms the animal cruelty that is part of our meat and dairy production; the lax oversight by the FDA and USDA as well as their corporate ties to our dairy, meat, and processed-food industries; and the dangers of pesticide residue on our foods. Indeed, they argue that their primary interest is in changing our food system and that the title *Skinny Bitch* is simply a "marketing ploy" to get readers' attention.[27] It's difficult to be convinced by their disclaimer, however, when they begin their introduction with "Are you sick and tired of being fat?" Describing fat as "lumpy shit," they promise to "empower" readers with the food knowledge necessary to become a "skinny bitch" (said with endearment and envy) in a "perfect, skinny world."[28] In other words, the fat denigration in *Skinny Bitch* is tightly bound to the discussion of food quality and purity.

Unlike PETA, the *Skinny Bitch* series, or Spurlock's *Super Size Me*, other popular food activist writers do not so blatantly rely on stigmatized and mocking images of fat people. They do, however, draw on the language of the "epidemic" to justify their ideas, and they ignore the complexities regarding nutrition, health, and body size. In the *Omnivore's Dilemma*, the detailed and nuanced best-selling book on the plethora of food options available to Americans, Michael Pollan refers to the United States as the "republic of fat" and relies heavily for his evidence on the scaremongering and chastising work of Greg Critser's *Fat Land: How Americans Became the Fattest People in the World*.[29] Likewise, in *Fast Food Nation* Eric Schlosser refers frequently to the "obesity epidemic," a loaded term with its connotation of sickness and contagion, and to our country as an "empire of fat."[30]

The orientation of food activists in this regard reminds me of the publication of Upton Sinclair's 1906 book *The Jungle*, which exposed the horrors of the Chicago meatpacking industries. Public outcry about the description of rancid meat, rat droppings, and human limbs churned into the sausage mix sped the passage of the Pure Food and Drug Act and the Meat Inspection Act of 1906. Somewhat disappointed, however, Sinclair famously quipped, "I aimed for the public's head, and I hit them in the stomach." That is, while he was not unconcerned about the quality of people's food, he was more concerned about the state of workers' lives—the child labor, the abuse of immigrants and black migrants from the South, and the violent and state-sanctioned squashing of protests and strikes. His vivid descriptions of food adulteration were there to lure readers to an understanding of the more abstract and radical tenets of socialism and workers' rights he advocated;

most readers, however, could never get past the nauseous feelings evoked by the grotesque descriptions of the meat factory.

Like Sinclair, food activists are aiming for one thing but have hit another. They want a complex overhaul of our food system, but they aim at readers' waistlines. It might just be a rhetorical device or a marketing ploy, but it is nevertheless significant.[31] With each image and reference like the "Obese in the U.S.A." billboard, the ideology of fat hatred and the realities of discrimination against fat people are reinforced. Moreover, the very diet-industrial system that food activists so abhor is strengthened, as fat denigration encourages people to turn to desperate measures to fight the stigma they experience. And, finally, by relying on the fat stigma motif, food activists alienate fat readers—it is almost as if they do not exist in the imagined readership of these texts. They are not, to use the language relevant to my overall argument on fat stigma, citizens of this reading republic.

Researching and Shaping Fat Shame

In order to write this book, I have drawn from a range of sources and texts. I've culled through hundreds of issues of *Harper's Weekly*, *Life*, and *Godey's Lady Book*, examining the first political cartoons about fat people and the first advertisements for weight loss products. I've spent time at the British Library and the Library of Congress, poring over the medical literature of the 19th and 20th century regarding "corpulence" and "obesity." I've studied hundreds of postcards depicting fat women, an odd but enlightening collection of ephemera found at a women's history archive. I've read in detail the work of Hilde Bruch, one of the first psychologists who identified eating disorders and considered obesity the result of a psychological drama within the family, particularly those of immigrant, ethnic, Jewish homes. I've examined in detail the suffrage propaganda published by both the pro- and anti-women's rights movements in the late 19th and early 20th centuries, and the ways that they both utilized "fatness" to mock their opponents. By searching the archives of the American Medical Association and attending Federal Trade Commission hearings, I've explored attempts to control the weight loss industries. I've spoken with physicians and personal trainers, experts on weight loss and body sculpting. Family, friends, and colleagues have provided an endless source of contemporary clippings about dieting and fatness all over the world. And, finally, I've read countless novels and essays by fat activists, and interviewed members of size acceptance organizations who have spoken movingly about their lives and their work.

Drawing from a wide range of medical and popular literature from the late 19th and early 20th centuries, chapter 2, "Fat, Modernity, and the Problem of Excess," explores the development of the stigma around fatness in the latter part of the 19th century through its full flowering in the 20th: the idea that fat is a mark of shame, a stain, something that discredits a person. It begins where Hillel Schwartz and Peter Stearns first pointed us, to the ways that anxiety over the fat body was linked to 19th-century cultural concerns about the excesses of industrialization and consumer culture within modernity. An exploration of cultural documents of the time—newspapers, magazines, political cartoons, and medical publications—suggests that the body became the site of struggle over other dilemmas that emerged during the modern period, particularly those surrounding consumer and political life.

Before the end of the 19th century, only the privileged—in terms of both wealth and health—could become fat. Just as industrialization and urbanization transformed every other aspect of life in the United States, it also transformed bodies. As the 20th century progressed, more people experienced sufficient wealth, lifestyles became more sedentary, the development of new farming methods and better transportation systems meant that food was more plentiful and relatively cheap, and health care improved. All of this meant that more people could gain weight and keep it on. At this point fatness became a marker dividing the rich and the poor, but now, unlike in earlier centuries, hefty weight connoted not high status but a person whose body was out of control, whose reason and intellect were dominated and overwhelmed by the weight of obesity. As the meanings of "fat" and "thin" shifted, moving up the socioeconomic ladder usually meant aspiring to a thinner body, even if that aspiration was unsuccessful.

This chapter explores the phenomenal shift, from fat being something associated with the rich and very prosperous to something associated with the middle class and then to the poor, an affliction of those who presumably could not control their bodies or their impulses. In the 19th and early 20th centuries, cultural representations of fat people shifted from the "fat cat"—the wealthy, powerful, and often greedy man—to the fat and undesirable ordinary person, who could not handle the riches and abundance of modernity. In exploring exactly who these "ordinary" people were, chapter 3, "Fat and the Un-Civilized Body," argues that the cultural hatred of fat emerged simultaneously with the construction of hierarchies of race, sexuality, gender, and class. Fat denigration was linked to overall processes of mapping political and social hierarchies onto bodies. The project of "civilization" meant not just racialization and gender and sexual hierarchies, but also the construction of certain types of body types as superior and others as inferior. Fatness became a significant marker of inferiority within cultural texts of all sorts, either as prima facie evidence of an already-existing inferior status or as a harbinger of an impending fall for those presumed to be higher on the "civilized" scale. In the intense conversations in the last decades of the 19th and the early decades of the 20th century about what—and who—constituted the most civilized culture and the most civilized people, fatness became another divide marking the differences between white people and people of color, between native-born, white American citizens and new immigrants, between the wealthy and the poor, and between men and women.

Chapter 4, "Feminism, Citizenship, and Fat Stigma," explores what these emerging ideas of the "civilized body" and the stigmatization of fat meant for women and for feminism. The linking of thinness and control, thinness and progress, and thinness and self-help, has made the "body project" a natural ally with many avenues of feminism, particularly liberal feminism. One women's studies scholar, for instance, discussed with eloquence the pride she felt in losing sixty pounds, despite her knowledge that "dieting culture" takes up so much of women's financial and emotional resources.[32] As one of my feminist colleagues said when I introduced my research interest in fat acceptance, "But, of course, you can't mean REALLY fat people." It is as if an invisible line separates the thin-enough feminist who is allowed to critique the excesses of the diet industry from the fat "other" who resides outside the boundaries of normative citizenship. "Feminism, Citizenship, and Fat Stigma" considers contemporary feminism's fraught relationship with fat by exploring its roots within the development of modernity and the first wave of feminism. It explores the complex ways that "fatness" has had powerful meanings for feminists claiming the stakes of citizenship, from 19th- and early 20th-century suffragists who needed to prove theirs were indeed "civilized" bodies, to the workingwomen of the 1920s and 1930s who were seeking to carve out a space of upward mobility. By exploring the links between notions of the civilized body and feminism, this chapter helps us to understand why women continue to bear the particular brunt of our culture's disgust with fatness, as well as the ways that feminism is implicated in that very disgust and stigma.

Chapter 5, "Narrating Fat Shame," focuses on stories found primarily within contemporary popular culture in which "fat" serves as an important motif. Exploring the popular narratives of people like Britney Spears, Kirby Puckett, Monica Lewinsky, and Oprah Winfrey illuminates the striking way that fat both signifies the "moral corruption" of particular individuals and reinforces hierarchies of race, sexuality, gender, and class. This chapter concludes with a discussion of Barack and Michelle Obama and the relentless media focus on their fitness and eating habits, exploring the ways that this attention is both typical and distinctive. As a sign of civilized behavior and inherent character, thinness is a desired—some would even argue necessary—trait for anyone reaching for the contemporary presidency. For the first African American with a serious chance at the office, and then for the first African American family living in the White House, thinness is, this chapter argues, particularly necessary.

The final chapter, "Refusing to Apologize," provides a compelling contrast to the saga of fat denigration told in the previous chapters. It takes as its title the words of Marilyn Wann's important and very funny book *FAT!SO? Because You Don't Have to Apologize for Your Size!* and explores the ways that fat activists have, since the late 1960s, challenged fat stigma and insisted on the full rights of citizenship. This chapter discusses the significance of fat activism's emergence in the early second wave of feminism, and the ways that this activism has dealt with the complex threads of race, sexuality, and class that are linked to fat denigration. Above all, it explores the ways that fat activists have rejected narratives of shame, often after years of dangerous attempts to lose weight, and pushed for an acceptance and celebration of the fat body, an end to fat discrimination, and the popularization of new health and medical perspectives on fat bodies. In their various campaigns and activisms, they have worked to "rewrite" the meaning of fatness. This chapter, then, brings us full circle, back to the earliest representations of the inferior fat body, as we see fat activists challenging dominant popular culture and medical discourse surrounding fatness.

Writing Fat Shame

When I began my project on the history of fat stigma, there was no clearly defined area in which it resided. The topic spanned women's studies, American studies, African American studies, disability studies, the history of medicine, and U.S. cultural and social history, and it still does. In the last decade, however, there has emerged a newly defined field in which my exploration of fat stigma clearly rests: fat studies.

Certainly prior to the development of this new field, research existed on the body, dieting, and fat. For instance, Hillel Schwartz's 1986 book *Never Satisfied: A Cultural History of Diets, Fantasies, and Fat* remains one of the most detailed studies of dieting and weight reduction in the United

States.[33] Research on the body and dieting has played a significant role within women's studies and women's history since the 1970s, resulting in important research that both bolstered the political agendas of feminist activists and furthered crucial theoretical understandings of how gender has worked across time and place.[34] My early research and writing on fatness did not exist in a vacuum, then, but rather as part of a range of work focused on issues related to gender, bodies, and power. This research, however, primarily focused on the meanings of *thinness* (as opposed to *fatness*) and on the problems associated with dieting. In addition, works such as the ones identified above were not necessarily in dialogue with one another; it remained up to readers to pull together and compare studies and points of view. Soon after I began the project, however, scholarly interest in fat began to converge into the academic field of fat studies. Books like Kathleen LeBesco's *Revolting Bodies?* and the earlier collection she edited with Jana Evans Braziel, *Bodies Out of Bounds*, explored the cultural meanings—and challenges—posed by the fat body. Don Kulick and Anne Meneley's *Fat: The Anthropology of an Obsession* compared across time and place the cultural significances attached to fatness. Andrea Elizabeth Shaw's *The Embodiment of Disobedience: Fat Black Women's Unruly Political Bodies* illuminated the ways that women across the African diaspora rejected Western ideals of thinness. Other scholars such as Paul Campos in *The Obesity Myth*, Glenn Gaesser in *Big Fat Lies*, and Eric Oliver in *Fat Politics* challenged the medical and biological perspectives on fat and health and urged readers to rethink the "obesity epidemic." By 2006 there was sufficient scholarly interest on fat that the psychologist Esther Rothblum and the legal scholar Sondra Solovay put out a call for papers for the volume that would become *The Fat Studies Reader*.[35]

All of this new research has at its core a political perspective, informed by the work done simultaneously and previously by fat acceptance writers and activists such as Marilyn Wann, whose 1998 *FAT!SO?* became a kind of early "classic" within the field. Just as women's studies, queer studies, Native American studies, African American studies, Chicano studies, and working-class studies emerged out of political movements and maintained their ties to those movements even as the scholarly work gained a life of its own, fat studies has clearly grown out of a political movement that promotes the acceptance of fat bodies and the elimination of the discrimination and shame that plagues fat people's lives. Unlike "obesity studies," which generally presumes the social and biological pathology of fatness and which poses fat people as the objects *of* study rather than the subjects who are engaging in the work themselves, fat studies challenges notions of pathology and encourages scholars to listen to the work and words of fat people themselves. The terminology itself is important. Rejecting the term "obesity" either as a euphemism or as a medical term that objectifies fat people, fat studies reclaims the term "fat," arguing that it should become a common term freed of negative connotation, no more controversial than describing someone as tall or brown haired. As I see my work as part of this larger field of fat studies, I too have chosen to use the term "fat" unless I am describing or analyzing the range of terminology—from "corpulent" to "heavyset" to "morbidly obese"—used in the primary texts I am exploring.

A friend recently asked me what all this research has done for my own body image. This was a fair question, and one that is certainly relevant to understanding my own "place" in this project. I've never been a thin person, nor have I ever been extremely fat. I hover in that gray area between "healthy" and "overweight" on those ubiquitous and dubious BMI charts. As a child I was chubby (though the pictures of me from that time don't really bear out how fat I felt), a victim of a lot of teasing and discomfort. As I grew older my weight evened out, or perhaps it was just that my cohort grew fatter, and my sense of self much less sensitive to teasing. As I've been immersed in this research I've experienced moments of great irony. When I was giving a talk on "Body Size/Body Image" for the opening of a women's health care clinic, and showed early cartoons mocking fat people, I looked over my shoulder to see that I was standing next to the Weight Loss Surgery wing. I am daily struck by the incongruity of the countless weight loss ads that pop up on my e-mail and Internet screen, even as I read the medical notices about the dangers of various pharmaceutical "cures." In a particularly poignant contrast, I once spent an evening speaking with a fat acceptance activist; the next day I watched as one of my neighbors was being helped out of her car by her parents after undergoing weight loss surgery.

I consider myself both a fat activist and a food activist, a pairing I hope will become more common in the future. I have been a "locavore" for nearly two decades, buying a share in a local organic farm when it was a tiny operation and purchasing grass-fed lamb and beef and locally raised chickens from our neighboring farmers. On the other hand, we don't own a bathroom scale, and I think it's much more important to encourage our kids to walk and exercise daily and to listen to their bodies than it is to weigh them. Yet my own awakening as a fat activist has not been without pain. Particularly in my interviews with fat activists I've had to swallow my pride many times as they have pointed out the manifestations of fat prejudice in my own thinking. In contrast, it has been very heartening for me to have family, friends, students, and colleagues come to me with examples of fat denigration and fat activism in our culture that they hadn't recognized before they began sharing my research on fat stigma. It is my hope that after reading *Fat Shame*, readers too will be able to recognize the deeply historical and complex layers of fat stigma at work in our culture.

Ads selling weight loss drugs and diet regimes—like these speaking to "stout people" for products like Corpus Lean, found in *Life* magazine in 1887—indicate the emergence of cultural anxiety over fatness. (*Life,* June 30, 1887, 373.)

2

Fat, Modernity, and
the Problem of Excess

In 1869, an article titled "Cure for Obesity" in the *San Francisco Daily Evening Bulletin* reported that an ammonium compound might be a cure for those who "suffer from an excess of fat." A longer article that appeared the same year, titled "How to Reduce Obesity," described the work of a Mr. Banting in England, whose popular pamphlet on the "dietetic means of reducing the superfluous fat" had supposedly drawn letters from two thousand people thanking him for their "emancipation from obesity."[1]

In 1887, amid *Life* magazine ads for resorts, whiskey, trouser stretchers, and products that promised to "ease digestion," was a small classified advertisement that read, "TO LADIES! ARE YOU CORPULENT? CORPUS LEAN is a safe, permanent and healthful flesh reducer—ten to fifteen pounds a month." Among those same ads, the Lynton Company advertised, "TO STOUT PEOPLE: OBESITY easily, pleasantly and certainly cured, without hardship or nauseating drugs . . . fat can be destroyed (not merely lessened) and the cause removed."[2] In 1891, a long article in the Kansas newspaper the *Emporia Daily Gazette* described a new "gymnasium," an exercise machine with complex pulleys and stretching devices, designed to "reduce obesity" and "make graceful forms."[3]

By the early 1900s, magazines like *Life* and daily newspapers across the country were filled with advertisements for weight loss products. Mrs. Adair's Salon promised that Ganesh Retardine, when applied externally, would "reduce the most persistent fat."[4] The Magic Figure Mold Co., from Columbus, Ohio, described a mesh elastic garment that reduced flesh by "evenly distributed, gentle pressure," which would "secure immediate reduction."[5] An ad for the same product read, "Keep your figure Lithe and Supple. You can reduce flesh without loss of time, diet or physical discomfort. Instantly reduces abnormalities and produces a smart, well-set-up appearance." This product, the advertisement suggested, was even for thin people who were anxious about the possibility of weight gain: "If you are fat or fear you are becoming so, if your figure is in any way abnormal, you need the Magic Figure Mold Garment."[6] An ad for a similar product, Dr. Jeanne Walter's Rubber Garments, explained that "the comfortable life for men and women alike means living free from the annoyance and unsightliness of disagreeable, unhealthful fat. Reducing your fat means not only better health but vastly improved appearance as well. You can rid yourself of superfluous fat easily, hygienically, safely, with Dr. Jeanne Walter's Famous Medicated Rubber Garments." These garments worked, the ad explained, "by inducing perspiration, causing the safe and speedy reduction of all unnecessary flesh."[7]

By 1912, commercial products sold as weight loss remedies constituted a large enough industry to worry the American Medical Association, which published the first list of dangerous or ineffective "Obesity Cures" in its *Nostrums and Quackery*, written by Dr. Arthur J. Cramp, who joined the AMA in 1906 to investigate deceptive medical practices, including weight loss remedies. Physicians and consumers from around the country sent the AMA dubious advertisements and products, which Cramp would then study. The AMA was particularly concerned about organizations that claimed medical affiliation where there was none, such as the "Society of Associated Physicians," which promised weight loss through an African remedy overseen by a panel of expert doctors. It turned out that the "expert" was a man by the name of J. A. Knox who held no medical qualifications, and the testimonials fake.[8] "Obesity Cures" included listings of these sham medical connections and identified dangerous weight loss products, from tapeworms to products like Corpu-Lean containing dinitrophenol, an industrial toxin that sped up the metabolism, to arsenic to thyroid extract in Kellogg's Safe Fat Reducer.[9]

General wisdom associates the origins of a "cult of thinness" with the 1920s, the era of skinny flappers who bound their breasts and whose short and sleeveless dresses exposed svelte arms and legs. As the publication of the AMA's 1912 "Obesity Cures" and the sampling of advertisements from the 1860s, '70s, '80s, and '90s suggests, however, concerns about fatness were already being articulated, companies were already profiting from those concerns, and consumers were already engaging in dangerous weight loss measures long before the 1920s. From the 1860s onward, savvy entrepreneurs perceived the growing cultural hatred of fatness and advertised products that both intensified the worries about fatness and promised to shrink the corpulent body. The idea that fat is a mark of shame, a stain—something, to use Goffman's phrase, that is a "discrediting attribute"—developed in the 19th century. What we see in the 1920s is the ability of the burgeoning advertising and corporate industries to fixate and elaborate on what had already been established: an overall anxiety regarding body size and fatness.

The advertisement for Dr. Jeanne Walter's Famous Medicated Rubber Garments, promising to rid users of that which was "superfluous" and "unnecessary," speaks specifically to the 19th-century anxiety about body size. A *fat* body came to be seen less as one that was successful, healthy, or wealthy, but rather as one that was ineffectively managing the modern world. That is, a thriving, upwardly mobile person needed to demonstrate those aspirations by controlling the wealth and abundance that came with an improvement in class status; and a fat body revealed an inability to handle that new wealth. Of course, these ideas never completely changed, so that one can find positive associations with fatness even as the general trend shifted toward fat as a disreputable trait, a sign of redundant and dangerous excess. Indeed, the processes of modern life created a set of cultural tensions that played out in people's conflicting experiences of their own bodies and in divergent and often inconsistent cultural representations of the body. By the early decades of the 20th century, however, fat had generally become Goffman's "discrediting attribute," a sign that one was not able to manage the prosperity and resources that came with upward mobility. This is a significant shift from earlier understandings of fatness as a sign of one's superior class status.

Fatness as Wealth

Until the late 19th century, fatness was generally a prerogative of the few. One had to have both wealth (meaning one had sufficient food and physical leisure) and health (meaning one was free of the diseases that wasted away bodily flesh) in order to maintain a hefty body. As such, fatness was often linked to a generalized sense of prosperity, distinction, and high status. The corpulence itself was not represented as bad, but rather was a sign of how much the rich person had, in the same way that a large mansion was a sign of their affluence. Political cartoons and satire in popular journals like *Life* and *Harper's Weekly* illuminate the ways that fatness marked well-being and wealth. A *Harper's Weekly* cartoon from 1881, for instance, portrays a farmer, with a protruding girth, commenting on the fate of a poor sailor who needs to ask for government handouts: "Here I, that have had *no protection*, am growing fat and rich, and can compete with the world, while my poor sailor brother, who has been *protected*, is obliged to leave and go to Washington."[10] My point here is not to comment on government policies for farmers and sailors in the late 19th century, but rather to point out that fatness itself was seen as a marker of prosperity and security—not of any sort of personal shortcoming or degradation. A 1908 *Life* magazine cartoon similarly links fatness with wealth and status. In this one we see a young white woman urging her beau to remove his arm from her shoulder, as she can hear her papa coming into the living room; all we see is his stomach peeking around the corner, and his arm holding his fine pocket watch. The opulent yet tasteful furnishings, the expensive jewelry, the obedient and desirable daughter—all these mesh with his formidable girth to represent a successful man.[11] The relatively late date of this cartoon—1908—reminds us that even as cultural ideas about fatness shifted, threads of earlier and often contradictory meanings remained.

Of course, prosperity could be taken too far, as we see in the commentaries of the 18th and 19th century that used fatness to lampoon greedy and unscrupulous characters—usually those holding political or economic power. In these cases, abundant flesh was seen as the prerogative of the

"OH, MERCY! GEORGE, DO TAKE YOUR ARM AWAY, QUICK! SOMETHING SEEMS TO TELL ME THAT PAPA IS APPROACHING"

The father in the 1908 *Life* cartoon (*opposite*) is the quintessential "fat cat," a rich, powerful man. The caption under the cartoon reads, "Oh, Mercy! George, do take your arm away, quick! Something seems to tell me that Papa is approaching." This particular "fat cat" appears benignly paternal, but in other cases, such as this 1881 *Harper's Weekly* cover (*above*), the "fat cats" can be sinister, greedy, and oppressive. Note that "merit" and "duty" are dumped in the trashcan, while the illustrations on the wall read, "Bloated Aristocracy." (*Life*, March 12, 1908, 273; *Harper's Weekly*, February 5, 1881, cover.)

wealthy—a direct result of their riches. Their greed and avarice allowed their bodies to grow corpulent. A late 18th-century British cartoon, titled "The Old Sow in Distress, or the Country Parsons Returns from Tithing," shows a very fat vicar, holding a pig and chicken, returning, presumably, from a successful trip to collect his "donations." The vicar completely overshadows the poor, small, horse on which he rides.[12] Cartoons in *Harper's Weekly* and *Life* in the late 19th century mocked the greedy undertakers by portraying them as fat and bloated; the rich and unfeeling aristocrats by picturing them as fat-cheeked and corpulent; and the avaricious capitalists by picturing them as overweight men, whose protruding stomachs nearly tore apart their suit jackets.[13] A 1916 cartoon by the artist John McCutcheon, published in the *Chicago Tribune*, portrayed a very fat man lounging in a chair. The buttons on his vest look like they are about to burst. Mistaking him for someone making money selling arms to European forces, a thin man points to the fat man, asking his friend, "Munition maker?" "No," the friend replies, "Thanksgiving dinner."[14] This image of the "fat cat" has endured sporadically throughout the 20th century. Think, for instance, of the evil, rich, fat Mr. Potter, played by Lionel Barrymore, in Frank Capra's 1946 *It's a Wonderful Life*.

For women, the "fat cat" image often took the shape of an older, rich, and no longer attractive matron. These women needed to be placated and pleased, however, as they held the purse strings. In 1883, for instance, *Life* magazine pictured a wealthy and fat woman, "Mrs. Stone," who brought her physician to see a bust taken of her as a young woman. She says, "Oh, how I've changed since then." The physician, "never one to let a wealthy patient swim in shallow waters," replies, "Oh, but eighteen is such a lanky age."[15] In a *Godey's Book* short story, a wealthy widow asked that her portrait be repainted in order that the likeness be more "exact." What happens is that the painter is only "successful" when he has turned her "fat face, thick lips, double chin, and anti-Grecian nose" into a painting showing a thin, attractive, younger woman. He finds his fortune increased as the widow's "fat, old, and ugly"—and very wealthy—acquaintances commission his work.[16] In all these cases, then, fat certainly indicated power, even if it was unattractive or disagreeable.

Fatness as Metaphor

Throughout the 19th century, then, fatness was a sign of a person's affluence, and, as such, might be respectable (the wealthy father, for instance) but also might reveal gluttonous and materialistic traits of specific, unlikeable, even evil individuals. By the end of the 19th century, fatness also came to represent greedy and corrupt political and economic systems. American ambivalence regarding the political and economic developments of the 19th and early 20th centuries—industrialization, monopoly formation, political corruption—were represented by, and projected onto, the bodies of fat people. In an 1881 cartoon from *Harper's Weekly*, a small man wearing a determined look attempts to sweep away political corruption using a broom marked "Hygiene." The corruption he's sweeping away, politicians linked to liquor interests, are fat, coarse, dirty-looking men wearing dollar signs. In an 1888 cartoon from the same journal, a cartoon portrays the problems that American veterans of the Mexican War were experiencing in receiving any kind of compensation from the government in the form of a very fat business man saying to a skinny and ragged veteran, "All I've got against you is that you survived." In 1900, the political cartoonist John S. Pughe portrayed Richard "Boss" Croker as a blown-up balloon of a man, about to be pierced by the slender, but strong, man running behind him, whose spear read "New York State Democracy." A *Daily World* cartoon from the turn of the century pictured an obese white man, wearing a full dress suit, a crown with the dollar sign atop it, and a large ribbon stamped "Capitalism" waving from his lapel. Skulls labeled "Child Labor," "Our Flesh," and "Blood Fattened Him" fill the field behind him, as well as a factory with smoke billowing out of the chimneys. Clearly, here the fatness represents a system that kills children and laborers to make some wealthy. A later cartoon, one from 1937 published in the *New York World-Telegram*, shows a bloated fat man, wearing a raincoat marked "Monopoly," reading a letter from Franklin Delano Roosevelt that said, "I'm going to bust you."[17]

What is interesting about these cartoons is that the fat person *represents* something that threatens the United States—monopolies, unbridled capitalism, child labor, political corruption linked to business interests. While mainstream American thought recognized business growth as the root of prosperity, there certainly was a recognition, not only among social reformers and critics but also among many "ordinary" Americans, that unchecked business interests would allow some to grow fat—literally and figuratively—while others could starve and grown thin, again both literally and figuratively. What is important to note, however, is that fat people themselves are not the threat; rather, they are the metaphoric representation of greed and corruption.

This metaphor of fat as greed and corruption continued to be used throughout the 20th century, even when the focus of greed shifted from private business to government itself. A *Saturday Evening Post* cartoon from the early 20th century, for instance, focused on the burden of high taxes. Picturing two people in a rowboat, the cartoon shows an extremely fat woman, in a dress labeled "Tax Burden," pulling the boat down into the water as her companion, a very thin man labeled "Taxpayer," tries to get the "Prosperity Engine" to go. The caption read, "I've got the engine started but . . . "[18] A 1953 cartoon commented on the Republican pledge to cut government overspending. Published in the *Memphis Commercial Appeal* by the artist Cal Alley, the cartoon shows a very fat, unhappy-looking man, labeled "Government Workers," with his belt cinched very tightly around his huge middle. One end of the belt, labeled "Additional Hiring," has been cut off. Much more recently, this same image of government as fat and gluttonous was revived in the September 2005 demonstration at the Pennsylvania State Capitol, where 1,500 people staged a "Pink Pig" rally to challenge the state legislators' secret and large pay raises they had given themselves in a midnight session immediately before adjourning for summer break. As late as the summer of 2007, billboards on the Pennsylvania Turnpike read, "Put the Pennsylvania Government on a Diet."[19]

Fatness as Spectacle

Though the fat person in 18th- and 19th-century culture usually represented wealth and prosperity, or by extension, either literally or metaphorically, greed and avarice, there was one situation in which fat people themselves were mocked and shamed. Since the early 19th century, the fat person—particularly the extremely fat person—had served as a spectacle in British and American urban and traveling amusements, such as fairs, circuses, and later, vaudeville. Their interest lay precisely in their oddity, in the way they differed from the size and look of "normal-sized" people. Extremely fat people were seen as a form of human grotesquery, similar to the spectacles offered by dwarves, "Siamese" twins, and bearded women. Late 18th-century and early 19th-century posters and billboards from Piccadilly's "Hall of Wonders" in London advertised both the fattest man, "Fat Dan," a fifty-stone (about nine hundred pounds) man named Daniel Lambert, as well as a Frenchman, Claude Ambroise Seurat, who was billed as the thinnest man alive, a "Living Skeleton."[20] Early moving picture films carried on the cartoon, vaudeville, and circus traditions of making fun of and humiliating the fat person. In a 1916 George Klein silent picture, for instance, titled the *Lightning Bell-Hop*, a very fat man gets stuck in the hand-powered elevator; the slapstick continues as the goofy bellhop seeks out a set of workhorses, and then an outdoor hoist, to heave the fat man upstairs. While the entire short film is predicated

Since the late 18th century, the extremely fat person has served as a spectacle of oddity, in fairs, circuses, vaudeville, and, most recently, on television programs such as *The Biggest Loser*. Here we see a portrait of Daniel Lambert, publicized as "Fat Dan" for Piccadilly's "Hall of Wonders" in London in the first years of the 19th century. Years later, the suffragist Elizabeth Cady Stanton, herself quite sensitive about her increasing girth, would disparage the well-known Lambert as certainly not "distinguished for any great mental endowments." (Portrait of Daniel Lambert [1770–1809] [oil on canvas] by Benjamin Marshall [1767–1835]. Courtesy of New Walk Museum, Leicester City Museum Service, UK/The Bridgeman Art Library.)

on slapstick and bodily humor—from the ill-fitting bellhop's suit to the room tailored for the extraordinarily tall and thin man, it is the fat man who suffers the greatest humiliation. His body is at once exposed and undignified. (We see the continuation of this kind of slapstick mocking the fat person in 1950s shows like *I Love Lucy*, in episodes such as the one where a fat woman sits on Lucy when she is on a Hollywood tour bus. Or, more recently, the scenes in the 2001 film *Shallow Hal* play on the spectacle of the fat person when Gwyneth Paltrow, wearing a fat suit to play the fat protagonist, nearly tips a canoe over into the water.) What links all these representations is the way that they play on the embarrassment of the fat body—how it literally and figuratively does not fit in with the built environment of chairs, doors, and vehicles, and with the world of other "normal-sized" people. What is important to note here is the way that the spectacle of the fat person engages its viewers precisely because it is perceived to be so different, so far removed from the bodily experience of the "average" person. This is not to deny the negative effect that these freak shows had on viewers who themselves were fat, or those who feared becoming fat, or certainly on those who were themselves the object of ridicule. The stigma in this case, however, is one of oddity and uniqueness. This emphasis on fat as a peculiar deformity, however, shifts by the end of the 19th century.

The Balanced Body

One might think that the negative connotations surrounding fatness emerged simply as a result of a recognition of the apparent health risks associated with fat. This idea—that we think poorly of fat simply because we know it is unhealthy—is particularly powerful within our contemporary context, when the health warnings surrounding fatness are ubiquitous, nonstop, and very alarming. What is clear from the historical documents, however, is that the connotations of fatness and of the fat person—lazy, gluttonous, greedy, immoral, uncontrolled, stupid, ugly, lacking in will power, *primitive*—preceded and then were intertwined with explicit concern about health issues. Throughout the 19th century and well into the 20th, physicians generally were rather lax in their concern about weight. "Wasting" diseases like tuberculosis and malnutrition made doctors much more concerned about encouraging their patients to eat than to lose weight. Physicians perceived it as "natural" that one would gain weight with aging. The ritual of the weigh-in, so key to our understanding of how physicians perceive and diagnose us as patients, was not at all a part of the medical lexicon until far into the 20th century. Even as late as 1949, records from the American Medical Association indicate that many doctors needed to be convinced of the relevance of weighing children.[21]

Significantly, two of the earliest marketers of diet programs and products—William Banting and Helen Densmore—rejected their own doctors' advice about the naturalness of their hefty and aging bodies. Considered the "father" of dieting, William Banting enjoyed a successful business as a casket maker in England. By the time he reached middle age, Banting was quite fat, despite continued attempts at vigorous exercise to reduce. Banting disagreed with the physicians who tried to persuade him that weight gain was a natural part of the aging process. "These doctors," he wrote, didn't understand the "parasite of barnacles" that promised to destroy him. He explained that from his "earliest years [he] had an inexpressible dread of such a calamity." In 1863 he published his "Letter on Corpulence," which became a best seller for decades, first in England and later in the United States, going through twelve editions by 1902.[22] "Corpulence" spoke in no uncertain terms about the "crying evil of obesity." "Of all the parasites that affect humanity I do not know of, nor can I imagine, any more distressing than that of Obesity," he wrote. Banting consulted doctor after doctor until he found one who offered a weight loss diet that worked for him: no starches, lean meats, few liquids, and a "morning cordial" that counteracted the constipation that resulted from a diet so high in protein and short on liquids. By the end of his pamphlet, he celebrated the regiment that had freed him from "that dreadful tormenting parasite on health and comfort" that caused such "bodily and . . . mental infirmity."[23]

Like Banting, Dr. Helen Densmore, another early marketer of diet products, also refused her physician's advice to "submit to the inevitable, and let well enough alone." She rejected the idea that it was natural, as her doctor told her, for some people to be fat, and she decried the "nameless something departing from me that every woman holds dear—the lines of beauty and grace of movement . . . " Working to update the Banting system, she began selling her weight loss tea (a laxative) in 1896, in both England and the United States. She explained that the problem with the Banting system was that readers frequently failed to take the "draught," "wrecking havoc with the system," as she explained. In other words, people suffered severe constipation. She began selling packets of her herbal tea laxative for two dollars and advertising for "agents" to sell her solution. It is no wonder that people might have lost weight with her new Banting system. Not only were they given what was supposedly a strong laxative, but they were also told to eat two small meals, skip breakfast, and limit liquids. If that failed, they were told to eat one small meal. If that failed, they were told to reduce the size of the solitary meal. And if that failed, she encouraged fasts of up to thirty days![24]

It is important to realize that it was at first middle-class patients who put pressure on physicians to take seriously the "crying evil of obesity," not physicians who urged their patients to lose weight. For decades—indeed, continuing into the present day—doctors have debated the significance of weight for a patient's health, but there was no such lack of clarity when it came to a popular consensus about weight and beauty. Fatness began to be seen less as a fine *embonpointment* than as Banting's "parasite of barnacles." Obesity as a "crying evil," a "dreadful tormenting parasite," a "calamity" that he wished to avoid—these were all the exact phrases that would recur in writers on fat and weight loss in the next seventy years. Many of the themes that we see in today's dieting literature and propaganda first appear in Banting's early material: the sense of fat as somehow a leach that doesn't belong to the "real" person (a "parasite of barnacles"), the sense of doom associated with fatness (a "dreadful calamity"); and finally, the sense of sin and immorality associated with fatness (a "crying evil"). Fat is not just a state of matter, or even a health risk factor, but is a sign of one's character flaws, even immorality. The harsh words of Helen Densmore painted in stark outline the cultural denunciation of the fat person. All that was needed to lose weight, she argued, was for patients to conform to a strict dietary regime, such as the one she provided. If they failed, her condemnation was swift and cruel: "There was a glimpse of sanity in the old Spartan practice of putting to death the weak, sickly and deformed children at birth. It was a dim perception of the truth that to be ill is a monstrosity."[25]

What is fascinating about this time period, however, was that the growth of fat denigration did not necessarily mean that a thin body was universally viewed in a positive manner. For many physicians, writers, and fashion experts of the 19th century, the key ingredient to an aesthetically pleasing and healthy body was balance. Just as thinness destroyed the "graceful curvings" of a woman's body, obesity destroyed "beauty by wrecking the basic harmonies of proportion," by filling up "those hollows which Nature formed to add highlights and shadows."[26] Fashion plates from magazines like *Godey's Lady's Book*, published in the 19th century, highlight women whose arms are round and cheeks plump. We even see the shadow of very full thighs under their voluminous skirts. The waists are thin, to be sure, but this was to be accomplished with a form-fitting corset, not through an overall reduction in weight.[27] As Peter Stearns so cleverly put it in his book *Fat History*, fashion required the *redistribution* of fat into desirable locations, rather than an elimination of fat.

Indeed, for many 19th- and early 20th-century physicians, the debilitating consequences of modern life, with its crowded urban settings and competitive office employment, could be seen in a *thin* body, not a fat one. In the latter half of the 19th century, a British physician, Dr. John Harvey, for instance, complained that too much attention was being paid to the "fatties." For Harvey, leanness was a more significant problem, caused not only by "errors of diet," but also by anxiety, care, too much brain work, an impure mind, and masturbation. Fighting against cultural forces favoring thinness that he already saw at work, Harvey urged readers to strike a balance between leanness and obesity. "In perfect health," he wrote, "the body should present a rounded appearance; there should be sufficient adipose deposit to give to the person grace and ease of carriage. No ugly prominence of bone should appear, no emaciation should exist. Leanness, like corpulence, produces physical deformity and is calculated to destroy beauty of person and elegance of form."[28] Physicians' pamphlets with titles like *How to Get Fat: Or, the Means of Preserving the Medium Between Leanness and Obesity* emphasized the importance of achieving and maintaining a "balanced" weight, neither too thin nor too heavy.[29]

Many physicians saw modern life as particularly challenging for women, whose bodies, they argued, were being deformed by the emphasis on too much physical and mental activity and a dangerous push for equality between men and women. The American physician Dr. S. Weir Mitchell, for instance, was famous for the "rest cures" he prescribed for women with hysteria and other nervous conditions emerging from the stress of living in a modern world. One of his most well-known patients was the writer, socialist, and feminist Charlotte Perkins Gilman, whose negative experience taking Mitchell's "cure"—which included no writing, no reading, drinking lots of milk, and resting in bed all day—was recorded in her autobiographical short story "The Yellow Wallpaper." As Mitchell explained in his 1877 book *Fat and Blood*, dieting was a "rarely needed process" for Americans. "As a rule," he added, "we have much more frequent occasion to fatten than to thin our patients."[30]

When exploring popular periodicals from the late 19th and early 20th centuries, one can see that manufacturers and advertisers often played to this uncertainty about proper weight, reflecting the concerns of Harvey and Mitchell for "balanced" weight. In 1890, the Chichester Chemical Company explained that "many women with fair faces are deficient in beauty owing to undeveloped figures, flat busts, etc." Their product, Adipo-Malene, promised to "permanently develop the bust and form." An ad in *Godey's Lady's*

Book described Neave's Food as "rich in bone-forming and flesh-producing elements." Many of the advertisements pledged to strengthen the body, the nervous system, and a person's energy, particularly within the context of urban life with its daily mental and physical stresses. Some of these ads were directed primarily to men, such as "Vigoral," a "concentrated nutriment of prime lean beef" that promised to be a "foe to fatigue." An 1898 ad for Dr. Williams' Pink Pills for Pale People, picturing a white woman in a low-cut evening gown, promised to help "Society Women and, in fact, nearly all women who undergo a nervous strain," those who "regretfully watch the growing pallor of their cheeks, the coming wrinkles, and thinness that becomes more distressing every day." The weakening and wasting effects of tuberculosis were explicitly discussed in advertisements, such as the one for Scott's Emulsion, a cod liver oil product, that offered to "build flesh anew." An 1895 ad for the same product described thinness as the cause, not simply the result, of various forms of ill health: "The diseases of thinness are scrofula in children, consumption in grown people, poverty of blood in either. They thrive on leanness. Fat is the best means of overcoming them. Everybody knows cod liver oil makes the healthiest fat." And as yet another ad for Scott's explained, "Good nature goes with plumpness; irratibility [*sic*] goes with thinness. Good friend, you need SCOTT'S EMULSION." Another ad, by the Oxygen Compound Company, told readers that out of "21,000 Beautiful Young Girls, 7,000 will soon die of consumption." While the ad exaggerated, it is worth nothing that in the 1800s, tuberculosis, "nervous diseases," malnutrition, and digestive problems made weight gain desirable for many Americans. The concerns about "excess fat" seen in the classified ads described above existed alongside deeply held concerns about the opposite body attribute—thinness—as a health and beauty hazard.[31]

Modernism, Fat, and the Problems of Excess

As an 1878 advertisement for Allan's Anti-fat Remedy in the Philadelphia African American newspaper the *Christian Reporter* demonstrates, there existed increasing concern about the significance of fat in the post–Civil War era. "Are Fat People Happy?" the ad asked. The text that followed read, "Why are fat people always complaining? Ask someone who entertains the popular though erroneous notion that health is synonymous with Fat. Fat people complain because they are diseased. Obesity is an abnormal condition and oleaginous elements of the food are assimilated to the partial exclusion of the muscle forming and brain producing elements. In proof of this, it is only necessary to assert the well known fact that excessively fat people are never strong, and seldom distinguished for mental powers or activity."[32] Upward mobility and success within the quickly changing conditions of modern life required health, strength, mental power, and a positive (happy) outlook. In contrast, advertisements like Allan's Anti-fat Remedy taught people that fatness was a disease, something that made people unhappy, weak, and stupid. These were the kinds of ideas that propelled the burgeoning of products promising weight loss that emerged by the second half of the 19th century. Significantly, the cartoons and editorials found in newspapers and periodicals complemented the many anti-fat advertisements, marking an early example of seamless commercial journalism where the editorial content matched and enhanced the advertisements.

The ad for Allan's Anti-fat Remedy is notable, then, as it is one of the earliest commercial articulations of fatness as a signifier of inferiority. It is also remarkable as one of the exceptional cases in which this idea of fat as a sign of inferior status is articulated in a forum speaking to African American readers. In general, the articles and advertisements within African American periodicals rarely focused on fat as a significant problem. Instead, concern about the *excessiveness* of fatness showed up primarily in publications geared toward a white, middle-class audience, marking a key instance in which we see how deeply racialized the concerns of the modern period were. The following chapter will return to this question of racialization, focusing on the ways that the anxiety about body size was not just a concern *among* white people but was precisely *about* the construction of whiteness. For now, however, it is important to notice how widespread the expression of body size anxiety was within "mainstream" periodicals and publications, such as *Life* and *Harper's Weekly*, which billed itself as the "Journal of Civilization." Periodicals such as these deeply assumed that their audiences were white, educated, and status conscious. Filled with articles and cartoons mocking African Americans and immigrants, the journals also included ads such as the one for Cuticura skin remedies, which so presumed an attitude of white supremacy that it could tout its product's quality by picturing two toddlers, a black female gazing kindly at a white male, under whom the words read, "As Different as Black from White."[33]

By the late 1800s and early 1900s, periodicals like *Life* and *Harper's Weekly* were peppered with cartoons commenting on—and mocking—the new phenomenon of the "average" fat person. These were different than those that caricatured the wealthy and greedy fat person, or those that used the fat person as a metaphor for some other national threat, or those that made a spectacle of the atypical fat curiosity. By the end of the 19th century, it was not just aging wealthy matrons and prosperous politicians and men of property whose bodies were marked with the sign of wealth—corpulence—in political cartoons and commentary. Nor did these newer cartoons focus on fat people as a human *oddity*. Instead, the cartoons in popular periodicals mocked fat people who were otherwise notable for their *typical* middle-class attributes. The objects of ridicule in these cartoons are not curiosities, but rather are emblematic of an entire new group of people, who are notable for their ordinariness: usually white, dressed in "respectable" clothing, and taking part in the lifestyles and rituals of the newly burgeoning middle class. There was no end of "fat jokes" about these people, portrayed as members of "mainstream" America who seemed to have partaken too much in the pleasures of their relatively easy lives.

The economic and social changes of the 19th century paved the way for these shifting ideas about corpulence. The growing middle class of the 1800s meant just that: more people experienced sufficient wealth or performed work that was either sedentary or less physically taxing than farmwork, so that bodies literally began to change, able to put on and keep on weight. Even factory work—dangerous as it was—often required less energy expenditure than farmwork as employees were required to stand in one place all day. In addition to a more sedentary lifestyle, food production began to change by the end of the 19th century. Mass production of foods on farms, factory-processed foods, and better transportation systems meant that more people had better access to more—though of course not necessarily healthier—food. As a result, people's bodies began to change in the late 19th century, growing more hefty and corpulent. And, ironically, it is at this point—when heftiness became more widespread and was not solely the prerogative of the wealthy—that fatness began to be seen as a *cultural problem*, worthy of public comment and concern. A new image of the fat person emerged on the scene. It is key to remember here that this image took hold long before the date that most historians argue the diet industries were firmly established—the 1920s—and that it had nothing to do with concerns about health, real or imagined.

These new middle-class "fat jokes" permeated U.S. culture by the end of the 19th century. A cartoon from the late 1880s, found in *Harper's Weekly*, for instance, pictures a fat man building his own swimming pool, certainly an extravagance that previously would have been available only to a select few. Despite owning his own swimming pool, however, he still doesn't know how to swim, so he "fills it with just enough water to come up to his neck by actual measurement." Due to the "immensity of his figure" he nearly drowns when he jumps in. Linking stupidly and fatness, the cartoonist has the fat man saying, "Don't see how I came to make such a mistake. Was positive I had only four feet of water; but when I jumped in I thought I had plumped down in the middle of the Atlantic Ocean."[34] Jokes about stupid fat men and women were a regular occurrence. In the early 1920s, for instance, we see the image of a fat man trying on a suit in a clothing store. The trick mirror makes the man look trim and fit, and his goofy wife exclaims, "Oh, take that one, Elmer! I love you in those slender college-boy effects!"[35]

A reader of *Life* and *Harper's Weekly* around the turn of the century could find many cartoons making fun of average "people with excess." In the 1880s, *Harper's Weekly* published a series of such cartoons, the first of which shows a balloon-like man, barely able to walk he is so fat; it's titled "A Heavy Mail."[36] One from the 1890s in *Life* pictured a very short, very round man in a tuxedo; the caption read, "A Full Dress Suit."[37] In 1915, we see a very fat man sitting on a bench that sags under his weight, reading "How to Develop a Slender Figure." In a play on words, the caption reads, "Corporation Counsel."[38] Another cartoon in 1915 pictures a bench with two large women and a large man sitting on it. The back of the bench says, "This seat accommodates five persons." "Does it?" reads the caption.[39] In another cartoon from the same year a very fat husband and wife sit in their living room, while their small dog looks on. "What's the use of being a lap-dog anyhow?" the caption reads.[40]

What is supposed to be funny about these people is their unbridled enjoyment of the privileges that had once been reserved for the upper class: travel, shopping excursions, theater, and, of course, good eating. In a 1908 *Life* cartoon, for instance, we see the back of a very fat woman who is walking briskly to a train, carrying a parasol and a number of satchels. Clearly, however, she is not going to fit through the set of double doors. The guard yells out to his coworkers, "Lively there now—both gates!"[41] A decade later, we see a middle-aged couple, both fat and resting uncomfortably against the side of a ship, presumably returning from a trip overseas. The caption reads, "Yes, indeed, travel does broaden one: was that the dinner-bell?" The same cartoonist, John C. Conacher, published a cartoon in the same decade that pictured a line to the theater; a well-dressed young woman exclaims, "Oh! Excuse me, sir! Did I step on your toes?" The extremely fat man, whose stomach protrudes far beyond his feet, responds, "sadly" the cartoon reads, "Ah! No, no, Miss, I'm afraid not!"

The cartoons prevalent in popular culture mocked middle-class white fat people for too excessively indulging in the pleasures and freedoms that had been ushered in during the advent of the modern era. These people, the cartoons appeared to say, did not know how to enjoy these new privileges without overdoing it. Unlike the older, wealthier classes, these "nouveau riche" seemed to be incapable of demonstrating the restraint and control necessary to experience these new liberties "responsibly." Moreover, the cartoons mocked this new class of people for even *daring to think themselves capable* of self-improvement and class mobility. One of the best examples of this is a 1908 *Life* cartoon that pictured a balloon-shaped man, dressed in an ill-fitting suit and vest, who was comically knotted up in exercise ropes. His round eyes seem almost to pop out of his head. Next to him is an "Anti-fat" potion, and a book titled "What a Man Should Weigh and Measure." The framed

SELF-TAUT

A FULL DRESS SUIT.

By the late 19th and early 20th century, cartoonists began to mock the phenomenon of middle-class fat people, suggesting the folly of their desires for the lifestyle of the rich. Opposite, "Self-Taut" derides a man's desire for education, while "A Full Dress Suit" above ridicules his enjoyment of urban leisure activities previously restricted to the upper class. Their fat bodies indicated how ill suited they were for the pleasures of the rich. (*Life*, March 12, 1908, 281; *Life*, August 19, 1897, 147.)

picture on the wall reads, "Knowledge Is Power." The caption, clearly making fun of his attempts at self-improvement, reads, "Self-taut."[42]

The work of scholars such as Hillel Schwartz in his now-classic *Never Satisfied* and Peter Stearns in his *Fat History* help us to understand why the middle class was mocked so extensively for their growing girths. Schwartz and Stearns argue that middle-class fat denigration in the United States emerged with industrialization and the birth of a consumer culture. The processes of industrialization and urbanization at the turn of the century depended on the expansion of this consumer culture. This meant buying more products, engaging in commercial leisure activities, and augmenting one's standard of living as a sign of one's success in life. This was the birth of the advertising industry—encouraging people to buy, not just that which was needed but also that which promised to provide pleasure, beauty, and fun.

As we moved from a primarily rural, farm-oriented nation to a primarily urban, consumer-oriented nation, many critics feared the loss of older habits of thrift and economy. These fears were exacerbated once again after the Depression, when new consumer options of buying on credit and spending beyond one's income became normative. Schwartz and Stearns argue that it was within this context, of concern over consumer excess and the potential for chaos created by the enjoyment of new freedoms and cultural pleasures, that both widespread fat denigration and the diet industries were born. This new imperative—to buy, to spend, to enjoy—came in direct conflict, however, with an older, Victorian, Anglo-Protestant ethic of deferred gratification, of containing one's impulses and desires, of working continually and diligently. Interestingly, this cultural conflict got played out—and continues to get played out—on the body. The individual bore the responsibility for maintaining control, for not exhibiting that abhorrent cultural excess. What Schwartz and Stearns argue, then, is that the United States' cultural fixation on the pursuit of thinness originated with the guilt induced by a society of excess that still harbored Victorian, Protestant ideals of restraint and hard work.[43]

One can see this most clearly in the religious connotations embedded within much dieting discourse; Banting said it most articulately when he referred to the "crying evil of obesity." By the late 19th and early 20th centuries, concerns about overconsumption and excessive desire in the newly industrialized, commercial culture found expression in the disparagement of fat bodies, both of the wealthy and greedy "fat cat" and of the middle-class fat person, unable to regulate the abundance of the modern world. In other words, the fat person stood as the symbol par excellence of the sin of gluttony. Interestingly, as early as the 1830s, some Americans perceived overconsumption of food with suspicion. At the time, however, the common idea was that the overconsumption of food led to a *thin* body, caused by the digestive problems of "dyspepsia." Too many rich foods, in other words, caused one to be thin, not corpulent. The most famous of those concerned with overconsumption was the Presbyterian minister Sylvester Graham, who encouraged his followers to reject "rich" foods like meat and tea, which led to overexcitement and self-pollution (i.e., masturbation), and to seek out instead a diet of plain vegetables and whole grain biscuits. (Today's graham crackers are a direct legacy of this minister's movement.)[44] By the late 1800s, others picked up on Graham's thinking; by this time, however, overconsumption—or gluttony—was clearly linked in the popular mind with obesity. Horace Fletcher, like Banting a wealthy businessman, became known as the "Great Masticator," encouraging his followers to chew their food one hundred times per minute, to consume less and to convert all the "pitiable gluttons" who populated the United States. Known for wearing white suits, symbolizing purity, Fletcher was obsessed with avoiding waste, and was even known to weigh his own feces. "Is there anything more sacred," he argued, "than serving faithfully at the altar of our Holy Efficiency?"[45] Popularizing even further the methods of Fletcher was the devout Seventh Day Adventist and physician John Harvey Kellogg. In his books and at his sanitariums he promoted what he called "Fletcherizing," intense and prolonged chewing of whole grain foods, as well as water cures and massage to treat his fat patients.[46]

By the end of the 19th century, Protestant dieting gurus like Fletcher and Kellogg emphasized the superiority of the thin body, one that showed restraint and control in the face of the excess of urban, commercial life. As Marie Griffith argues in *Born Again Bodies*, at the turn of the last century Protestants increasingly looked to the body for signs of a person's piety, a practice that dovetailed nicely with the more secular "science" of phrenology, which measured body parts (particularly the skull) for signs of a person's innate character and intelligence. As Griffith demonstrates, Protestant Christians increasingly saw fatness as an outward sign of both gluttony and a poor relationship to God, and thinness a marker of one's "chosenness." She concludes that the valorization of thinness and the development of fat stigma are the consequences of the continuing force of Protestantism's "craving for a perfectible, eternal, living, breathing, disciplined yet sensual body, along with its obverse, the sinister repugnance toward deficient, impoverished, or languishing bodies."[47] By the end of the 19th century, then, within mainstream Protestant thinking, fat became a sign of a deficient body, one that was not sufficiently demonstrating the restraint and control that God required.

Gender, Fat, and Modernity

For many cultural commentators at the turn of the century, the very hallmarks of civilized culture—new freedoms, urbanization, and work that was increasingly mental rather than physical—posed a threat to both men and to women, albeit for different reasons. As Gail Bederman argued in *Manliness and Civilization*, physicians, ministers, politicians, and writers began to worry in particular that civilization was endangering white middle-class men. These men, it seemed, were threatened both by "neurasthenia," a nervous disorder, and by the risk of becoming an "invert," the term used at the time for homosexuals.[48] In response to these concerns, cultural thinkers urged middle-class men to build up their strength, to regain the prowess that had been lost within the context of urban life and office work. An 1888 article in a Kansas newspaper, for instance, argued, "Men grow fat eating good lunches and club dinners and sitting in offices the rest of the time, when they ought to work or exercise strenuously full five hours a day."[49] The fat male body began to be seen as evidence of a man who had succumbed too much to the pleasures of civilization and whose constitution was too weak to withstand the pressures of modern life. Cultural critics began to see the fat male body as dirty, impure, and unchristian in its abundance. Instead, the ideal male body was firm, muscular, strong, able to participate in outside sport and recreation. As Elliot Gorn and Warren Goldstein argue, by the middle of the 19th century "Muscular Christianity" was making its mark, first in England and then in the United States. Mixing "morality, religion, and sport," this movement—of which the Young Men's Christian Association, or YMCA, is a product—focused on the importance of "masculinity, assertiveness, control over [the] environment."[50] Fatness was the antithesis of this masculine control, evidence that one was weak in both willpower and physical strength. As Henry Finck argued decades later in his very popular *Girth Control: For Womanly Beauty, Manly Strength, Health, and a Long Life for Everyone*, published in 1923, the perfect weight was "essential" for "efficiency and vitality in men." It was simply a matter, he argued, of gaining control over a "flabby will."[51] By the turn of the century, then, fat was viewed suspiciously for middle-class white men, evidence of the enervating force of modern life. A man needed to battle fat if he was to survive in modern culture.

The risks of modern life were different for middle-class men and women, according to Anglo-American cultural commentators of the time. Dr. Leonard Williams, for instance, in a 1926 text argued that men were naturally "katabolic" creatures, meaning their metabolisms were inherently active and energetic. He contrasted their "katabolic" metabolisms to women's "anabolic" systems, ones that were slow, designed to store energy for the necessary rites of pregnancy and lactation. He explained that "Man is intended by Nature to hunt his game, or to exercise his muscles in an equivalent sense. When he fails to do this, preferring an arm-chair, hot baths, cooked foods, and woolly undergarments to an outdoor life, he is behaving as though he were an anabolic creature, and in the majority of cases he suffers the anabolic penalty of storing fat and becoming corpulent."[52] In other words, by partaking too much in the comforts of modern life, men became like women: anabolic, fat, corpulent. In this line of thinking, civilized culture, with its hot baths, cooked foods, and cozy underwear, clearly damaged men. Fatness was both a result and a sign of this weakening culture.

According to cultural commentators like S. Weir Mitchell, who prescribed his famous "rest cures," and Dr. Williams, modern life posed a risk to middle-class white women for reasons widely disparate from the creature comforts that so risked the strength of modern men. Instead, it was the transformed cultural environment, with its newly established freedoms available to women in both politics and consumer life, that threatened the well-being of modern females. Since the middle of the 19th century there had been in both the United States and England a lively women's movement. Women agitated for property rights, educational opportunities, religious power, legal rights, and, most explicitly, suffrage rights. Women gained the vote in 1920 in the United States, and in 1928 in England. By the early decades of the 20th century, there was also a growing movement for women's education, including both the beginnings of women's colleges and the opening of men's schools to women. Consumer culture quickly latched on to the rhetoric of what has since become known as the "first wave" of feminism, bringing with it the possibilities for heterosocial mingling in urban dance halls and movie theaters, a new style of clothing and hair—the flapper's dress and the short hair bob, both of which revealed more of women's bodies than ever before—and new forms of recreation for women, from bicycle riding to cigarette smoking. For Williams, as for other conservative commentators in this period, these changes of modern life were explicitly damaging to women:

There is nowadays a great deal of ignorant and pernicious nonsense spoken, written and preached about the essential equality of the sexes. It is said that the differences now observed are due entirely to suggestion and environment, and that consequently if the woman's mental atmosphere and physical environment are caused to approximate more closely to man's, the differences will disappear. These stupid, unnatural, and wholly vicious attempts to tamper with the mental and physical differences between the two sexes can only lead, as indeed they are fast leading, to serious disaster. . . . It is no more possible to convert a normal anabolic creature into one who is effectively katabolic than it is possible to convert a plum-pudding into anything resembling a gun.[53]

Although Williams, like many of his contemporaries, was sure that it was impossible to convert a woman into a man (or a plum pudding into a gun), he was concerned about the forms of physical education and sporting events available to women that seemed to be aimed in this direction:

The violent exercises, the athletic contests, the combative games (we were at one moment threatened with a display of female boxing) provoke the emergence, and, in many cases, the ultimate predominance of the kata-bolic side of women and the consequent abasement of the normal ana-bolic side, with the result of converting what would have been a good wife and mother into a homosexual who fails in every normal adaptation and becomes a byword and a shaking of the head among her neighbours. Save to their sister homosexuals, who, though daily on the increase, are still happily in the minority, lesbians are not lovable.[54]

There is, of course, much to comment on in his thinking about the development of lesbians, not least of which is to point out his convoluted logic that first poses the "impossibility" of making women into katabolic beings, and then suggests that such attempts make women into lesbians, who are "daily on the rise." But the point relevant to this discussion is that one would think that Williams, considering women "anabolic creatures," would perceive women's corpulence as natural and normal. This was S. Weir Mitchell's point of view, and why he prescribed rest cures and milk diets for his female patients. Williams makes an abrupt shift, however, arguing that *fat* in women was also evidence of the ways that the excesses of modern culture—too much comfort for the men, too much freedom for the women—had warped their minds, their bodies, and their sexualities. In the following quotation he speaks of the "dangers" of modern forms of child raising and education that allow young men too many comforts and young women too much exercise and too many rights and freedoms:

The dangers involved include the development of a *very intractable type of obesity*, and, what is far more serious, such a degree of failure of adaptation to social environment as may ultimately lead either to the prison or the madhouse. Thus are perfectly innocent and potentially useful citizens sacrificed on the sorry shrine of a purely imaginary equality of the sexes.[55]

"Intractable obesity" becomes seen as both a result of the excesses of modern life and as a sign portending other problems—homosexuality, criminality, and mental illness. In Goffman's terms, fat becomes a form of stigma that in itself is bad but that also conjures a whole host of other troubling issues as well.

Women, Body Size, and Class Culture

While the commentators who worried about the problems of modern life saw negative consequences for both men *and* women, there was particular concern about women. As Joan Brumberg argued in her classic historical study of anorexia, *Fasting Girls*, women were often the targets for cultural fears about excess consumerism in the latter part of the 19th century. Indeed, as the philosopher Susan Bordo so elegantly reminds us in *Unbearable Weight*, the late 19th and 20th centuries inherited from the Enlightenment an "agonistic relationship of mind/body" that linked an abhorrence of the body with the female while associating the male with rationality. As Bordo explains, the prevailing cultural idea was that women lacked sufficient rational qualities and were therefore especially weak in will, unable to control the impulses of corporal desires, and susceptible to the siren call of consumer culture. At the same time that females were seen to be at most risk for exhibiting body and cultural excess, however, the dominant ideology of "true womanhood" also presumed and expected women to "maintain civilization" through their behavior, their clothing, and their exchanges both with men and with children. In terms of fatness, this meant that women were considered more likely than men to exhibit "bodily excess" because their rational qualities were not sufficiently developed to control their appetites for food and comfort. At the same time, however, for white women fatness was a bigger transgression than it was for men, because women were expected to maintain that line of civilized culture. For middle-class men, a certain level of sexual desire, violent impulses, and healthy appetite for food was a sign that they had not been too weakened by modern life; women, however, were not only expected to show no evidence of these traits but were also expected to keep in check those same impulses in their husbands and children.[56]

By the beginning of the 20th century, then, fatness for women became associated less with matronliness, healthful fertility, or attractive sensuality than it had in earlier decades. A very humorous 1885 short story, written by Luke Lovart, illuminates the tensions resulting from this shift regarding beauty, women, and fat.[57] Lovart's protagonists are a husband and wife in their mid-thirties, married for fifteen years, who face a "growing" problem: the wife's weight gain. Important to recognize in this story is that Lovart's protagonists are part of a newly established and expanding middle class; as such the husband would have found himself in particular need of a "slim" wife in order to augment his own social status. As Susan Bordo wrote about the late 19th century:

> In the reigning body symbolism of the day, a frail frame and lack of appetite signified not only spiritual transcendence of the desires of the flesh but *social* transcendence of the laboring, striving "economic" body. Then, as today, to be aristocratically cool and unconcerned with the mere facts of material survival was highly fashionable. The hungering bourgeois wished to appear, like the aristocrat, above the material desires that in fact ruled his life. The closest he could come was to possess a wife whose ethereal body became a sort of fashion statement of *his* aristocratic tastes. If he could not be or marry an aristocrat, he could have a wife who looked like one, a wife whose non-robust beauty and delicate appetite signified her lack of participation in the taxing "public sphere."[58]

Lovart's short story illuminates this very desire for the "ethereal" wife that Bordo describes. At the beginning of the story, the husband explains that he had "married an angel" but "instead of developing wings, she began to develop adipose tissue. Instead of soaring about the earth, she pressed day by day more heavily upon it. In other words, she grew fatter and fatter." The confrontation he has with his wife about her weight reveals not only his anger at her weight gain, but also the changing connotations of cultural vocabulary regarding weight. When he refers to her "growing corpulence," she replies, "You are very rude, Edward. What a horrid word to use!" She prefers that he call her "matronly" or "comfortable."[59] When he accuses her of cheating on the Banting method (one of the first published "diets"), she replies, "You asked what was impossible. It was easy enough for you. Men are so wiry. Women have such a sinking feeling sometimes." Extremely angry, the husband retorts, "No law, human or divine, can compel me to remain with a woman who is constantly swelling. Where would the world be if this were tolerated? It would have to be reconstructed on a larger scale." She answers, "You are foolish and unreasonable. I shall get a divorce for cruelty and I shall go to my mother at this very moment." "Her house is too small. . . . Do give her time to enlarge it," he replies. Their final exchange sums up their feelings for each other: "Edward, you don't deserve the name of a man." "And you are really too much of a woman for me," he replies.[60]

Even the mother-in-law, herself a large woman, gets involved. She wonders why he is making such a fuss over her daughter's "fullishness," another kind reference to weight: "What folly! You can't expect her to remain a girl forever."[61] She further explains that her daughter's *embonpointment* is a "sign of her unfailing good temper." He bitterly replies that he wants a "less visible" sign.[62] He even asks his wife to "lay" herself out for "a little misery" if that would make her more lean.

By the end he realizes, through a twisting plot and a series of mixed-up identities, that he does not like to have his own appearance mocked and is happy to have his chubby wife back. While he concludes that her "original sin" of corpulence remained, "What does it matter, after all," he asks the readers, "a little more or a little less of the envelope when the letter remains the same and such a charming one?"[63] What is interesting about this story is the tension it reveals between the older, gentler terms referring to body size and the new, "rude" ones; between an older perspective valuing "matronly" women and a new preference for slim wives even in midlife; between domestic fidelity and a new cultural aesthetic of thinness and upward mobility. While it at first glance seems the domestic fidelity and older values win out, notice that he never concludes that he likes the looks of her more portly body. Moreover, throughout the story, the jokes are primarily at his wife's expense. And finally, in the end, he doesn't have to tolerate a fat wife, because she loses over forty pounds in the shock of thinking her husband dead. Lean has triumphed in this story, even if there is a passing applause given to kindness and tolerance.

Newspaper clippings from the same time period as Lovart's short story suggest that angst over "matrimonial weight" was not just fictional. The *Raleigh Register* in 1884 printed a lengthy article describing the weight loss efforts of a young woman who wanted a young man to propose to her. When the doctor asked if she was willing to "follow a prescription" to deal with her "adipose tissue," she responded, "Willing! Willing! I would be willing to go through fire, or have my flesh cut off with red hot knives. There is nothing I would not be willing to endure if I could only get rid of this condition."[64] Decades later the *New York Times* reported on a similar case to the Lovart short story, describing a Swiss divorce case where the husband sued his wife for divorce based on "abnormal obesity." He complained that she "ate as much as four adults and his savings were squandered buying food for her." In response, the wife defended herself by saying that she had taken a "dozen different medicines to reduce her appetite and weight without effect." Although the Swiss court found in favor of the wife, this did not mean there was a generous attitude toward fat women.[65] Writers often urged middle-class women to emulate the self-control of the upper-class women who were already accustomed to managing wealth and abundance. For instance, in 1923 an early weight loss "expert," the British writer Cecil Webb-Johnson, encouraged readers to be more like aristocratic women:

> Women of the British upper classes are known to practise the sternest self-denial in order to retain their youthful looks even into middle-age. The middle-class woman in comfortable circumstances, however, is not accustomed to deny herself anything in the way of gastronomic indulgence, and has never been taught the value of exercise. Wherefore when she reaches the age of forty or thereabouts, she is liable to be a shapeless mass of fat. Middle-aged women of the lower middle-classes, whose means allow them to indulge in practically unlimited eating and drinking, often tend to become enormously stout.

Elsewhere in his book *Why Be Fat?* he describes with contempt those who failed his diet program:

> They cannot deny themselves their feasts, and go back to their gorging and guzzling again. Their end is unenviable; but if they prefer some succulent dish to life and comfort that is their own affair. They are veritably among those who dig their graves with their teeth. This is a free country, and if people choose to eat themselves to death, as some poor wretches drink themselves to death, there is nothing to stop them.[66]

Abundant food and physical comfort threatened middle-class and poor women. According to the logic of many conservative commentators of the time, however, a new wealth of political and consumer opportunities threatened women of all classes.

By the turn of the century, fatness often became a sign that a woman had taken part in activities that typically had been reserved only for men, whether in politics, consumer culture, or family life. We see this critique of women who had pushed the boundaries of acceptable behavior particularly well in the increasingly popular tourist postcards sent in the first half of the 20th century. Often sent from beach resorts or national parks, these cards were comic in nature, and frequently arrived with clever sayings from the sender.[67]

Many of the cards pictured cartoon images of fat middle-class women traveling on trains and ships, often after large shopping sprees; others pictured fat women at resorts, bathing in the ocean or resting on the beach.

Interestingly, these postcards reveal an important irony in the history of women in the United States. They clearly mark the growth of tourism and the emergence of an increasingly mobile population, one that travels not only to follow work (which had been true for centuries) but now, with money and new opportunities, also for pleasure. These tourist postcards—so often written by women—also provide evidence of the increased mobility and independence of women, particularly those who were white and middle class, enhanced by the strong feminist movement of the first decades of the century as well as the advent of car travel in the 1910s and 1920s.[68] (African American women still faced the danger and discrimination of Jim Crow laws, which made travel very difficult and staying at resorts reserved for whites impossible. Poor and working-class women had less money available for leisure travel, though many of the beach resorts and national parks did indeed cater to the working class.) At the same time, however, these tourist postcards also provide evidence of the ways that new controls can quickly move in to replace the old ones that had disappeared. That is, at the same time that these cards illuminate the ways that certain women in the United States now had more freedoms—to travel, to enjoy leisure time often with money of their own, to take part in a public life of commercial culture—they also mocked those very women for their unbridled enjoyment. Through their biting ridicule these cards formed part of a backlash that constructed a new set of bodily restraints on women, replacing the old constraints that had hindered their access to public life. These postcards suggest that as women gained more political and geographic freedom in the early 20th century, they were increasingly curtailed by a set of body disciplines that mocked and denigrated all those who did not seem to display proper modes of bodily control.

Many of the postcards ridicule middle-class women who have, according to these images, clearly indulged too excessively in the growing consumer culture of both tourism and purchased goods. A consistent saying found on the postcards announces, "Travel Really 'Broadens' One." In one we see a fat woman as she perches precariously on a stool at a soda fountain, her bottom hanging off both sides, as the waiter hands her a huge ice cream sundae. In a similar image we see a woman with an enormous behind sitting on a stool at a soda fountain eating a multilayered sundae; she says to a slim companion, drinking only a cup of coffee, "Travel really 'broadens' one!" In another postcard we see a car stopped on a road out west, with the same caption, "Travel

I am an innocent Pin
Cushion. !

Certainly *Broadens* One!" A fat woman is trying unsuccessfully to wedge herself into the passenger side of the car. The woman's huge behind, accentuated by the size of her tiny feet, barely fits through the car of the door. The trunk is stuffed with suitcases, making it too full to close, suggesting that this woman clearly has bought too much stuff. Her slim male companion, presumably her husband, looks on with big eyes. She cannot fit, just as the trunk cannot fit with all the suitcases. Both her eating and her shopping, the cartoon suggests, are out of control.[69] In another card making fun of the traveling middle-class woman, we see a fat woman dressed in furs and hat sitting astride a train, hanging on unsteadily. A skinny man, presumably the conductor, looks out at her with big eyes. The caption reads, "I expect you've treated yourself so well they'll have to put you on top of the train when you come home!"

Other cards focused less on travel and more on shopping itself. "Sorry I had to rush away—and leave so much BEHIND!" reads one that shows a fat woman with protruding buttocks, wearing nothing but a lacy undergarment

Postcards in the first half of the 20th century often poked fun at fat, white, middle-class women enjoying travel—whether on bicycles or in cars. The buttocks on the bicycling woman in this early 20th-century postcard opposite was plumped with fill and could serve as a pincushion. The caption reads, "I am an Innocent Pin Cushion!" Above, the fat woman getting into the car has overindulged in both eating and shopping according to this later postcard. (Courtesy of Alice Marshall Women's History Collection, Penn State Harrisburg, Middletown, Pennsylvania.)

and high heels, running out of a tailor's shop, after she has been frightened by a mouse. A shocked tailor, well dressed in his suit and tie, looks on. In another we see a well dressed woman bending over, her huge bottom taking up nearly a quarter of the card. She points to a chair in a furniture store but tells the salesman, "It won't do, it's not large enough for my big sittin' room." We're supposed to laugh at the double entendre, referring both to her big buttocks and to her huge living room, a sign of her luxurious lifestyle.

Many of the cards focused particularly on the humor of traveling women enjoying beachside resorts. In these postcards we see that women who did not toe a line of bodily control were presented as so comically huge that they literally overcome the elements, blocking out the sun, stemming the tide, or causing tidal waves of their own. In one a male and female couple kiss under a hammock that holds a fat woman, whose bottom protrudes down and on whose stomach rests a pitcher marked "ginger ale." "We are keeping out of the hot sun here!" the man says. Another shows a fat woman wearing a bathing suit at the edge of the ocean; a baby rests in the shade of her bottom as a thin male and female couple look on. "Found a shady spot here! Take the sun a bit to get through this!" the caption reads. In another, two

Cartoonists mocked fat women who enjoyed new travel and leisure opportunities—such as bathing at the beach—as so extraordinarily large that they could even block the sun or stop the tide. (Courtesy of Alice Marshall Women's History Collection, Penn State Harrisburg, Middletown, Pennsylvania.)

dogs rest under the bottom of a woman bending over to pick up a beach ball. "Found the shadiest spot on the beach!" the card reads. In other cards fat women wade into the ocean, usually bending down to fill a bucket or pick up a shell. We see huge buttocks, usually with some sort of petticoat; the captions read something along the lines of "high tide," and we often see thin people nearly drowning in their wake. In one a policeman lectures a fat woman who lounges on the beach in her swimsuit and bathing cap, "Get up, Missus, and let the tide come in!" Certainly one can understand from these postcards that the fat female body is not supposed to enjoy the pleasures of the beach and sunbathing that were newly available to middle- and working-class Americans in the first half of the century. Moreover, they suggest that the fat female body is so gross (in both senses of the word—disgusting and huge) that it literally has the dangerous power of controlling natural forces of sun and sea. The fat female body is not welcome in *this* geographic space because it takes up too *much* geographic space.

Ironically, then, even as more women were able to enjoy new freedoms—of travel, of leisure, of tourism, of money available to be spent at their own discretion—they also experienced a diminishment of space. Any woman who could not or would not maintain control of her body size had less figurative and literal space available to her. In other words, these postcards illuminate the establishment of a symbolic *place*—or rather, *no-place*—of the fat woman in the 20th century. It is no wonder that the diet industries began to flourish within the cultural context of a burgeoning fat stigma.

The Power of Fat Stigma

One of the books most regularly advertised in *Life* and *Harpers' Weekly* was Vance Thompson's *Eat and Grow Thin*, published in 1914 by E. P. Dutton in both England and the United States. Using language very similar to that of Banting fifty years earlier, Thompson described the "the tragedy of fat!":

> One could write books, plays, poems on the subject. One thinks of the beautiful women one has known—loved perhaps—who have vanished forever, drowned in an ocean of turbulence and tallow; of actresses who filled one's soul with shining dreams—and now the dreams are wrecked on huge promontories; of statesmen and rulers who lumber the earth, now mere teeth and stomach, as though God had created them, like Mirabeau, only to show to what extent the human skin can be stretched without breaking. The tragedy of fat![70]

While Thompson goes on to discuss the health benefits of weight loss, this is almost an afterthought, a way to legitimate the need to eliminate the possibility of drowning in an "ocean of turbulence and tallow." The key risk, in Thompson's articulation of the dangers of fat, was a cultural one: a loss of status, of beauty, and of power.

As Peter Stearns so astutely points out in his *Fat History*, the diet industries did not create the culture that privileges thin and denigrates fat. Neither the tourist postcards, the critical commentary on the effects of modern life, nor the political cartoons in magazines like *Life* and *Harper's Weekly* were products of the diet industries. Nevertheless, individuals, physicians, and companies quickly began to pick up on this emergent fat stigma, articulating it back to consumers and exacerbating the cultural fear of fatness. As the cultural anxieties induced by the processes and excesses of modern life fixated themselves on the body, the early advertising industries found a perfect new set of products and services to sell, ones designed to diminish our bodies into a size that could deflect any recrimination. This concern about modernity and excess, however, is only a partial explanation for the increasing denigration of fat and policing of body shape that we see in popular magazines like *Godey's Lady's Book*, *Harper's Weekly*, and *Life*. As the cartoons, short stories, and diet tracts discussed in this chapter demonstrated, the sign of one's competence at navigating the modern world and successfully moving into the upper classes became a slim figure. But this does not adequately explain why the slim figure would become the sign of control and wealth. Indeed, the *fat* figure had previously been the sign of wealth and power. The following chapter takes up this question, exploring the ways that concern about the excesses of modernity dovetailed with powerful ideas about race, evolution, and civilization that were popular at the time. The fat body, I argue, became seen as unable to manage the modern world *precisely because* of its association with inferior bodies, or, to use the language of the "obesity experts" of the time, with the primitive, the abnormal, and the uncivilized.

3

Fat and the Un-Civilized Body

In 1864, one of the earliest anti-fat physicians, Dr. Watson Bradshaw, wrote that in "advanced nations" (and by these he meant England, the United States, and France) a "multiplied chin and an abdomen of enormous periphery do not entitle the possessor of any distinction." He compared this to "primitive cultures" where, he argued, a big stomach continued to bestow cultural status.[1] In the early 20th century, an American physician, Dr. Leonard Williams, also pointed to the supposed link between civilization and obesity: "It is to be admitted that there exists a settled belief among the uneducated, and even among many of the educated, that it is a man's duty to eat as much as he possibly can, in order to keep up his strength. This belief probably reaches back to the most primitive days when food was scarce and its enjoyment intermittent."[2] According to this theory, lower-class people harbored unconscious memories of famine and hunger, thus prompting them to eat in excess even in times of plenty. In contrast, wealthy people literally had this tendency to enjoy food in great quantities "bred out" of them. Williams went on to explain that men of "savage tribes" preferred women who were fat and round; in England and the United States, however, Williams noted approvingly, women were fighting their "endocrinal" tendency to gain weight because they knew that fat women were "repulsive sights, degrading alike to their sex and civilization."[3] Published in both the United States and England, Henry Finck's popular 1923 dieting book *Girth Control* took up a similar refrain to that of Williams and Bradshaw. In elaborate detail Finck described the various fattening processes and beauty standards of fat appreciation among Africans, Polynesians, the Turkish, and the Aborigines of Australia. In his list of those who valued fat, however, no European or "Western" countries were included. Indeed, he quickly reminded his readers that they were "modern British and American citizens" whose "standards of good looks are different from those of Hottentots, Moors and Turks."[4]

The comments of Bradshaw, Williams, and Finck, covering a span of more than sixty years, point us to a rationale for fat stigma that has gone surprisingly unexplored, indeed even unremarked, in both the study of the modern period and the exploration of the history of fat and dieting. Many scholars have observed that fat denigration seems to have had less hold among people of color in both the United States and England, usually citing either the existence of more pressing issues of survival or simply a different standard of beauty. In other words, a greater tolerance for corpulence has something to do with the racial identities and experiences of people of color. What has not been explored, however, is the way that the denigration of fatness is intricately linked to the racial identities and experiences of white people in the United States and England. The moral outrage against fat that developed in the 19th century and that was firmly in place by the time Finck wrote his book in the 1920s had everything to do with the construction of whiteness and the racial identities of white "mainstream" Americans and Britons. Writers like Schwartz, Stearns, and Brumberg have clearly outlined the ways that a cultural hatred of fatness emerged in order to cope with the ambivalence and anxiety that the excesses of the modern period brought. This chapter will explore yet another, deeper layer of this emergent denigration of fat: the ways that fat hatred was linked to cultural, religious, political, and scientific thinking regarding civilization and evolution. Nineteenth-century thinking about the "natural" evolution of human races into stages of civilization meant not just the complex articulation of racial, gender, and sexual hierarchies, but also the construction of certain types of body types as superior. Marie Griffith argues that by the end of the 19th century, white Protestants began to see a fat body as a "deficient" body, due primarily to its associations with gluttony, and a thin body as one closer to God, as evidenced by the control and constraint one presumably had to demonstrate to maintain that body. By exploring the thinking of 19th-century scientists and philosophers, however, one begins to see that fat was a sign of a deficient body for the white Protestants whom Griffith describes because it was already linked to the typographies and detailed descriptions of those designated as "inferior" on the human classification schemes of evolutionary scientists. In other words, fat was not white.

The words that Williams, Bradshaw, and Finck use in their writings—"advanced nations," "modern citizens," and "civilization," as contrasted to "primitive," "degrading," and "Hottentots"—are fundamental to understanding the worldview in which fat denigration became linked to racial and gender hierarchies. These terms are all references to beliefs common in the 19th and early 20th centuries about science, evolution, and the "perfectable" body. Drawing on a variation of Aristotle's "Great Chain of Being," Western philosophers had for centuries categorized all of existence in a line toward the great perfection of God—from the minerals that constituted the lowest rung of the chain, to the flora and fauna that constituted the middle rungs, and finally to the highest rungs on which existed human beings. Within each grouping, differentiations of gradations existed; for instance, philosophers placed some animals, such as domesticated cats and horses, higher on the list than wild bores or rats. Europeans always emerged on the highest rungs of human beings, and, not surprisingly, those doing the classifications generally placed their own "type" highest on the list. European explorers, traders, and naturalists of the 16th, 17th, and 18th centuries wrote at length of their observations on the "inferior" types of humans, from Asians to Africans to Native Americans. Their travel writings became more "evidence" for the hierarchy and also served as philosophical justification for oppression, imperialism, and unjust social orders within their own environments.

By the 19th century, however, the power of Enlightenment thinking, with its focus on rationality and individual rights, the emerging Industrial Revolution, and widespread democratic revolutions challenged the power not only of monarchies, the Catholic Church, and imperialist governments, but also the legitimacy of slavery and unequal relations between servants and masters, adults and children, and men and women. Significantly, as scholars such as Londa Schiebinger have argued, within this political, social, and economic upheaval of the 19th century, new justifications for vastly unequal hierarchical arrangements and oppressions emerged to replace the old ones that were being so fundamentally undermined. The rising institutions of science and medicine now provided "objective" evidence of "natural" inferiority among women, the poor, and colonized people. Thus the lack of political, economic, and social rights were now justified on the basis of "inherent" differences rather than unfair political systems.[5]

Within this context, early 19th-century naturalists focused intensely on cataloging the different peoples of the world, including in their descriptions extensive details on "distinctive" bodily traits and cultural practices. By the end of the 19th century, the emerging fields of anthropology and sociology had picked up the cataloguing habits of the naturalists and, earlier, the travel writers. Anthropologists and sociologists drew from the evolutionary theories proposed by Charles Darwin in his 1859 *On the Origin of Species* and 1871 *The Descent of Man*, adapting and often revising his ideas as explanations for the same Great Chain of Being now described as the "advancement of civilization." Christian theologians, far from rejecting Darwin's work, instead tailored it to their own thinking, emphasizing the role of God's will in determining the abilities of various peoples to evolve to the highest position near Divinity.

As Gail Bederman has argued in her far-reaching study *Manliness and Civilization*, dominant thinking at the turn of the last century positioned white males at the very pinnacle of the evolutionary hierarchy. The 1893 World's Columbian Exposition in Chicago, for instance, portrayed this picture of the "advancement of civilization" quite literally through its major exhibits, the White City and the Midway. Fair planners designed the White City as a utopian version of the perfected future, highlighting all the highest achievements of man's ingenuity, engineering, and scientific discovery. Women's rights activists such as Susan B. Anthony complained vociferously to Congress that all the women's applications for inclusion in the White City had been rejected, suggesting that women had no role in the rise of civilization. The response was the creation of a "Board of Lady Managers," who were authorized to create a Woman's Building on one edge of the White City, implying, its creators rather sadly pointed out, that women were within civilization but not really of it. The Midway was the location for the international exhibits, which the official on-site historian of the fair described as consisting of "Dahomey, Indian, Chinese, Turkish, German and other villages, tenanted by living representatives of savage, civilized, and semi-civilized nations." Indeed, the order of exhibits moved upward from the most "savage," the Dahomey—a West African group—and Native Americans, to that of the most "civilized," the Irish, then the German, and, finally, as the official historian explained, the "best site being allotted to Great Britain, near the northern inlet." Despite the objections of well-known activists like Frederick Douglass and Ida B. Wells in their internationally circulated pamphlet *The Reason Why the Colored American Is Not in the World's Columbian Exposition*, no American people of color were included in the White City, the vision of perfected civilization, other than two small exhibits in the Woman's Building.[6] In a striking visual fashion, then, the Columbian Exposition in 1893 represented the common thinking about race, gender, and civilization. White, northern European cultures were at the top of the hierarchy, African and Native American at the bottom, Asian and southern European in the middle. Women constituted yet another complexity in this picture, for within each of these groups females clearly existed a step down from whatever heights of civilization their male brethren could reach. Indeed, by definition within this evolutionary scheme, women could never reach the pinnacle of humanity as they were by definition intrinsically inferior, and, as some argued, not quite human.

Interestingly, within this line of thinking the differentiation between women and men was most pronounced the higher one rose in the "civilized ranks," and least pronounced among the more "savage" people, whose size, clothing, and cultural roles appeared scandalously close according to contemporary observers. Indeed, a mark of a civilized nation was, according to prevalent 19th-century thinking, clearly demarcated roles, dress, deportment, and even physiognomy between men and women. Scholars Nicole Rafter and Mary Gibson explain the typical 19th-century belief about gender differences and evolution: "Among lower races, women resemble men in their strength, intelligence, and sexual promiscuity. Through sexual selection, however, males—whether animal or human—choose mates for feminine qualities like beauty, modesty, passivity, and domesticity. Evolution, therefore, increasingly differentiates the sexes, with men dominating the public sphere of politics and work and women relegated to motherhood in the home."[7] This helps to explain the protagonist in Luke Lovart's short story, who so desires a thin, compliant wife to complement his own strength and assertiveness. Her corpulence and her vivacity not only mark her as unfeminine, but also mark him as part of an inferior, "less evolved" class for having a partner so similar to himself in both body size and temperament.

The scientific and religious experts who constructed these theories of racial and gender hierarchies based their ideas on the classification and differentiation of peoples according to a multitude of factors: geographical location, cultural practices such as foodways and clothing, and social norms regarding gender, the elderly, and children. Above all, it depended on the minute observation of bodily attributes: skin color, hair texture, the shape and size of skulls, ears, noses, and lips, and the appearance of genitalia. Experts "read" the body for signs and evidence of primitive status or, conversely, for signs of genius and aristocratic breeding. They created complex charts that linked racial typing, evolutionary status, and bodily characteristics, collecting the skulls, skeletons, and preserved body parts of cadavers to further their investigations and provide evidence of their often-competing evolutionary theories. The developing fields of anthropology, sociology, and psychology all incorporated theories of evolution and body typing, codifying and popularizing the work that had begun centuries earlier with the writings of naturalists and travelers. One of the best known of these is Lewis Henry Morgan's 1877 *Ancient Society*, in which he postulated that there were three major stages of social evolution: savagery, barbarism, and civilization. In his influential *Studies in the Psychology of Sex*, Havelock Ellis explained in detail the development of beauty. He argued that the bodies and faces of Europeans displayed spiritual beauty while Africans exhibited and enjoyed bodily characteristics that were animalistic and, basically, ugly.[8] For many 19th-century social reformers, the body served both as evidence of inferior status and as the key to improving the lives and conditions of inferior people. In his campaign to educate and thus "save" Native Americans, for instance, the founder of Carlisle Industrial Indian School, Richard Henry Pratt, focused not only on eradicating students' indigenous languages and on teaching them "gender-appropriate" work skills. As John Bloom explained in *To Show What an Indian Can Do: Sports at Indian Boarding Schools*, Pratt also focused intensely on teaching "proper" body etiquette: physical education with flags and marching for the girls, and strength-building American sports like football for the boys. By changing their bodies, Pratt hoped to change their "primitive" culture and identities.

One of the key bodily signs of inferiority for scientists and thinkers of the 19th and early 20th centuries was fatness. Interestingly, this has gone relatively unremarked in the literature on 19th -and early 20th-century thinking on evolution and civilization. Yet much of the writing in this time period described in detail the fatness of "primitive" peoples and of all women, using that trait as evidence of inferior status. Fat became clearly identified as a physical trait that marked its bearers as people lower on the evolutionary and racial scale—Africans, "native" peoples, immigrants, criminals, and prostitutes. All women were also considered to be more at risk of fatness, another sign of their status lower on the evolutionary scale than men. Thin, in contrast, became identified as a physical trait marking those who were higher on the evolutionary and racial scale—aristocrats, white people, men. Fatness, then, served as yet another attribute demarcating the divide between civilization and primitive cultures, whiteness and blackness, good and bad. When Williams urged his "British and American" women readers to avoid fatness because it was "degrading" to their "sex and civilization," he meant just that. In other words, to become fat, for these white British and American women, meant that one had moved down—had degraded—on the scale of civilization.

If European men held the highest place on the scale of civilization, far below were the "Hottentots, Moors, and Turks" whom Henry Finck alluded to disparagingly in his popular diet book *Girth Control*. At the very bottom of the scale of civilization were the Hottentots, which was the Western, denigrating name given to the Khoikhoi people of South Africa. Ever since the 17th century, travel writers and naturalists had focused on the Khoikhoi as the possible "missing link," the connecting "species" between apes and humans. Thus, not only were the Khoikhoi described as the bottom of civilization, experts also studied them for evidence of animal-like traits and behavior. The most famous of the Khoikhoi was Sara Baartman, known more popularly as the "Venus Hottentot." Historians speculate that Baartman was either a slave or an indentured servant in Cape Town, who fell into the hands of a Dutch trader, Alexander Dunlop. (Indeed, Saartjie Baartman is her Dutch name; we have no evidence of her real name.) Dunlop brought her to England in 1810, where he sold her to Hendrick Cezar, who exhibited her for nearly four years. The public could pay a few shillings to see Baartman, who was presented as one of many exotic specimens and curiosities on display in London at the time. One could see tropical birds, African animals, and Indian artifacts along with dwarves, fat people, and other human "curiosities" on a typical visit to London in the early 19th century. According to Sadiah Qureshi, Baartman was one of many Khoisan women who were brought to Europe, exhibited, and studied. Baartman herself was shown on a "stage two feet high, along which she was led by her keeper, and exhibited like a wild beast; being obliged to walk, stand, or sit as he ordered." These popular shows eventually caused a public outcry, as abolitionists in England (where the slave trade had been banned since 1807) doubted the veracity of her "signed" acknowledgment that she was working of her own will and being fairly paid. Cezar then moved her to Paris, where he continued exhibiting her until 1815, when she died, still a young woman.[9]

Like the displays of other "exotic" humans, the exhibits of Baartman focused on her physical distinctiveness and differences from presumably "typical" Europeans. What drew most attention were her large buttocks (referred to as her steatopygia) and pendulous breasts, both on view for the public. In addition, there was endless speculation about her supposedly enlarged labia, often referred to as a "Hottentot apron." When Baartman lived in Paris, the eminent scientist Georges Cuvier became interested in her, observing her naked for three days at the Muséum national d'Histoire naturelle. After she died, Cuvier and his colleagues had her body transposed immediately to the museum for an autopsy, bypassing all the normal laws of the city regarding cadavers, in the name of important scientific inquiry. He dissected her body, focusing on her brain, her genitals, her breasts, and her buttocks, writing up the results in an essay that provided "definitive" evidence of her low-level status on the scale of civilization.[10] Visitors to Paris could see a plaster cast of Baartman (in profile to emphasize her buttocks), her skeleton, and her labia (preserved in a jar of formaldehyde) at the Musée de l'Homme until the 1970s, when criticism from feminist and African activists forced the museum to remove the items from public display. After years of pressure from the South African government, her remains were finally repatriated to her home country in 2002, where she received a formal burial.[11]

Many scholars have written persuasively about the way that Sara Baartman, as the "Venus Hottentot," has served as the iconic "proof" of black women's excessive and licentious sexuality, legitimizing not only the horrific treatment of black women under slavery but also the continued discrimination against black women in 20th- and 21st-century Western cultures. Cuvier's autopsy report of Baartman, as well as the countless other European writings on women from southern African, reduced black women to their sexual parts—the buttocks, the breasts, the labia. What is key to recognize in terms of considering the development of fat stigma is the emphasis that the "experts" placed on the *fatness* of these body parts.

Indeed, besides writing that her face had a "brutal" appearance and that her lips were like those found in the "orang-outang," Cuvier spent numerous paragraphs explaining that "l'ennorme protuberance de ses fesses" (the enormous protuberance of her buttocks) was not muscle but an elastic and trembling mass of fat under the skin. Likewise, he described her knees as fat and blubber-like. Her neck, Cuvier wrote, was shorter and fatter than those of the white women he had studied. Her breasts he described as "grosses masses pendants" (a fat hanging mass).[12] In thinking about the legacy of Cuvier's work, then, it's important to recognize that he, like other experts of 19th-century science, focused not just on the sexual attributes of Baartman, but on *fat* as a distinctive attribute of those sexual attributes. This was not just seen as a normal variation of human bodies, but as something abnormal, deficient, degraded. Indeed, the very term "steatopygia" conferred a medical, objectifying sense for a normal bodily development, and, as such, suggested that bodies that exhibited it were somehow sick. Janell Hobson in her book *Venus in the Dark: Blackness and Beauty in Popular Culture* points out how contemporary scholars replicate an imperialistic, racist, and sexist language of scientific objectivity when they refer to Sara Baartman as "suffering from steatopygia."[13] In addition, I would argue, they replicate the idea that *fat* itself is something to "suffer" from. In a similar vein, the *Merriam-Webster's Unabridged Collegiate Dictionary* still defines steatopygia as an "excessive" development of fat on the buttocks, as opposed, of course, to a normal accumulation that happens on some people.

Cuvier's writings, confirming the observations of earlier naturalists, became the accepted wisdom about Hottentot women far into the 20th century.[14] The writings of Bradshaw, Williams, and Finck clearly draw from his ideas in their pronouncements about primitive cultures and fatness. These connections between primitivism and fatness also carried over into other fields of 19th-century science. One of the most important and influential experts to note here is Cesare Lombroso, an Italian anthropologist who focused his work on the "natural" criminal—that is, the character and traits of those whom he argued had inborn tendencies toward criminality. The book most widely known in the United States was probably his *Criminal Woman*, published first in Italy in 1893 and then translated and widely available in English by 1895. In it he focused on his theory of the born criminal, who "constitute throwbacks to earlier evolutionary stages—atavisms whose primitive nature dooms them to violate the laws of civilizations in which they unwittingly find themselves." He focused particularly on the "stigmata of degeneration," bodily signs of a person's atavistic, primitive nature.[15] Criticized for his earlier work in phrenology, which focused solely on the skull for signs of one's interior nature, Lombroso focused on a full range of bodily signs in *Criminal Woman*, including but not limited to the skull. Lombroso's study categorized hair texture and color, jaw shape, eye formation, breast size and shape, and the contours of the vulva, ear lobes, and thighs, comparing those of "criminal" women to those of normal women. (He had trouble getting "normal" women to submit to examinations of the thigh and vulva, so his studies focused primarily on the forced exams of "criminal" women for those attributes.)

Among all these bodily traits, weight was an important factor. Of course, his interest in phrenology led him to compare the weights of "normal" versus "criminal" women's brains, preserved through the autopsies of select women. But he also measured women's thighs and calves, noted the heft of breasts, and weighed and measured their entire bodies. In the end, he argued that criminal women were shorter and fatter: "Female criminals are shorter than normal women; and in proportion to their stature, prostitutes and female murderers weigh more than honest women." While his comments here refer to both prostitutes and murderers, most of his findings regarding weight and women's criminality focused on prostitutes. "Prostitutes' greater weight is confirmed by the notorious obesity of those who grow old in their unfortunate trade and gradually become positive monsters of fatty tissue," he wrote. Even before they become the "positive monsters of fatty tissue," their "thighs, too, are bigger than normal women's," he argued.[16]

For Lombroso, white criminals exhibited behavior that was commonplace among lower levels of civilization. He argued that prostitution was a "normal fact of life" for savage people. Among whites, it "survived only as a morbid and retrograde phenomenon in a certain class of people." One could recognize those who had these "morbid" qualities by studying their bodily traits, which because of their resemblance to "savage" people would reveal their primitive characters. Prostitutes often cleverly hid their physical faults with deceptive makeup and artifice, but fat was a telltale sign of atavism. As he explained, there was a "marked development of connective and fatty subcutaneous tissues so often found in inferior races." Interestingly, Lombroso argued that one of the main pieces of evidence that women were "childlike" and inferior to men was their "greater wealth of connective and fatty tissue." Fatter than what he called "normal women," prostitutes and savages were even more "childlike." A fat body, then, was a primitive body, lower on the scale of civilization and highly sexual.[17]

The White Man's Burden: Disciplining the Venus Hottentot and the Fat, Female Body

Cuvier's and Lombroso's ideas about the fat Venus Hottentot and the fat prostitute did not die out in the 20th century, but rather threaded their way into various forms of popular culture. White women were expected to toe a very narrow line, neither "denying" their sex—and sexuality—by becoming too thin, nor "betraying" their sex by becoming too fat. As standards for thinness changed in the early decades of the 20th century, commentators frequently reminded women that a "certain plumpness" was necessary to attract men: it indicated health and fertility. As Henry Finck argued, "Don't try to look like the lean and lank caricatures in the awful fashion plates. *Men laugh or shudder at those.* They never laugh at a plump girl, even if she overdoes it a little." He continued to note, however, that it was important to stay on the thin side: "If she is wise, she will not overdo but read my chapters on how to reduce the moment she crosses the divide. A stitch in time saves nine."[18] "Crossing the divide" was a dangerous move, and many commentators reasoned that "plumpness" would soon be solely a vestige of more primitive cultures. As Dr. Williams wrote in 1926, "civilization" was changing men's "natural" sexual instinct. They were beginning to realize that they preferred thin women. And to accommodate this preference, he explained, women were taking part in slimming campaigns in order to fight their natural—that is, primitive— "endocrinal" tendency to gain weight. As Williams approvingly commented, white women in "civilized countries" were beginning to realize (and presumably, men were "learning" it themselves) that men preferred slim women. As Williams concluded, fat women were "repulsive sights, degrading alike to their sex and civilization."[19]

It was not just early 20th-century dieting books that explained this "civilized" shift to thinness. Postcards from the first half of the 1900s also promoted the idea that a fat white woman's body was a body out of control, attractive only to those men who were themselves less civilized. The postcards not only showed women who were unable to manage the wealth of consumer goods that a new middle-class life afforded (such as the fat woman unable to fit her packages or her body into a car, which I described in the previous chapter), but also showed fat women who presumably simultaneously evoked sexual desire and sexual repulsion in the male viewers. One postcard, for instance, shows a young fat woman on the beach. She asks, "Have I been places? See the labels on my trunk?" Instead of a suitcase with stickers, we see her bathing suit clad body filled with tags, her stomach labeled "Danger Point, U.S.A.," her breasts labeled "Petter's Paradise, U.S.A.," and her very round bottom marked "Lover's Seat, U.S.A." Often the cards mock women's fat breasts or stomach, as in this postcard, but more frequently the incessant focus is on the women's behinds. In postcard after postcard we see women bending down—to look for a shell, to do the laundry, to reach over the railing of a ship, to put on her stocking. We see the round cheeks of her bottom, often clad in some absurdly decorated and lacy undergarments. The butt of many of the postcards' jokes, literally and figuratively, are women's voluminous, fat buttocks. The poses of many of the women—bending down, huge buttocks on display—suggest the position of female animals in heat, who

Cartoons and postcards often mocked fat women as simultaneously sexually loose and sexually repulsive, as this woman whose body is marked with destinations just as a traveler's trunk would be. (Courtesy of Alice Marshall Women's History Collection, Penn State Harrisburg, Middletown, Pennsylvania.)

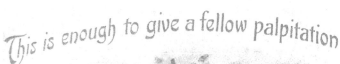

Only "hobos," working-class men, and strangely dressed figures such as the man in this 1907 postcard enjoyed the sight of a fat woman, according to popular and scientific literature. The caption reads, "This is enough to give a fellow palpitation." Note the voluminous buttocks and the position of the woman in this card, typical of the many images that evoked the style of the "Venus Hottentot." (Courtesy of Alice Marshall Women's History Collection, Penn State Harrisburg, Middletown, Pennsylvania.)

"present" themselves to interested males. More specifically, of course, their huge buttocks are reminiscent of the early 19th-century representations of the "Hottentot Venus" that Cuvier and others drew. Cartoons from the time often showed men viewing Baartman from behind, as she bent down and exposed her buttocks. These popular postcards encouraged viewers to laugh, since they were highlighting a bodily characteristic and position similar to those that were already familiar as "Hottentot." Fat white women showing off their fat buttocks meant that they were primitive, "black," and overly sexual.[20]

Sometimes this overabundant sexuality seems to please the men pictured in the travel and comic postcards. Indeed, we often see the face of some amused—presumably aroused—usually small man, spying on the woman with a twinkle in his eye. In a 1907 postcard, a tall, thin man, holding onto his crotch, looks anxiously away from a fat woman who, while bending down, has split open her skirt. "This is enough to give a fellow palpitation," the caption reads. In a 1930s postcard we see a raggedy hobo sitting on railroad tracks, with a big blonde sitting on his lap and nearly knocking him over. "I'm on the right track—and everything is going along on schedule!" the caption reads. In one from the 1940s, we see a smiling plumber, with a very large housewife sitting on his lap. "They told me to take care of the big tub in the kitchen!" the caption reads. In another from the same decade we see a small man, hearts above his face, hugging a very large and buxom woman. "The days are long and dreary," the caption reads, "but I get *around a lot* at night." One particularly interesting—and menacing—postcard shows a tropical island where a U.S. marine, grin on his face, grabs a fat "native" girl, who looks shocked and worried. "The U.S. Marines Get Around A Lot! Leave the Heavy Work Up to Us!" In this postcard the fat, the sexual, and the primitive are all clearly linked.

With the exception of the U.S. marine, whose exuberant manliness presumably excludes him from the niceties of "civilized" behavior, the men in these postcards who look happy with fat women are either poor (the hobo), working class (the plumber), or exceedingly silly (the absurdly small or thin). In contrast, most of the men in the comic "fat women" postcards look overcome by the fat women in their lives and on their laps. Postcards from the first years of the 20th century show fat women sitting on thin men's laps, with captions like "On account of a pressing engagement" and "I *must* try to get around." In one from 1909, a beleaguered man sits on a chair, with a very fat, large-buttocked woman on his lap. "Our eyes have met / Our lips not yet / But O, You kid; I'll get You yet," the caption reads as the woman presses forward toward the man's face. In a postcard from 1911, the woman sits on the chair, her buttocks extending far beyond the edges of the seat. The man sits atop her, holding on for dear life. "Just able to get around" the caption reads. A dog sitting next to the couple sighs and says, "Oh me, oh my." In one from the 1930s, a fat young woman sits atop a man who is sweating with exertion. "There's a girl up here who's goin' for me in a great big weigh" reads the headline. In another 1930s postcard we see a fat woman with her arm around a thin, balding man, who looks nervous and unhappy. "Don't worry about me. None of the guys up here can get around me," she says. Clearly this fat woman both threatens to crush the man in her life *and* is oversexed, allowing numerous men to "try" to get their arms around her.

It's important to note that within these "fat women" postcards, the working-class and poor men seem to enjoy the fat women, while the middle-class men are overwhelmed, suffocated, and distressed by these fat women's bodies. Indeed, one can see these postcards as cultural tools used to *teach* Americans to see fatness in women as a sign of primitive, out-of-control impulses. Yes, perhaps men do find fatness attractive, these discussions and images seem to note, but if the men are civilized, are middle class, are "white," then they shouldn't. Only the hobos among us would find a fat woman attractive. These postcards and cartoons, then, were part of a larger cultural discourse that increasingly valorized the superiority of the thin body as one showing "correct" attitudes of control, both in terms of sexuality and appetites for food. According to this literature, the "thin ideal" needed to be taught to the "primitive," meaning immigrants, the working class, and certainly people of color, and it needed to be embraced by all women.

Indeed, some of the postcards represent visually the same kind of rhetoric that the physicians were using at the turn of the century. Going beyond a suggestion that middle-class men should hold fat women in contempt, they imply that it is men's responsibility to discipline fat women and what is seen as their overabundant sexuality. Certainly the marine postcard could be read in this light, as his actions—and her look of fear—indicate an imminent rape. In a different postcard, we see a big-bottomed young women bending down to garden, her lacey underpants and stockings showing. A young man looks like he's about to paddle her with a board from the fence he's fixing. "Obey that impulse!" the postcard reads. "Come on down here and have a *smacking* good time!" In an earlier and more erudite card, from 1906, we see a photo of a white, well-dressed man sitting in a well-appointed drawing room, with a heavy woman perched on his lap. Under their feet is an animal-skin rug, suggesting safaris and travels to exotic locations. The caption reads, "The White Man's Burden." Evoking the title of Rudyard Kipling's

A married man's burden

In contrast to the palpable enjoyment of fat women expressed by working-class men, middle-class men appeared crushed and shrunken by the fat women in their lives. The caption on this card, "A married man's burden," calls to mind Rudyard Kipling's "The White Man's Burden." Other cartoons were even more explicit about the need to discipline fat women. (Courtesy of Alice Marshall Women's History Collection, Penn State Harrisburg, Middletown, Pennsylvania.)

famous 1899 poem, this postcard suggests that not only does a more civilized white man not appreciate a fleshy and sexually exuberant woman, but also that it is his "responsibility" to tame her. In Kipling's poem, he urges the United States to bring colonial rule to the Philippines, as it is necessary for "the best ye breed" (white Americans) to control the "Folly" and "Sloth" of the Filipino people, whom he describes as heathens, "half-devil and half-child." It will be a savage war, he says, but it is necessary.[21] Of course, just as the British imperialists, with whom Kipling grew up in India, enjoyed the privileges of their rule, the men in these postcards also seem to enjoy their "responsibility" of taming these fat women. The marine postcard shows the agent of U.S. imperialism—the marine—setting out to rape a fat "native woman"; the second postcard promises a "smacking good time"; the final shows a man whose face does not express his pleasure, but whose cheeks press into the woman's fleshy body and whose hands seem ready to reach for her breasts. Dr. Williams suggested in his earlier treatises that civilized men were learning not to "enjoy" fleshy women; perhaps what they were learning instead, these postcards suggest to me, is to frame and express their conflicted enjoyment as a duty to discipline the "primitive."

In a fascinating way, the connotation of fat as female, primitive, and sexual has often evoked a mixture of attraction and repulsion, as suggested by the "White Man's Burden" postcard. The popularity of the bustle in women's fashion in the second half of the 19th century is a prime example of this attraction and repulsion. The bustle can be seen as a false "steatopygia," an artifice that creates an excessive protuberance of the buttocks. On the other hand, it's important to note that it was a *false* set of buttocks that was fashionable, an allusion to the shape of the iconic Venus Hottentot but not an actual development of real fleshy buttocks. In a similar vein, the empire dress, a style popular following the bustle, also linked sexual attraction and repulsion. It featured a high waist with a flowing, loose skirt, which allowed plenty of room for the stomach and the hips, a sensuality that evoked discomfort among a white audience. As one fashion commentator in the *New York Times* argued in 1913, "Largely following Turkish ideas in dress, the big, lazy waist on some of the best models is indicative of the form of the women of the harem, who spend their days lounging, eating fruit, and consequently putting on flesh. In that country, the first requisite of beauty is obesity. . . . Women in Paris are very tired of this aiming to be like the Turk. At first it was novel and highly amusing, but, realizing that their own good forms have been spoiled, they are revolting."[22] In a fascinating way, this passage links a fashion style that allows the female body to exhibit its *fat* to a site of decadent sexuality and primitive cultures, the harem. Presumably, however, the good (white) readers of the *New York Times* were like the women of Paris, who were revolting against this fashion, refusing to allow their bodies to be *spoiled*, an interesting choice of terms connoting both *fat* and *sexually loose*.[23]

Although it is important to recognize the complex meanings that representations of fatness evoke, it is also essential to note the way that large body size has been consistently linked to notions of the primitive. Much has been written about the importance of cultural representations of African Americans within dominant white culture and the ways these images historically have legitimated and reproduced racial hierarchies and subordination in the United States. As Patricia Hill Collins has argued, "controlling images" of black women as mammies, jezebels, and matriarchs have been central to the reproduction of racism and oppression. The mammy and the jezebel figure are, of course, in opposition to each other; the mammy is the quintessential asexual figure, loving to her white family but in no way a sexual threat to the (white) woman of the house. The jezebel figure, in contrast, is the black woman *as* sexual threat, who exudes and elicits sexual desire. What links these two images, however, is the focus on the body, one that is "out of control" and certainly in "excess" of white normative standards. Collins points out that the mammy figure is "overweight, dark, and with characteristically African features."[24] Barbara Christian further explains that the "functions of mammy are magnificently physical. They involve the body as sensuous, as funky."[25] Important for us to note here is the way that the *body in excess* is key to these representations of racial inferiority—the fat mammy, the jezebel figure with protruding buttocks, or, in contemporary American life, the image of the fat (and over-sexed and over-fertile) black "welfare queen."

The fat and stupid black man has also served as an important controlling image, one used to legitimate racial oppression. He is seen as less a sexual threat than an ill-fitting butt of a joke, worthy of the degradations and humiliation he faces. Such representations were common in vaudeville, blackface, and minstrel productions. In the poster for "William West's Big Minstrel Jubilee," printed in 1900, for instance, we see a very fat black man, stomach protruding over his belt, wielding a long rifle while protecting his watermelon patch. Clearly his stomach has the best of him, however, as a small child is able to use it as cover while she steals a watermelon right from under his feet.[26] We see a continuation of these fat images on television and film in the 20th century—Mammy in the 1939 film *Gone with the Wind*, Fat Andy on the TV version of *Amos 'n' Andy*, the overweight maid Beulah in the 1950s eponymous television show, and Fat Albert in the 1970s. These controlling images link blackness, fatness, and the "uncivilized body," making it easy for (white) viewers to read these characters as silly and inferior.

The Fat, Immigrant, Ethnic Body

The use of fatness as a marker of the less civilized body not only could be found in late 19th- and early 20th-century comic representations of white women and of black men and women, but also in cartoons ridiculing "ethnic" Americans, particularly recent immigrants. Within the hierarchy of civilization articulated by anthropologists and sociologists at the turn of the last century, which was so powerfully illuminated by the World's Columbian Exposition in Chicago, white Anglo-Saxons held the position of most civilized, and indigenous and African peoples the position of least civilized. While all Europeans held higher positions than the "Hottentots" or "Moors"

Cartoonists around the turn of the century began to link fatness and ethnicity, as in this 1907 postcard titled "Irish Descent," showing a fat Irish servant falling down the stairs and breaking a tray of dishes with her clumsiness. (Courtesy of Alice Marshall Women's History Collection, Penn State Harrisburg, Middletown, Pennsylvania.)

within this line of thinking, there was certainly skepticism about the culture and nature of Irish, eastern European, Jewish, and southern European immigrants. Within the context of increased waves of immigration from southern and eastern Europe and migration from the U.S. South, nativist critics and health professionals argued that everything from health and fortitude to intelligence and character were inherited traits, in low supply among the immigrants and migrants, and in high supply among native-born Americans of northern European stock. There was significant attention paid to those supposed signs that would clarify the identity of the "superior" from the "inferior," the "civilized" from the "primitive," or, to use Lombroso's terms, the "normal" from the "atavistic."

Cartoonists who published their work in periodicals like *Harper's Weekly* and *Life* frequently drew immigrants as fat, a quick way to signify to readers their inferior status. In an 1880 cartoon, for instance, we see a fat, coarse-looking Irish woman, who tells Mrs. Smith, presumably her Anglo-Saxon (and thin) employer, that "a simple Republican votes once, an interprising Dimmycrat'll vote tin toimes!"[27] In 1897, a beleaguered, poor man talks to a thin, upright lady, presumably some sort of social worker, who asks, "Have you any visible means of support?" The man points behind him to an immense woman, wiping her hands on her apron. "Oi'd loike to'know phat ye call thot!" he replies.[28] In another, a thin farmer announces to a very fat German man lounging in a bar, "I don't know what will become of us if this dry spell lasts. Not a drop of water." The German "gentleman" replies, "Oh, I dond drouble myself. De Peer always holds out."[29] In another cartoon we see a very fat Irish man, with a face that looks more like an ape's and who wears a suit of stars and stripes. He's telling his fellow Irishman, Mick, that in the United States he is a "Landlord and a Gentleman."[30] Clearly, he is confused as to what a gentleman looks like, as we see in another cartoon the picture of a "true" gentleman—thin, trim, well dressed—who comments on the "impudence" of a fat man who has stolen his cigar.[31] In all these cartoons, *thin* signifies the upstanding citizen, *fat* the cheating, stupid, and coarse immigrant.

Not only do we find such "fat ethnic" jokes in periodical cartoons, but also in postcards sent at the turn of the century, such as one of a middle-aged woman with a fat face, whose large breasts are straining her blouse. The back reads, "Wish you success in getting a good hired girl." In another, the sender shows some self-deprecating humor as she writes to her niece that she had "better send my picture before I came or you would not know me and not let me in." The postcard shows a very fat and short woman, missing teeth, wearing a ragged dress, and sporting a kerchief over her head. Like the beer, she is labeled "Stout and mild."[32] One of the postcards, from 1907, by Irvin Kline, pictures a very fat maid who has fallen down the stairs, breaking a tray of china dishes and knocking her head so hard she sees stars. She has thick lips, a huge buxom chest, very thick arms and ankles, and a bloated stomach. As the owner of the house looks on, the maid looks confused and perplexed, as if she has no idea what happened. Mocking her ethnic identity, her immigrant status, and her clumsy, stupid persona, the caption reads, "Irish Descent."[33] These comic postcards use *fatness* as a strategy to typecast and mock these immigrant workingwomen. Connecting "ethnic," working class, and fat, the women pictured in these images are far from the ethereal, thin, white women who signified status and upward mobility.

By the early 20th century, medical research on the role of the endocrine system added strength to the "civilization and obesity" theory. Physicians began to focus on the role of hormones in regulating metabolism and weight, and researchers drew on earlier theories of the "primitive" body to speculate about the connections between ethnic and racial background and body size. In 1915, Dr. William Preble, in his article "Obesity and Malnutrition," noted that there was much authoritative work focused on the "racial factor" associated with fatness, particularly "as the Jewish people seem inclined to adiposity." He suggested, however, that this had more to do with eating habits than with metabolism.[34] Nonetheless, the idea that Jews and other "racial groups" (meaning nonwhites) had a biological propensity to obesity remained powerful throughout the first decades of the 20th century. One of the most famous weight researchers to challenge this racial link to obesity was Hilde Bruch, a Jewish psychologist who came to the United States in the 1930s after fleeing persecution in Germany. Although she is best known for her later work on anorexia, Bruch began her U.S. career studying obesity. At the time, much medical attention focused on the supposed pituitary abnormalities of fat children, specifically a condition called Froehlich's syndrome, in which boys exhibited a lack of genital development, an effeminate appearance, and obesity. Bruch's first study focused on hundreds of children in New York, mostly Jewish and Italian, whose bodies she examined in detail at her Columbia University clinic. She also spoke at length with their mothers, and often conducted home visits, observing the children playing, eating, and interacting with other family members. Noting their normal height and genital development, Bruch concluded that none of the children demonstrated any "glandular" problem. "In spite of all evidence to the contrary," she wrote in a paper she gave in 1946, reflecting on her 1930s research, "fat children continue to be burdened with this misleading diagnosis. Not one of the youngsters who have been sent to me as 'typical Froehlich' was entitled to the name." Resisting the racist, eugenic theories that fueled the rise of Hitler in her home country, Bruch argued that there was nothing physically inferior about her largely Jewish and Italian patients that led them to be fat.

Challenging the notion of the inferior immigrant body, Bruch did not, however, discard entirely the theory connecting civilization and fatness. Instead, she transposed the theory of ethnic physical inferiority onto the children's immigrant culture. "Obesity seems to occur with greater frequency in children of immigrants than in those of settled American background," she argued in a 1942 conference paper titled "Psychiatric Aspects of Obesity in Children." The children were fat, she argued, because they ate too much and exercised too little, a result of the smothering behavior of their strong-willed immigrant mothers. These mothers simultaneously resented and clung to their children, trying to make up for both their conflicting emotions and poor living conditions by providing excessive food and physical comfort. Bruch described the fathers of these fat children as weak willed, often absent, and "yearning" for the love that their wives devoted to the children.

In a 1941 paper, "Obesity in Childhood and Personality Development," she describes these pathological parents:

Many fathers of obese children were found to be weak and unaggressive persons, with little drive and ambition. They are unable to give positive manly guidance to their children and to counteract the overindulgent and retarding influence of the mothers. With few exceptions the mothers are domineering in the life of the families. Many mothers had suffered from great poverty, and often hunger in their childhood and had been thrown upon their own resources at any early age. They had reacted to their early experiences with self-pity and were unable to loosen their ties to their past. In a primitive way they try to create for their children that "normal" and carefree childhood of which, they feel, they had been deprived and which is represented for them in a life of idleness and in abundance of food.

Described as "retarding," "unable to loosen their ties to their past," and "primitive," these mothers were not just guilty of improper gender roles but of uncivilized behavior. As a result of their regressive conduct, their children became psychologically stunted in an infantile state.

The fact that he does not rebel against the excessive feeding and prolonged overprotection may be considered the basic weakness in his make-up. . . . He indulges in the continued and excessive gratification at a primitive level and is unwilling to give up the pleasures and safety of infancy. He does not conform to the changes which growing-up implies. It is as if he sells his birthright of becoming an independent and mature person in his own rights [sic] for the continued abundance of nourishment and protection.

Indulging in "continued and excessive gratification at a primitive level," the fat children demonstrate a psychological weakness, one that merges pathologically with the "retarding" behavior of the mothers.

To further her research into the cultural aspects of obesity and other problems, Bruch proposed an additional study, one that would explore evidence of "disorder, illness or defect among children" who could be identified as "coming from some recognized racial, ethnic or nationality group with a distinctive culture and pattern of childrearing." Minutes from committee meetings in 1944 indicate that officials from the Tuskegee Institute and the Harlem Hospital rebuffed her proposal. They were "not inclined to be cooperative and seemed to feel that the project was going to prove something unfavorable about the negro group," the memo read. Bruch and her colleagues seemed surprised at these officials' perspective, and certainly were critical of their unwillingness to take part in "science." But the officials from Tuskegee and Harlem Hospital were wise in their reluctance to participate. Both the medical and the psychological research on fatness at this time always wound up "proving" the inferiority of the fat person.[35] For Bruch, it was the families' inferior *culture* that created the fatness; for physicians like the ones Preble described, it was their inferior *bodies*. What remained the same, however, was the belief that modernity and civilization were inextricably linked to thinness, and that the primitive and uncivilized were linked to fatness. If the fatness was hormonal or endogenous, a term used to describe fat that was "associated with the disturbance in one of the endocrine organs such as the thyroid, pituitary, adrenal or gonads," then the person's inferior body was to blame.[36] If a person became fat for "exogenous" or "alimentary" reasons (e.g., overeating), then the person's uncivilized culture and inferior will were to blame. The stigma attached to this type of fatness was equally powerful, as the words of Dr. Leonard Williams, quoted at length earlier in the chapter, suggest. "Alimentary" obesity, he further argued, was "contemptible and disgusting" because it denoted "self-indulgence, greed, and gormandizing; and most are disgusting because they represent an unsightly distortion of the human form divine, and a serious impairment of the intellectual faculties."[37] Exogenous or endogenous, hormonal or alimentary, physical or cultural, the blame continued to reside with the person, whose body or culture revealed an inferiority and lack of civilization.

The idea that "lower" races and ethnicities tended toward obesity remained salient well into the 20th century, even when the supporting evidence was vague or nonexistent. Paula Saukko, for instance, described the work of a physical anthropologist in the 1940s who "found to his surprise that the obese women he studied came from 'old' American families." Undeterred, the anthropologist pointed out that most of the fat women had German, Irish, and Italian backgrounds, which "indicated that they presented the 'alpine' and other 'rugged' stocks of Europeans, who were '"survivors" of Upper Paleolithic' populations that evolved during the last glacial period." He contrasted these to the later European arrivals who brought "farming and urban civilization." As Saukko points out, this anthropologist "went all the way to the Paleolithic period to establish a connection between a robust body shape and lack of civilization."[38] Strikingly, this ideological connection between fatness and notions of the primitive continues today. In their extensively researched study on the last twenty years of obesity research,

Michael Gard and Jan Wright point out how frequently "evolution" is used to explain some people's fatness, such as the currently popular "thrifty gene" theory, despite the fact that there is little to no scientific evidence to support that conclusion.[39] Theories of the "uncivilized body" remain powerful today, though they show up in new and scientific forms.[40]

In 1891 a St. Paul, Minnesota, news article described the "predisposition to fat" as similar to "all other morbid tendencies that come down to us from past generations, multiplying and gathering force with the lapse of ages."[41] Fat was seen as a "stigmata of degeneration," to use Lombroso's terms, a sign that one either was *from* an inferior group, or that one was an individual *throwback* who inherited and exhibited primitive tendencies. The chapters that follow will address the ways that the *idea* of fat as a morbid, primitive tendency has indeed multiplied and gathered force, creating a powerful barrier for those who wish to claim their own rights as citizens, as "fully civilized" bodies worthy of rights, respect, and freedom.

4

Feminism, Citizenship, and Fat Stigma

On the 1910 cover of the American humor magazine *Judge* we see a fat white woman staring at us menacingly.[1] She has a mean face with protruding eyes, a thick neck, large muscular arms, and a wide girth and ample chest that are belted tightly with an unbecoming apron. Her feet, planted wide apart, are adorned with men's oxfords; her thick ankles sport red socks. She is surrounded by pots and pans, and holds tightly to a huge wooden spoon in one hand and an oversized rolling pin in the other. Clearly she threatens to hit the viewer with these kitchen tools. The caption reads, "Speaker of the House." What a joke to suggest that women need more rights! Look what the desire for public citizenship has done to this woman, the cover says: it has turned her into a primitive, coarse beast, too ugly, too big, too fat to be a woman. In contrast, a 1912 pro-suffrage poster, published on the cover of the *Sunday Magazine of the Philadelphia Press*, pictures a young white woman with soft, curly hair. She is leading a suffrage parade. Clad in white gloves, her dainty hands hold her "Votes for Women" sign, while her coat shows the outlines of a slender figure. Young men march behind her, transfixed, it seems, by her beauty. The desire for suffrage, for the rights of public citizenship, has made this young woman all the more beautiful, all the more attractive to the gentlemen in her midst. She deserves, the poster suggests, the support and attention she has garnered.

As these two propaganda pieces suggest, competing representations of the *body* were critical within the campaigns for and against women's rights in the first wave of feminism, from the mid-19th century through the 1920s. As we saw in the previous chapter, this time period, which marks the parameters of modernism as well as early feminism, saw the development of anthropological and sociological justifications for racial and class hierarchies, based both on earlier beliefs in the stages of civilization and the harnessing of newer scientific understandings of evolution. Within this explosion of scientific, religious, and philosophical discussion regarding civilization and evolution, the *body* served as key evidence of one's place within these complicated hierarchies. Skin color, hair texture, facial features, sexual traits, and body size all served as signs of one's evolutionary status and hinted at any hidden atavistic traits. Fatness became both a sign of greedy and uncontrolled impulses—a sign that the excesses of modernism could not be handled—*and* of inferior, primitive bodies, a sure indicator of one's low position on the evolutionary scale.

First-wave feminists worked within a cultural and social milieu where sociological, anthropological, scientific, and religious ideas about bodily traits and their links to stages of evolution and civilization dominated. Women's rights activists had to battle the firmly entrenched belief in the inferiority of women's bodies, whose reproductive capacities and weaker physical physique served as justification for unequal social, political, and economic status. Not surprisingly, then, the *body* became a locus of attention in the political cartoons, propaganda, and literature of both those who agitated for and those who agitated against women's rights. This was particularly true once the more widespread women's movement of the 19th century narrowed its focus to the fight for suffrage, perhaps one of the most powerful symbolic claims for the right to participation in the *public* sphere. Anti-suffrage activists used the motif of the big and fat woman's body to lampoon suffragists, whose struggles threatened to ruin the social order and "unsex" both men and women. In contrast, first-wave feminists lampooned the female anti-suffragists as fat, inferior, and resistant to progress, and the male anti-suffragists as selfish fat cats, greedy, dangerous, and stomping on the rights—and bodies—of their thin, civilized sisters. In their cartoons, posters, and other visual propaganda, white suffragists in the early part of the 20th century frequently used body typing. Their tactics emphasized not only their white skin, a racist practice that has been analyzed in detail by other scholars, but also their thin and wispy body size as physical evidence for their rights to full citizenship.

The Anti-suffrage Movement and Fat Denigration

Throughout the 19th century, women's rights advocates found themselves under attack by ministers, physicians, and politicians who argued that their activism stood in direct contradiction to God, to nature, and to civilization. Higher civilizations, as I discussed in the last chapter, were supposedly marked by distinct separation between the sexes. Men and women were supposed to look, behave, and dress differently from each other. Cultural roles and responsibilities were equally distinct, with men taking on the positions

This 1910 *Judge* cover was typical of anti-suffragist propaganda that ridiculed suffragists as fat, overbearing, and mannish. (*Judge*, June 14, 1910, cover.)

Anti-suffragists relentlessly mocked suffragists as being ugly and fat, while the suffragists countered with their own propaganda campaign, representing themselves as young, white, and alluringly slim. (*Sunday Magazine of the Philadelphia Press*, November 3, 1912, cover.)

in the public world, and women those in the domestic realm. "Lower levels" of civilization, however, were marked by less distinct, and sometimes overlapping, cultural roles, styles of dress, behavioral standards, and, essential to note for the purposes of this study, bodily characteristics. That is, within "higher levels" of civilization, male physiques were notably different from female ones. In contrast, men and women within "lower levels" might demonstrate somewhat similar strength, agility, sizing, and even some comparable sexual characteristics. Those writers, preachers, and physicians who railed against the women's rights advocates contended that women's attempts to speak in public, to challenge male privilege within marriage, and to seek educational and economic power were direct attempts to thwart the "natural" order of higher civilizations, to blur the essential differences between men and women, or to turn women into men and men into women. Indeed, the term used most frequently was that women's rights advocates threatened to "unsex" women. As a derogatory, all-purpose, ubiquitous insult, "unsexed" could of course contain a multitude of meanings and insinuations, but generally it meant that the movement threatened to strip away that which was distinct to women—usually defined as either maternal traits or (hetero)sexually alluring characteristics—turning women into freaks of nature, bullying tyrants, or ugly creatures with vaguely masculine physical features.

One of the most tangible and easy pieces of "evidence" that contemporaries used to demonstrate that women's rights reformers sought to "unsex" women were the "bloomer" outfits popularized by Amelia Bloomer in her journal *The Lily* in the early 1850s. Billowing pants worn under shortened skirts, bloomers were a more comfortable and practical alternative to the long, layered skirts and tight corsets worn by most middle- and upper-class women. Bloomer-wearing women proved a powerful target for anti–women's rights advocates, who pelted the women with food and rocks and ridiculed the women as "fe'he males" for wearing male attire.[2] The reaction against bloomers was so powerful that most women's rights advocates, including Bloomer herself and Elizabeth Cady Stanton, quickly abandoned them. Even the venerable Susan B. Anthony eventually returned to her ordinary clothing, "despite," she wrote, "the terrible bondage of these long skirts." Although Anthony said she lacked the *"Moral Courage"* to continue wearing the bloomers, one has to be more generous in judging her today, noting the ways that the harassment was unrelenting, the attacks fierce, and the diversion from other issues discouraging.[3] Returning to the protective clothing of long skirts, however, did not protect the women's rights advocates from ongoing ridicule. Nor did the argument that they were thwarting the normal order of civilization die with the passing of bloomers. The attacks simply shifted to other means to mock the women and their bodies as "unsexed" and "uncivilized."

One of main critiques lobbied against women's rights advocates was that these women who urged changes in law and custom were simply embittered spinsters who were unable to find or keep a man. Generally portrayed in caricatures as tall and gaunt, with "masculine" features and severe clothing, the spinster's personality supposedly mirrored her body: lacking in warmth, sensuality, or maternal instinct. As with the "fe'he male" described above, the sexuality of these spinsters was also called into question, especially with the popularization of Freudian thinking by the end of the 19th century. "Lesbian" and "invert" were frequent epithets used against women's rights advocates, terms that coexisted and then replaced the concept of "unsexed." It was difficult to lampoon Elizabeth Cady Stanton as one of these gaunt, mannish spinsters, as she was married, the mother of seven children, and a woman of increasingly corpulent proportions. Her lifelong friend and comrade Susan B. Anthony was another story, however. Single, tall, thin, with an angular face, Anthony fit the powerful stereotype used to mock women's rights advocates. Significantly, in the biographical piece that Stanton wrote about Anthony, she carefully explained that Anthony's physical features did not correlate with the usual personality traits outlined in the phrenology textbooks. Indeed, Anthony was even more womanly than other females, Stanton suggested. She wrote, "Miss Anthony, though not beautiful, has a fine figure and a large, well-shaped head. The world calls her sharp, angular, cross-grained. She has, indeed, her faults and angles, but these are all on the outside. She has a broad and generous nature, and a depth of tenderness that few women possess."[4] Despite whatever defense Stanton and others provided to counter the spinster stereotype, this caricature of a dry, thin, tight-lipped, mannish woman continued throughout the long battle for suffrage. In one cartoon, published in the early 1900s in Great Britain and in the United States, for instance, we see a skinny white woman, with a long face and buckteeth, wearing a mannish hat and a tight, sleeved dress.[5] As she enters a courtroom all the men—the judge, the lawyers, the stenographer, and the police officer—turn to look at her. "I protest against man made laws," she says; one can almost hear her squawky voice coming through those buckteeth. Behind this shrewish woman stand her supporters, one of them holding a "Votes for Women" sign. The one closest to her is very large, with big hands, a very wide body, and a square, jowly face. Wearing a brown suit and a crazy hat, she looms over the men in the courtroom, taking up more space than any of them. Here, then, is the counterpart to the spinster woman's advocate: the unsexed, *fat* woman's advocate.

Caricatures and cartoons of fat women, portraying them both as unable to handle the bounties of modern life and as uncivilized, primitive beings, found their way into popular journals like *Harper's Weekly* and *Life* by the last decades of the 19th century. This use of the fat motif, then, could be harnessed quite powerfully to attack those women who were fighting for more rights within both the private sphere—rights to education, to child custody, to ownership of property within marriage—and the public sphere—rights to work, rights to reform municipal and state policies, and, above all, the right to vote. Those who attacked women's rights argued that women both were clearly unfit for the hardships and pleasures of public life, and thwarted the "normal" hierarchies of civilized behavior. By portraying these suffragists as fat, these cartoons and caricatures symbolically argued that they were *unfit* for public citizenship. Moreover, their fatness suggested the extent to which they posed a significant *danger* to the social order, pulling men and women into a chaotic, primitive world. If the spinster suffragist seemed scared of matrimony, sexuality, and men, the fat suffragist seemed the opposite. Angry and overpowering, these fat suffragists had no reason to fear men. These were large, strong women, out-of-control beasts who threatened to suffocate the men in their midst. They were simultaneously comically ugly and threateningly dangerous.

The fat, masculine woman, such as the one pictured on the 1910 *Judge* cover, was a staple caricature in anti-suffrage propaganda. In another poster published first in Great Britain, then reproduced frequently as a postcard in both Britain and the United States, we see a suffragist on a stage, shouting her speech to an audience of white women, many looking at her with round, vacuous eyes. The suffragist is very fat, wearing a red suit, mannish shoes, and a hat bedecked with a feather that stands erectly. She points wildly in the air as she yells, "*What* are men? *who* are they? *where* are they? &c &c." The signs on the wall read "Votes for Women" and "We will never give in." Sharing the stage with this angry, large woman is another fat woman, whose large breasts, double chin, and grey hair loom at us in the foreground of the poster.[6] In a 1908 *Life* magazine spread, we see six well-dressed people sitting on a bench, each reading a book or novel that covers their faces. Clearly each person is supposed to represent a "type." The small boy with his boot untied reads a comic. The fancy women with their billowing hats read a celebrity tabloid and a romance novel. The matron with her packages reads *Suburban Life*. A dapper man in a top hat reads the *Morning Telegraph*. And, finally, we see the suffragist. Reading the newspaper *Equality*, she is sitting with her fat thighs far apart, and her thick ankles and mannish shoes are planted firmly on the ground. Her hat sports that same phallic feather seen in the previous poster. Her *Equality* newspaper includes articles like "Rights" and "Suffrage" as well as a sketch of a fat woman with very thick, broad shoulders, a double chin, and wide, thick cheeks.

Clearly, in both these posters the suffragists' fatness represents the way that their bodies and their desires—for votes and for power—are out of control. Theirs is not the corpulence of fertile, feminine matrons, but rather a fatness that is brutish and animal-like. Indeed, their insatiable appetites have made them into monstrous, mannish women. They have truly perverted the normal order of civilization. Cartoonists often drew on this image of the beastly, mannish, fat woman to mock the suffragists' argument that women needed the vote as protection against the men in their lives. How in the world did the woman on the *Judge* cover, the suffragist reading the *Equality* journal, or the angry, fist-pounding speech-maker need any protection from men? Some cartoonists carried this point even further, emphasizing the way that men diminished in size as suffragists gained power—and heft. In one from 1908 we see a very thin, older man sitting in the shadows of the living room, while a scowling, very large woman sits reading a newspaper, again titled *Equality*. Both her voluminous size and her newspaper block the light coming from the only lamp in the room, so that the husband sits meekly in the shadows. The caption reads, "The Eclipse: A Husband of Woman Suffrage."[7] Clearly, in this case the woman's fat is associated with a political movement that not only threatens the "normal" balance within the home but also the very vitality of men. In a 1915 *Saturday Evening Post* cartoon we see a huge woman, with a big stomach, large arms, and thick face, walking next to a very thin, diminutive man. Gently holding on to a pair of gloves, he puts his arms through hers as they walk. His feet barely touch the ground. In contrast, she walks firmly, her stomach leading the way. She is so mannish that we don't even see the outline of any breasts, just the wide girth of her stomach and a square, jowly face. The caption reads, "Married women with the ballot will be able to protect themselves against the brutality and oppression of their husbands." Like the *Judge* cover, this cartoon makes fun of the idea that brutality against women even exists. The cartoon implies that we really know who rules the home. Moreover, through body size play—the fat woman, the thin man—we learn that suffrage will upend the normal order of civilization, creating monstrous, mannish women and effeminate, weak men. The images of these fat suffragists portray visually what Dr. Leonard Williams, the early 20th-century dieting guru quoted in the last chapter, wrote about fat women—that they were "repulsive sights, degrading alike to their sex and civilization." These cartoons use fatness as a means to portray the suffragists as primitive and as threatening. It doesn't really matter if the suffragists are actually fat in "real life"; this lampooning is a tool to teach readers how repulsive these women actually are.[8]

By portraying these fat white women suffragists as an affront to the gendered order of higher levels of civilization, these cartoons implicitly suggested that the suffragists posed a challenge to the entire order of civilization, threatening to bring white people down to the lower levels of primitive culture. Other cartoons were more direct, suggesting explicitly that the movement for more gender equality threatened to bring chaos to the orderly hierarchies of racial and ethnic civilizations. In a postcard published in both England and the United States from the early part of the 20th century, for instance, we see a suffragist who is giving money—bribes presumably—to two other women. The caption reads, "Electioneering." While the suffragist herself is white, thin, well dressed, and conventionally pretty, the other women are not. Indeed, one is the overly thin, gaunt, spinster type, the other fat, lumpy, and disheveled, with very strong arms. Both the women taking the money wear ragged shawls and mismatched clothing, obviously suggesting that they are working class, uneducated, and, for an American audience, "ethnic" immigrants. The devious tricks of the good-looking suffragist, then, threaten to contaminate the rites of public citizenship with deceit, fraud, and the inclusion of the lower classes.[9]

The disordering of civilization caused by women's suffrage was particularly clear in an 1893 cartoon about the state of Kansas. Kansas was especially notable when it came to female suffrage, as it was the first state to consider a women's suffrage referendum, in 1867. Although a referendum for women's suffrage did not pass until 1912, the state had a liberal reputation regarding women's suffrage, with Kansas women winning the right to vote in municipal and school elections and many "almost" successful statewide campaigns for women's suffrage, including one in 1893.[10] Significantly, the cartoon portrayed the disarray of civilization caused by women's suffrage through the confluence of fat and blackness. Titled "All on Equal Footing in This Line" and captioned "Female Suffrage in Kansas," the cartoon pictured a long line of people waiting to vote. We see a fat black woman, with a big smile on her round face, dressed in a head-scarf and a baggy dress. She is the quintessential uneducated black mammy figure. Next to her is a white "gentleman," a white policeman, a white army general, and a few fashionably dressed, white society women. Next to these women, at the back of the line, is a fat white woman, with ugly, stretched facial features. What an absurd situation, the comic says, suggesting that all these people are "equal." Clearly they are not—and clearly they should not be—equal. Yet in the state of Kansas, this is what female suffrage would produce: an upheaval of the "normal" order of gendered and racialized civilization.

Throughout the long struggle for women's suffrage, anti–women's rights activists argued that the suffrage movement both attracted and created women who were primitive and out of control. For instance, the *London Daily Mirror* in 1914 ran a piece titled "The Suffragette Face: New Type Evolved by Militancy," in which photographs of "militant" suffragists—usually close-ups taken from odd angles—were used as evidence of the women's psycho-pathology, ranging from "impotent rage" to "emotional" and "ecstatic."[11] The suffrage movement, within the logic of this article, had developed, or "evolved," these new forms of mania and insanity. Weak women with hidden unwomanly traits would be attracted to the movement, which would then "evolve" them into the new militant types. We can see this type of logic in cartoon imagery as well. Indeed, many of the anti-suffrage cartoons explicitly portrayed white suffragists as fat black women, suggesting, of course, that the suffrage movement was pulling white women down to the lowest strata. In a postcard distributed in both Britain and the United States, for instance, we see a fat white woman standing by a suffrage campaign table labeled "Votes for Women." "We only want what men have got!" she spurts out from a red, blotched face. Her skirt, also red, is hitched tightly across her middle, emphasizing her very big stomach and big breasts. Her face is so fat that there are no defining lines, just a fat neck straining at the shirt collar that moves upward toward her bulging, vacuous eyes. What particularly stands out are her thick, red lips, a distinct reference to blackface minstrelsy. The suffragist's name? "Miss Ortobee Spankdfirst." This is a particularly fascinating cartoon, as it explicitly connects the stigma of fatness and blackness with the woman's desire to end gender inequality. The cartoon, however, does not refer to suffrage or women's rights, but rather has the woman saying, "We only want what men have got," a clear allusion, of course, to the penis. Like the Venus Hottentot on display in Paris, like the women who shopped too much, like the fat woman in the "White Man's Burden" postcard, this woman should be punished for her desire. She ought to be spanked first, as her name tells us. Her desire for the rights of male status mark her as primitive, as out of control, as fat and black and in need of discipline.

WE ONLY WANT WHAT THE MEN HAVE GOT!!!

This anti-suffrage poster caricatured the suffragist as fat and big-lipped, two signifiers of a primitive body. Adding to the ridicule is her name, "Miss Ortobee Spankdfirst," which, like the "White Man's Burden" postcards, legitimates the punishment of women who transgressed normative roles. The fat body provided visual, physical representation of the way she overstepped political boundaries. (Courtesy of Alice Marshall Women's History Collection, Penn State Harrisburg, Middletown, Pennsylvania.)

This 1906 anti-suffrage document, with its emphasis on the black fat woman, drew explicitly on the stigmatized image of the Venus Hottentot, suggesting that voting was primitive, uncivilized, and undesirable. (Courtesy of Alice Marshall Women's History Collection, Penn State Harrisburg, Middletown, Pennsylvania.)

While the links between fatness, blackness, primitive status, and women's rights are clear in the "Ortobee Spankdfirst" postcard, the woman suffragist still literally has white skin. In a 1906 postcard, the white suffragist has actually become a fat black woman, whose shape and form are strongly reminiscent of the Venus Hottentot image. In this black-and-white postcard, we see a woman pointing down the hall, presumably in the direction of the "Womens Suffrage Convention," the sign for which we see hanging on the wall. The woman herself is completely black, as a cutout silhouette would be. She is fat, with a tremendous, drooping bosom, thick lips, oversized hands, and large, round, white eyes. Her bottom is very fat, pushing upward toward her thick arm and wavy hair.[12] "This is merely a matter of form," the postcard reads. There is an interesting double meaning here. One presumes that this quote is most obviously in reference to the common argument put forth by suffragists that voting was simply the enactment of rights that women already had in principle as citizens of the United States and as human beings with natural, God-given rights to self-sovereignty. Voting, so went this argument, was "only a matter of form." The woman's image on the postcard, of course, is also "just a matter of form." But what a form it is: black, fat, and gross in shape, like the Venus Hottentot.

To draw on the stigmatized image of the Venus Hottentot was a direct, easy-to-decipher form of ridicule. Voting for women may just be a "new form," but it will be primitive, uncivilized, and undesirable—just like the fat black suffragist in the cartoon. By linking the suffrage campaign and the image of the Venus Hottentot, this postcard suggests that granting women voting rights is unappealingly "low," degenerative, a direction too dangerous to take.

Suffragists in both the United States and Great Britain did not let these caricatures of women's rights advocates go by without notice or response. Indeed, as the use of visual propaganda increased in the first two decades of the 20th century, suffragists responded directly, creating a counterimage of the women's rights advocate as beautiful, white, youthful, and thin, such as the woman on the cover of the *Sunday Magazine of the Philadelphia Press*. These women were cultured and educated, the epitome of civilization. The suffragists themselves engaged in pageants and parades that highlighted their beauty and youth. Moreover, their more militant actions—the stampeding of Parliament in England and the protests held outside the White House in the United States—ended in hunger strikes during their imprisonments, yet another sign of their bodily control and *fitness* for citizenship.

The anti-suffragists did not let these new tactics develop without comment. Indeed, some of the most biting ridicule they laid on the suffragists dealt with these new images of the beautiful, white, and thin suffragist. One cartoon, for instance, pictured a group of older, jowl-faced suffragists, with thick waists, heavy bosoms, and rolls of fat covering their necks. They wear an assortment of oddly decorated dresses. "The only way we can gain woman's suffrage is by making our appeal through our charm, our grace, and our beauty," announces the speaker. What a joke, the cartoon obviously suggests, to think of these women as charming, gracious, or the least bit beautiful. Another is even more insulting and even vicious, considering the extraordinarily harsh treatment and brutal forced feedings the women prisoners received when they went on hunger strikes. Published first in the English humor journal *Puck* in 1913, this six-frame cartoon, titled "The Steadfast Suffragette: There Was Method in Her Starvation," shows a very fat suffragist, wearing one of the masculine hats with a phallic feather, sitting precariously on a stool within her cell. The jailer tempts her with a plate of steaming food and drink. In each frame we see him tempt her with more and more food. She refuses to eat, leaving the full trays on the floor. Obviously, she becomes thinner and thinner, her clothing draped loosely about her with that phallic feather beginning to droop. Finally, in the last frame we see that she is so skinny she can slip out through the bars on the window. Her fat and masculine suffrage comrades hoist her on their shoulders, ready for another suffrage parade.[13]

Ridicule such as that found in these last two cartoons failed to stop the suffragists from the powerful campaign they had fashioned to sell the vote to the British and to the American public. Representing the female body as *fit* for public citizenship was key to their campaign. *Fatness* was a body type that was antithetical to this fit body. Ironically, then, the suffragists disagreed with the anti-suffragists about the vote and women's rights, but they shared the use of *fat* as a tool to denigrate the opposition.

Fat Denigration as Feminist Tactic

When the youthful American suffragist Alice Paul returned from England in 1913, fired up by the Pankhurst family's militant strategies of storming the Parliament and hunger striking, she was disappointed by the carefully measured approach of the National American Woman Suffrage Association. Breaking off from the NAWSA, Paul began the National Woman's Party, whose goal was a women's suffrage amendment to the Constitution. One of Paul's first "hires" was Nina Allender, a watercolor painter whom she persuaded to begin work as a cartoonist for the Woman's Party new journal, *The Suffragist*. Picturing thin, white, good-looking women often being overpowered by burly policemen or rough crowds of men, Allender's cartoons graced the cover of every issue of *The Suffragist*. Her work typified a shift that had happened in both England and the United States by the first decades of the 20th century, as consumer culture and the advertising industries influenced the tactics and strategies of the suffragist movement. In this shift, the *body* became the key sign of one's worthiness, of one's *fitness* for citizenship. To be sure, the work of 19th century suffragists had also dealt extensively with the body. Think, for instance, of Sojourner Truth's impassioned discussion of the womanliness of her own body, of Stanton's detailed rationale for educating women's mental and physical selves, of Amelia Bloomer's attempts to popularize a form of clothing less hazardous and confining for women's bodies than the traditional corsets and long skirts. Think as well of the taunts, threats, and danger that women faced as they inserted their very physical bodies into public spaces of civic halls, churches, and town squares, previously reserved for men. As the anti-suffragists intensified their visual ridicule, and as the tools and technology available to feminist cartoonists expanded, however, the *visual representation of* and the *meaning attributed to* the body gained more significance. As Margaret Finnegan argued in her book *Selling Suffrage*, suffragists began to use the "new arts of publicity and propaganda" and "public displays that used beauty and sentimentality to overwhelm onlookers' negative impressions of women voters." Moreover, Finnegan explained, "suffragists used physical appearance, dress, and personality to suggest that woman suffragists (and thus potential woman voters) were attractive, stylish, charming, dignified, and virtuous. They used such representations symbolically, implying that women's enfranchisement was a positive goal because woman suffragists were personable, likable, and modern individuals."[14] Like the anti-suffragists, the suffragist cartoons used the available lexicon of fat as degenerative and thin as civilized in order to represent—in a visual, bodily way—the suffragists as dignified, virtuous, and modern.

Of course, the suffragists could have challenged the very use of the body to demonstrate fitness for citizenship. But the idea that the body somehow *meant* something was central to the mainstream thinking of white suffragists. Suffragists knew that they were being lampooned as fat, masculine, and primitive. (One British suffrage organization, for instance, printed a postcard of a "jackass anti-suffragist" that paints a portrait of a svelte suffragist; the image looks nothing like her, but instead shows a fat, short woman, bearing the title "Britannia Unsexed.")[15] When faced with the very powerful anti-suffrage propaganda that visually represented the suffragist as beastly, fat, and uncivilized, the suffragists chose not to challenge these notions but, instead, to deny the charges, to assert that suffragists were *more* beautiful, more slender, more attractive, and more civilized than their opponents. A 1913 cartoon in *Judge* illuminates the dichotomous typing of suffragists. In this cartoon, titled "Even Santa Claus," we see a youthful white woman stretching as she awakes on Christmas morning. She is still in the jumble of her luxurious sheets and comforters. In her Christmas stocking is tucked a copy of a newspaper called *Woman Suffrage*. The cartoon includes a poem, by J. A. Waldron:

> There are two sorts of Suffragettes,
>   Although they have one plea.
> One kind resembles dragonets,
>   And from these all men flee.
> They are ungracious and they vex
>   With shrill and angry note,
> While others so adorn their sex,
>   They surely ought to vote!
> And thus when Beauty asks for rights
>   That Voting will confer,
> E'en Santa Claus himself delights
>   To hand them out to her.[16]

Based on the visual campaign materials of the suffragists, it appears that they too chose Beauty to fight the suffrage battle. And Beauty, it seems, was white, thin, and young.

One of the most iconic photographs from the suffrage movement was that of Inez Milholland Boissevain, the young, beautiful white woman who, atop a striking white horse, led a thousand women in the 1913 Washington DC suffrage parade. Historical accounts of this parade, as well as those of other suffrage pageants and marches, often refer to the racism of their white organizers, including Alice Paul, who thwarted the efforts of African American suffragists to participate. Historians frequently explain this discrimination as resulting from the white suffragists' reluctance to anger their white Southern constituents. This certainly is part of the explanation. What has not been as well addressed, however, is the way that white suffragists were also engaging in a battle of symbols with the anti-suffragists at this point, one that played on the iconic status of the body and its fitness for citizenship. That is, the parades of women marching in unison in white outfits; the pageants featuring beautiful white women as liberty and justice; the posters, postcards, and billboards that highlighted young, rose-cheeked, well-dressed, and thin white suffragists: all these were part of a campaign to demonstrate the bodily fitness of women for the full rights of citizenship. This iconic figure of Beauty was the sign of progress, of the future. Beauty was white, thin, tall, and athletic. Northern white suffragists, I would argue, had as much stake in the creation of a particular iconic image of the suffragist, and thus in the exclusion of African American suffragists, as did their Southern partners. And, of course, *thinness*, like whiteness, was key to this iconic representation, as it stood in opposition to the primitive. Just as white skin was a fundamental sign of the highest level of civilization, so was thinness. "Thin" was a visual, bodily indication that one was highly evolved, able to manage the bounty and pressure of the modern world.

Suffragists in both England and the United States repeatedly portrayed the vote-seeking woman as beautiful, young, white, stylish—and thin. A British poster, for instance, showed a young, rose-cheeked suffragist wearing a low-cut, red, fur-trimmed coat cinched tightly on her tiny waist. "I'll vote for a woman any day," says a bright-faced man winking at the audience. While not all pro-suffrage material focused on the heterosexual allure of the young suffragists, the pro-suffrage cartoons did emphasize the youthful, thin, white body of the suffragist. Nina Allender's work on *The Suffragist* probably best represents this. In cartoon after cartoon, we see a slender woman in a stylish dress and hat. We can always see her thin ankles and narrow feet, clad in dainty, high-heeled pumps. Definitely dressed as a "lady," this suffragist nevertheless protests outside the White House, fights off burly guards, and argues with Uncle Sam. She is the picture of the civilized body, who in seeking out the vote is simply asking for what should already belong to her.

What is striking about the body size typing in pro-suffrage material is the extent to which the thin suffragist is paired with a fat body that serves as the anti-suffrage antagonist. Often this enemy of the suffragist in these cartoons is a "fat cat," that image of the greedy, gluttonous, rich, and powerful individual I described in chapter 2. Frequently the "fat cat" represents something larger than himself, such as a corrupt political system, crooked business organizations, or simply power run amok. In a National American Woman Suffrage Association cartoon titled "On Which Side Do You Stand?" we see two slender white women paired with two different sets of people. The woman on the right, whose elegant and simple dress reads "Suffrage Mother," is holding a baby. She is standing next to a visiting nurse, a professional woman, a child, a college graduate, and a laboring woman. All the women are white, and all are thin. In contrast, the woman on the left wears an overly fancy dress that reads "Anti-suffragist." With her stands a brothel keeper, a fat man whose suit reads "Liquor Interests," and a very fat man whose suit, bedecked with dollar signs and reading "Big Interests," holds a bedraggled baby on whose shirt is inscribed "Child Labor." One of Nina Allender's *Suffragist* covers shows a similar juxtaposition of the thin suffragist and the fat cat. In this 1918 cartoon we see a young white woman on a streetcar. She has a youthful face and rosebud mouth, a stylish dress, and those dainty pumps on her slender feet. Speaking to the conductor, whose hat has the initials W. W. on them (standing for President Woodrow Wilson), she points to a very fat passenger, whose protruding girth almost covers his briefcase, labeled "Democratic Senator." "Make that man move along," the suffragist says to W. W. Clearly here the fat man represents the Democratic Senate, which was targeted by the National Woman's Party as an obstructionist, reactionary body, working in tandem with those same "big interests" pictured in the NAWSA cartoon. In a poster from the New York State Suffrage Party we see a group of four men hanging around a table at a bar. Smoke from their pipes and cigars fills the air, and their round glasses of liquor sit atop a newspaper announcing "Woman's Suffrage Defeated in New Jersey." The bulbous-nosed men are very fat, with protruding girths that strain their vests. "Well, boys, we saved the home," the caption reads. This cartoon manages to capture both the fat cat and the fat ethnic stereotype. Clearly the fat cat anti-temperance interests have defeated the vote, but so have the working-class, uneducated, ethnic men, those who drink so much they have misshapen bodies and noses. Although the thin, white, civilized suffragist

The standard protagonist in Nina Allender's cartoons for the National Woman's Party was a tall, slender, youthful white woman, often shown in contrast to a "fat cat" who literally—or figuratively—threatened harm. (Courtesy of National Woman's Party Collection, Sewall-Belmont House and Museum, Washington DC.)

is not literally in this cartoon, she is referenced—the women at home who are now more oppressed than ever by these fat, ignorant bullies. Similarly, another cartoon, titled "Why This Ever Present Detachment in the 'Anti' Parade, If Suffrage Wouldn't Accomplish Anything?" juxtaposes the fat cats with the invisible oppressed woman. We see rows of men marching, carrying a banner that reads, "Our Motto: Woman's Place Is in the Home." Most prominent are the "Crooked Politician," the "Dive Keeper," the "Vice Protector," and the "Political Reactionary." Not surprisingly, all these men are fat. And in a cartoon explaining how a

Nebraskan newspaper editor came to realize his mistake in opposing woman's suffrage, we see a beautiful, young, female figure—"Suffrage"—being struck down by a very fat man, whose stomach hangs precariously low. On his lapels are two labels, "Liquor Interests" and "Vice Interests," and in his hand he carries a large stick labeled "Despotism." "Truth crushed to earth will rise again," Suffrage says as her long slender fingers rest against her breastbone.

Men were not the only ones lampooned as fat by the suffragists. Suffragist literature also frequently juxtaposed thin suffragists with "unevolved" female anti-suffragists. What is quite interesting here is that the suffragists were using the same typology as that within anti-suffrage propaganda: the motif of fatness to represent the primitive, undeveloped, less civilized body. In suffrage literature, however, it was the anti-suffragist who represented the degenerative force, thwarting progress with their old-fashioned ideas. Feminist activists at the turn of the century, such as Charlotte Perkins Gilman, strongly endorsed the idea that humans were racially grouped into hierarchical arrangements of civilization and evolution. It was true, they argued, that in "less evolved" groups men and women resembled each other more than in the more evolved groups of Europeans and white, native-born Americans. Their push for suffrage was not, however, in any way to be seen as a reevaluation of the "lower" civilizations of Native Americans and Africans. Instead, women's rights among Euro-Americans represented the *next* stage of civilization, in which women would catch up with the physical and mental development of Euro-American men.[17] Anti-suffragists, then, were portrayed as holding European and white American civilization back from this next step of evolutionary development. A British poster created by the Suffrage Atelier, in which an anti-suffragist dressmaker pictured as a jackass designs out-of-date and poorly fitting clothing for a young woman, clearly illuminates this idea of the "modern" suffragist. The dressmaker exclaims, "Out of date and a bad fit? *Impossible* madam! I assure you it must suit you, for I made it exactly after your grandmother's pattern." A piece of campaign literature by the New York State Woman Suffrage Association drew on the same theme, though this time adding the fat motif. Under the headline "Do You Use a Sewing Machine?" this brochure juxtaposes two women, one sewing by hand, the other at a modern sewing machine. The older, *fat* woman—a grandmotherly type—sewing by hand frets that she has no time to vote, because she spends so much time on housework caused by the filthy streets and high price of food. The younger, *thin* woman has plenty of time to fight those causes of housework, *precisely* because she is modern, up-to-date, and familiar with the newest technology of the sewing machine and the newest piece of civilization, the vote for women.[18]

Other pieces of suffragist literature were not so polite about the "grand-mothers" who fought the vote. One, for instance, showed a whole carload of the "Anti-suffrage League" women stuffed into their seats, rolls of fat brimming over their necklines. "We have *all* we want. No votes for women," the sign on the car reads. Even the dog that runs alongside the car is short and fat.[19] In an American cartoon satirizing the anti-suffrage movement for its hypocrisy, we see a group of women on a stage as they present their arguments against the female vote. "Suffrage would demoralize women by thrusting them onto public stage," announces one of the anti-suffragists. Behind her sits an older fat woman, with a thick girth and portly arms. Her nose turned in the air, she appears to be simultaneously sleeping and assured of

Suffragists did not simply represent themselves as youthful and slender; they also mocked the antis as aging, fat, and old-fashioned, as in this image of the fat conservative women driving. Note that even their dog is fat. (Courtesy of Suffrage Societies Collection, The Women's Library, London.)

her superior stance. Adding the fat cat to the fat anti-suffragist, the cartoon-ist sketched in some fat men in the front row of the audience, enjoying the women's presentation.[20] The suffrage cartoonist Nina Allender also drew on the image of the outmoded fat anti-suffragist. In a 1917 cartoon, for instance, we see a young woman, with slender legs and a petite face, holding a suffrage banner in front of her. Next to her stands a matronly dressed older woman, whose wide girth, thick arms, and long jowls are accentuated by the willowy body of the suffragist. "My child!" the older woman says to the suffragist, shocked at her political stance.

Clearly these suffragist tactics that mocked the older, fat women reveal the birth of a new youth culture, one that was being fashioned and promoted by the consumer and advertising industries of the early 20th century. It's impor-tant to remember, however, that the fat anti-suffrage women in the suffrag-ists' campaign literature were *symbols*; the ranks of anti-suffragists, like those of suffragists, were made up of older and younger women, fat women and thin women. Indeed, the historian Susan Marshall has argued that what pri-marily divided suffragists from anti-suffragists was class. Wealthier white women, both young and old, tended to reject the call for the vote, as the potential for large groups of working-class, immigrant, African American, and socially conscious voters threatened the privilege of their gendered class status.[21] Suffragists chose to latch on to the "older," "fatter" typology to rep-resent the anti-suffragists, I would argue, not because that's how the anti-suffragists actually looked. Rather, those two physical characteristics—old and fat—could be powerfully harnessed to "say" that the anti-suffragists were out-of-date, regressive women whose points of view threatened progress. Being older meant that one was outmoded. Being fat meant that one had degenerative characteristics. Neither was good in a modern world.

One of the British Suffrage Atelier postcards, popular in the United States as well, showed a short, stout "Anti-Suffrage League" woman strutting (and "tut-tutting") in front of a group of tall, slender, dignified women who are holding a "Woman Suffrage" banner.[22] This was an important contrast that the suffragists emphasized over and over again in their literature and activi-ties. The slender body was one of progress, of women who demonstrated resolve, rationality, and civilized behavior. Suffragists were dignified and in control, women of progress who were more than worthy of the responsibili-ties and privileges of the vote. Nowhere do we see this as clearly as in the hunger strikes taken on by the suffragists imprisoned for their participation in "votes for women" demonstrations. British suffragists like Marion Wal-lace Dunlop refused to eat even when tempted with an array of foods. When coaxing failed, prison wardens resorted to forced feedings, brutal acts that suffragists presented as more evidence of the atrocious tactics of the state and the bullied bodies of the women. Emboldened by what their experiences in England, the U.S. suffragists Alice Paul and Lucy Burns organized demonstrations in front of the White House, and, like the British suffragists, they refused to eat once they were in prison. Descriptions of their forced feedings suggest rape rather than a medically necessary, humane procedure, as prison wardens forcibly held the women down while medical personnel clamped open their mouths, thrusting tubes up their noses and down their throats. If these suffragists could survive the starvation and the forced feedings, then clearly, their act of resistance suggested, they had wills of steel that could match any man: they were strong enough to survive the "dangers" of the political sphere.[23] Certainly political hunger strikes had a long history before the battle for women's votes, one that the suffragists clearly sought to evoke. The decision to resist in a way that emphasized their controlled, thin bodies also resonated with the body politics of their campaigns. In contrast to the portly, "unevolved" anti-suffrage women, the fat cat special interests, and the burly prison wardens, these thin women were the worthy citizens, those whose powers of rationality and resolve proved them worthy of the vote.

Elizabeth Cady Stanton and the Rejection of Fat

The use of body trait denigration as a tactic among first-wave feminists seems at first incongruous, considering that a major battle for these activists was challenging the physical stereotyping regarding female bodies and brains that provided the legitimization for the social, political, and economic oppression that they faced. Like all humans, however, these early women's rights activists were not immune from contradictory thinking and limited vision. The case of Elizabeth Cady Stanton clearly illuminates the paradox inherent in the thinking of some of the most well-known early feminist activists in the United States. Her case also points to an early case of feminism's fraught relationship with fat.

Born in 1815, Stanton is, along with her best friend, Susan B. Anthony, probably the best-known 19th-century women's rights activist in the United States. Stanton was a keen thinker about the way that knowledge was constructed and power wielded. Her work on behalf of women spanned almost a century, focusing on a wide range of issues, including property rights, marital laws, suffrage, clothing restrictions, and the oppressive force of religion. As a young woman, she attended the World Anti-slavery Convention with her abolitionist husband in 1840. Angered at the conference organizers' refusal to seat women, Stanton returned home determined to work with other activists to organize the first U.S. women's rights convention. Family obligations delayed the conference (Stanton eventually had seven children), but in 1848 it was finally held in Seneca Falls, New York. Drawing a diverse crowd of abolitionists and women's rights activists, men and women, black and white activists, the Seneca Falls Convention resulted in a Declaration of Rights and Sentiments for women. Closely modeled after the Declaration of Independence, the Declaration listed a wide range of grievances and demands, of which voting is the best known and at the time was the most controversial. It's important to recognize how intertwined at this point the abolitionist and the women's rights movements were. Activists spoke on behalf of both causes, white women's rights activists housed runaway slaves on the Underground Railroad as they traveled north, and reformers' arguments for the elimination of slavery and of unjust laws for women rested on the inadequacy and unfairness of using body typing—skin color and sex—to justify oppression. When the Civil War ended and Congress proposed the 14th and 15th amendments, giving suffrage rights to all *male* citizens, however, the coalition of activists broke down. Although there were some African American activists, such as Sojourner Truth, who agreed that if one group should gain suffrage prior to another it should be *women;* and some white activists, like Lucy Stone, who argued that women should graciously support black men's rights and then continue to press for women's rights, for the most part the line was drawn on the basis of race.[24] The historian Bettye Collier-Thomas pointed out the extent to which African American women remained chary of the organized white women's rights movement and of white activists after this point; other scholars, beginning with Eleanor Flexner, argued that in their refusal to accept second-class citizenship, Stanton and her allies began what can be seen as the first true women's rights movement.[25] While I see the breakup of the alliance as a tremendous loss, my point here is to illuminate the extent to which Stanton's decision to narrow her focus on the rights of white women was deeply rooted in her beliefs about the significance of phrenology and physiognomy in measuring fitness for citizenship. For Stanton, certain people were simply more fit for citizenship than others. Anglo-Americans were more fit than people of African descent, and English-speaking native born Americans were more fit than recent immigrants, especially those who were either Irish or non-English speaking. These ideas about fitness for citizenship even emerged when it came to her own body.

Stanton's writings on issues unrelated to suffrage demonstrate the extent to which she challenged dominant thinking about the body in many ways. Raising seven children, she encouraged outdoor, active play for the health of both the girls and the boys, despite official advice that admonished physical activity for girls and discouraged outdoor play for all children in bad weather. She refused the advice of her children's doctors if she thought it wasn't working, proudly describing at one point the arm splint she had devised for a child's broken shoulder, much superior, she argued, to the one "officially" prescribed. She roused herself to exercise after giving birth, ignoring her physician's advice to stay in bed for weeks. Her essays on clothing spoke in detail about the physical harm done to women's bodies by the tight corsets that hindered breathing, the long skirts that risked catching fire in the kitchen and that prevented freedom of movement, and the wide-brimmed hats that obscured vision as well as making one look foolish. When faced with the argument that men were obviously superior because of their large size, she responded with characteristic wit, "The power of mind seems to be in no way connected with the size and strength of body."[26] Despite her awareness of the limitations of dominant thinking about women's and children's bodies, however, she was strongly influenced by Herbert Spencer's thinking on sociological evolution, and she embraced the "wisdom" of phrenology and physiognomical readings.[27] In her autobiography she described the ways she chose her servants based on "scientific" methods, reading them "phrenologically and physiologically" before hiring them. In one particular case, she chose a woman with a "large head" and "bumps of caution and order." She was dismayed to find that the servant became drunk one day and burned the baby's foot on the fire; apparently those "cautionary" bumps were not enough to overcome what Stanton saw as her general constitutional weakness as an Irish girl. Stanton particularly embraced the idea that the Irish were inferior in both body and culture, lamenting the licentious sexuality and drunkenness of the "large Irish settlement" in her hometown of Seneca Falls: "Alas! alas! who can measure the mountains of sorrow and suffering endured in unwelcome motherhood in the abodes of ignorance, poverty, and vice, where terror-stricken women and children are the victims of strong men frenzied with passion and intoxicating drink?"[28] Stanton could simultaneously reject explicit legal oppression at the same time that she embraced ideas about hierarchies of civilization. She spoke movingly about the horror of English brutality against the Irish, for instance, but also accepted wholeheartedly the "inferiority" of Irish culture and bodies. She worked tirelessly against slavery in the United States, but later wrote about the folly of degraded classes of citizens, meaning African American men and recent male immigrants, gaining the vote before women like herself. Her belief in Anglo-American superiority, then, coexisted in a complicated way with her fight against injustice and her piercing understanding of gendered inequities.

Stanton's embrace of Anglo-American superiority and the significance of phrenology and physiognomy became a bit of a touchy situation as her weight increased tremendously with age. Fat was a sign of a primitive, weak body, of atavistic tendencies, not of a civilized, rational being. Indeed, from her earliest writings Stanton used fatness to mock her opponents. In supporting her points about the size of women's bodies relative to their intelligence, for instance, she described the ways that a small, intelligent child can easily beat up a "big, fat boy." She even referred to Daniel Lambert, the extremely fat man who was part of the London curiosity circuit I described in chapter 2, exclaiming, "I have never heard that Daniel Lambert was distinguished for any great mental endowments."[29] For Stanton, then, her growing body weight posed a problem. One can see this in the careful way that her supporters wrote about her body size. In the 1868 *Eminent Women of the Age: Being Narratives of the Lives and Deeds of the Most Prominent Women of the Present Generation*, Theodore Tilton explained that, although he was "ungallant as to hint it," Stanton no longer rode a horse, "a lady of very elegant but also very solid proportions is somewhat more at her ease in a carriage than on a saddle." He continued to describe her corpulent body, though he took pains to explain that it suggested a good nature and hid an English strength; in other words, that her body fat did not in any way suggest criminal tendencies or any atavistic traits. "I may now paint her features and sum up her character," he wrote:

Mrs. Stanton's face is thought to resemble Martha Washington's but is less regular and more animated; her hair—early gray, and now frosty white—falls about her head in thick clusters of curls; her eyes twinkle with amiable mischief; her voice, though hardly musical, is mellow and agreeable; her figure is of the middle height and just stout enough to suggest a preference for short walks rather than for long. In reality, however, she can walk like an English-woman,—though, if, during a stroll in the street, some jest sets her to laughing, she is forced to halt, cover her countenance with her veil, and shake contagiously till the spasm be past. The costume that most becomes her (and in which her historic portrait ought to be garmented) is a blue silk dress and a red India shawl,—an array, which topped with her magnificent white hair, makes her a patriotic embodiment of "red, white and blue."[30]

In writing the preface to the 1922 edition of her autobiography and published letters, her children Theodore Stanton and Harriot Stanton Blatch equally took pains to downplay her weight, saying "to the last she set an example of care of the body, and always laid an emphasis on the importance of appearing at one's best in the family circle."[31] Yet we know from Stanton's letters that she considered her weight a "humiliation and sorrow." She enrolled in a six-week program at an upstate New York sanatorium, where she "tried all the rubbings, pinching, steaming; the Swedish movements of the arms, hands, legs, feet; dieting, massage, electricity" to lose weight and to recover from her overall depression. In her original autobiography, published in 1898, she reported that she "succeeded in throwing off only five pounds of flesh." Still, she said she "felt like a new being" after her time in the sanatorium.[32] Interestingly, her children in republishing her autobiography in 1922 carefully omitted the part of the sentence where she explained that she lost only five pounds.[33] One has to wonder if by that time the imperative to be thin, and the connection between a thin body and a civilized body, were so firmly entrenched that they did not want to discredit their mother with a failure to "control" her body—or what looks today like an early hint of a fat acceptance perspective.

Toward the end of her life, Stanton became a controversial figure within the suffrage movement. She had been the most articulate writer and speaker on behalf of women's rights, and she held numerous offices within the movement, including positions with the Women's Loyal National League during the Civil War, the American Equal Rights Association, the National Woman Suffrage Association, and the National American Woman Suffrage Association in the 1890s. Her African American suffrage colleagues had been reluctant to associate with Stanton for decades, as her belief in Anglo-American superiority and her support of the educated vote (meaning that citizens should have to demonstrate they could read and write in English before being eligible to vote) resulted in racist writings and activism. The publication of her *Woman's Bible*, in which she excised all passages from the Bible that supported male supremacy or denigrated women, was what pushed her white suffragist colleagues, with the exception of Susan B. Anthony, to abandon her. The controversy stirred up by this publication gave her fellow suffragists the final and sufficient rationale to bar her from sitting on the stages of suffrage events. Knowing the extent to which anti–women's rights activists were using body politics to ridicule the suffrage movement, however, one also has to wonder whether it was the combination of *fat*, outspoken, and incendiary that was just too much for her mainstream white colleagues. At any rate, Stanton's body size, an attribute which distressed her and which her supporters sought to minimize, certainly did nothing to legitimize this radical, aged activist. This was particularly true within a context where the ridiculing of fat women's bodies was already a major tool of the anti–women's rights faction and was becoming an essential tactic of pro-women's rights groups themselves.

The Independent Woman

The thin, flat-chested flapper is of course the iconic figure of the 1920s, the decade after women had finally won the vote. Many scholars have pointed out the extent to which this wiry, youthful figure corresponded to the exponential growth of advertising and consumer culture. Others, like Joan Brumberg, have argued that the cultural mandate for a thinner body was part of a larger "body project" that deflected women's attention from maintaining, let alone improving on, the political, cultural, and social rights they had gained in the preceding decades. (Susan Faludi made a similar argument in *Backlash* when she argued that the increase in eating disorders coupled with the decrease in models' sizes was part of a larger attack on the feminist gains of the 1970s.) While both points are certainly true—advertising industries did capitalize on selling the new thin body, and this cultural mandate did certainly pull women's attention away from other concerns—it is also essential to remember the extent to which feminist activists had helped to propagate this thin figure in the decades preceding the roaring twenties. The body had served as a cultural battleground during the suffrage battle, with each side wanting to claim "thin" as its own. For anti-suffragists, lampooning the female activists as fat provided a means to illuminate their idea that suffrage created primitive monsters that had upended the normal racial and gender order of civilization. For suffragists, portraying the activists as thin was a way to "prove" that they had civilized bodies, ones that had all the capacities necessary for entry into the public sphere. Moreover, these thin bodies were key to reassuring the public that the gendered order of civilization would actually be improved: women would be even more heterosexually alluring with the vote. In a cultural context in which one's physical, psychological, and moral characteristics were presumed to be tightly linked, "thin" was an essential attribute to prove one's right to move into the public sphere.

After the 19th amendment passed, granting women the vote, the Woman's Party journal the *Suffragist* became *Equal Rights*. This new journal focused on the party's decision to press for the passage of an Equal Rights Amendment. Nina Allender continued as the journal's cartoonist, and the same wispy, white, youthful figures dominated those images. On the June 1923 cover, for instance, we see a tall white woman pointing toward a banner labeled "Seneca Falls, 1848–1923." "Our best tribute is to finish the work they began," reads the caption. Surrounding the woman holding the banner is a group of equally wispy women, all wearing either stylish 1920s dresses and bobbed haircuts or vaguely Greek-style flowing robes. Even the young girl, to whom the adult women are clearly passing on the fight, is thin, with slender hands and tiny feet and ankles. In another image from the same year, we see a woman handing a surprised Uncle Sam a document for his signature. The document, of course, is for the Equal Rights Amendment. Not surprisingly, the woman is thin, tall, and white, with her hair pulled back in a neat bob. She has carefully groomed eyebrows and is wearing a dab of lipstick. She has all the attributes of a "civilized" body, and although Uncle Sam may be surprised, it's clear that she is on the side of progress.

Interestingly, after Allender retired from her position as cartoonist, *Equal Rights* did not continue to use the thin, attractive woman to publicize their ideas. Instead, they turned to "news photos" of activist women from around the world, generally head shots of important women or photos of groups of women signing key petitions and documents at international conferences. (Likely this tactic was chosen because it mirrored the style typically used to represent important male public figures.) Instead, it was the journal for the National Federation of Business and Professional Woman's Clubs, the *Independent Woman*, that continued the thin woman motif. Less radical than the National Woman's Party, the NFBPWC, founded in 1919, was nevertheless feminist, insofar as it pressed for the improvement in workingwomen's lives. By its very definition, the NFBPWC focused on women in the public sphere, those who earned a wage and were as likely to identify themselves by their work as by their family ties. Also important to note about the NFBPWC was its focus on upwardly mobile women; while the jobs the women held were often low-level office and professional jobs, they distinctly were not the jobs frequently held by women, such as factory workers, domestics, or farm hands. The imagined readers for this journal were relatively well-paid women workers who desired to own their own businesses, do well in their professions, and move into higher-tier positions previously denied to women. In the 1920s and 1930s, the journal provided information on laws dealing with women's employment, discussed job opportunities, and featured stories on successful business and professional women (all of whom, with the exception of some international figures, were white). It also included regular columns on health and living tips designed to improve their work success, such as the 1927 article that explained, "Part of the businesswoman's stock in trade is her smart, trim appearance."[34] Indeed, the "trim" body played an important role in the narrative of the successful "independent woman," from the lithe, slender cartoon figure traipsing over the world often featured on the covers, to the ongoing advertisements for weight loss products. Interestingly, the focus in some of the articles is more on bodily strength than on a slender body. A 1923 article, for instance, explained that "the woman with good health radiates strength. . . . Physical fitness is a business asset." The point of this article was to encourage women to show nerves of steel by developing robust physical bodies. And in 1927 an article quotes at length the head of the Physical Education Department at Barnard College, Agnes Wayman, explaining that young workingwomen were often *undernourished*, giving up nutritious meals to pay for overpriced housing and entertainment.[35] For the most part, however, these types of articles were aberrations in an unrelenting focus on the importance of a thin body. Regular advertisements featured the Davis Chin Strap, a device that strapped onto the chin and looped over the head. "A drooping mouth, flabby cheeks, a double chin—these need not be, as thousands of businesswomen wearers of the Davis Chin Strap have found," the advertisement promised. Articles with titles like "She Found a Pleasant Way to Reduce Her Fat" and "The Gentle Art of Reducing" provided details on menus, calorie counting, and exercise.[36] For $6.95 one could buy Reducex, a "systematic" guide to exercise that promised to shrink a woman from the size of the big woman on the right of the advertisement to that of the slender woman on the left.[37] As an article promoting the benefits of cosmetic surgery explained, it was important to feel "presentable" so that one could "conquer the world." And part of being "presentable"—able to present oneself to the public world with confidence—was a thin body. "The present mode," explained another article, "demands slenderness."[38] As one advertisement explained, "women of discrimination" were reducing.[39] In other words, if one sought status, upward mobility, and a better place within the business and professional world, it was necessary to develop a thin body.

As mentioned above, with the exception of some international women featured in the *Independent Woman*, all the women in the articles were white Euro-Americans. One has to ask, then, whether this imperative for thinness and fat denigration affected other groups in these same decades. The *Girls*

Guide for the National Association of Colored Girls suggests that body size per se held less importance among African American women. Formed in 1898, the National Association of Colored Women, whose motto was "Lifting as We Climb," had as its focus racial uplift and improvement in African American children's lives. As such, it was a complex organization, which blended practical homemaking advice with a political agenda that included women's suffrage, legal challenges to discrimination, and a keen focus on the power of education. In 1928 the organization formally organized its offshoot, the National Association of Colored Girls, whose emblem was a four-leaf clover representing "Mind, Soul, Body, and Race." The NACG published its first *Girls Guide* in 1933, a lengthy and detailed manual on everything from the organization's philosophy to the extensive requirements for earning various badges of distinction, all of which were designed with "uplift" in mind. As the manual explained, "Every bad fellow not only lowers himself but lowers the group." It was important for girls to learn to help others move up, "without rolling in the mud with them." One of the main thrusts was healthy living, in body, mind, and soul. As such, the manual focused on learning basic nutrition information and cooking tasty, inexpensive meals, not on body size reduction. Indeed, with the exception of one suggestion to "choose clothes that make one look neither stout nor too thin," most of the body information focused on making the body, character, and mind "strong."[40] In contrast to this focus on balance and strength, however, were the college records from Spelman College, a historically black college for women founded in 1881. Although the National Association of Colored Girls was decidedly an "uplift" organization that pushed for upward mobility for its members, it also was a national organization, open to anyone who could demonstrate that they went to church regularly and avoided places of ill repute. Many of their members would have been from poor or modest homes, in rural as well as urban areas. In contrast, Spelman was a decidedly elite institution, catering to the very few African American young women who would have had the financial and educational resources to attend, at a time when few young men or women of any racial or ethnic background went to college. Records indicate that for Spelman College students in the late 19th century and early 20th century, gaining weight or indulging in food boxes sent from home was strictly forbidden.[41] Students got around these college policies by hiding food boxes and sneaking in treats. The policy itself is important, however, as it suggests an awareness of the body politics of the time period, in which upward mobility and notions of the "civilized body" demanded a rejection of fatness. For Spelman College, which was cultivating an elite class among African American women who would be poised to break into the white, male-dominated world, it was important also to cultivate what was considered an "elite body"—the thin body.

Advertising and Consumer Feminism

The feminist activity in the beginning of the 20th century did not, of course, happen in a vacuum, removed from the broader context of consumer culture. Indeed, numerous scholars, such as Nancy Cott in the *Grounding of Modern Feminism* and Nan Enstad in *Ladies of Labor, Girls of Adventure*, have detailed the ways that feminism and consumer culture intertwined in complex ways in these early decades. What is key to note for thinking about fat stigma is the way that, regardless of whether certain feminist organizations dropped fat denigration as a tactic, as the National Woman's Party did, the advertising industries had picked up on and exacerbated the narrative of the "civilized body" as a thin body. Women who wanted a place in the public world needed to have a thin body, according to the mantra of these ads. Since the early part of the 20th century, advertisers for weight loss products have elaborated the theme that the suffragists expressed so explicitly in both their posters and their hunger strikes: a thin body is one that represents a person who has tamed primitive instincts, who has become fully civilized, and who thus deserves entry into the public sphere. For instance, an ad in the early 1900s for Marmola, described as a "harmless tablet" (actually a thyroid substance), pictured a side view of a woman with an extraordinarily large bosom. The ad read, "Most women suffer much humiliation because of great quantities of fat, so located that no matter how they dress, everybody sees that they are abnormal. This is the day of the slender figure, and fat women are simply not tolerated either in *business or social affairs*."[42] Far different from the image of the "slender figure," successful in business and social affairs, was the picture of the fat woman, laboring and sweating through her wrinkled, dowdy dress under the weight of a heavy black box, which was found in the advertisements for "Every Woman's Flesh Reducer," a bathtub remedy consisting of camphor, baking soda, and Epsom salts. The ad read, "You cannot be happy while you carry around with you that load of useless, energy using fat. Until you rid yourself of that burden you will not be capable of getting out of life the enjoyment you are entitled to. Be Rid of Your Handicap. Every Woman's Flesh Reducer Is the Easy Way." In this case, fat is literally represented as the weight keeping women down. That fat woman might be able to be a housewife or a domestic, but she certainly did not "fit" in the new urban and managerial world.[43] In *Slimming for the Million*, published in 1939, Eustace Chesser explained, "Fat folk have a thin time these days! Quite apart from the prejudicial effect which excess weight has upon health, these are times in which lean men and slender women are favoured. In all kinds of occupations, other things being equal, the lean are preferred to the fat. They look, and in fact are, more alert, fitter, better prepared for providing the quick results which are demanded of us to-day, both physically and mentally." As Chesser pointed out, fatness was a liability for both men and women in the business world. For women, however, the stigma of fatness, with its connotations of laziness and impulsiveness, was yet one more charge that could be used to deny them entry into "masculine" spheres.[44] (Chesser's solution for fatness was the Bergonie electrical chair, which he argued unfairly brought "to many minds the apparatus used for the execution of murderers.")[45] Less expensive than the electric chair, Ponzoff Reducing Cream was sold as the "easy way to reduce" in the early 1940s. Picturing a slender white woman in both a swimsuit and a business suit, the ad read, "Why give FAT another day's chance? A Stunning Figure Always Commands Attendance. . . . . The Business Woman Must Always Be Neat in Appearance." It continued, "Competition is very keen in all walks of life. . . . Why let fat rob you of what should be rightfully yours? Start remodeling at once! Delay can profit you nothing!"[46] What all these ads played on was the idea that in order to compete in the newly structured public world, women needed to eliminate signs of inferiority, including the marks of primitiveness and impulsivity that fatness symbolized.

The question that the ad for Ponzoff Reducing Cream posed to readers, "Why let fat rob you of what should be rightfully yours?" encapsulates in many ways the body size ideology confronting first-wave feminists as well as those who continued the fight for equal rights and professional advancement after the 19th amendment had passed. The thin body was the civilized body, fit for the full rights of citizenship, worthy of a place in the public sphere, poised for upward mobility. Fatness, a powerful cultural sign of degeneracy, threatened to undo all the difficult work feminists had done to prove their worthiness. Rather than *challenging* the ideology of fat denigration, first-wave feminists for the most part battled for their rights *within* the ideology, painting themselves as slim and fit for citizenship and drawing on fat stigma to humiliate their opposition.

Contemporary Feminism's Fraught Relationship with Fat

The tactics of these first-wave feminists suggest why so many contemporary feminists continue to have such a fraught relationship with fat, both challenging the valorization of the thin body but also supporting and participating in a culture of fat denigration. Feminist scholars have been at the forefront of critiquing the cult of thinness that pervades U.S. media and culture. Susie Orbach's *Fat Is a Feminist Issue*, published in 1978, first articulated the idea that a thin female body was desirable by patriarchal standards because it took up little space—the deferential body that did not claim too much. In *Fasting Girls: The History of Anorexia Nervosa*, the book that motivated my own research into fatness, Joan Brumberg laid out the historical roots of women's preoccupation with weight. In *Unbearable Weight: Feminism, Western Culture, and the Body*, Susan Bordo articulated the links between Western culture's mind/body dichotomy and the cult of thinness. She brilliantly analyzed the ways that the body/mind duality, which posits the physical as inferior and feminine, the mind as superior and masculine, inherently constructs an ideology in which the female person is seen as physical and thus substandard. In *Backlash* and *The Beauty Myth*, Susan Faludi and Naomi Wolf, respectively, explored the ways that American women faced the restrictions of raised expectations for a beautiful and thin body despite, or in reaction to, the gains women had won during the second wave of feminism in the 1970s and early 1980s. In *Losing It: False Hopes and Fat Profits in the Diet Industry*, Laura Fraser demonstrated the ways that the U.S. diet industry plays on women's fears about fatness, all in order to increase their profit margins. In addition, feminist scholars such as Sharlene Hesse-Biber have challenged in great detail the cult of thinness and the way that it harms women both physically and mentally. And, of course, feminist activists like Marilyn Wann and Sondra Solovay are at the forefront of fat activism and the size acceptance movements.

The powerful synthesis of feminism and fat activism is a combination that I will explore more fully in the final chapter of this book. This chapter, however, suggests the extent to which feminism as an ideology has also had a stake in fat denigration and thin valorization. The anecdotal evidence of feminists' lack of immunity to the desire for a thin body are plentiful. As the title of one article by Esther Rothblum on body size and feminism so aptly put it, "I'll Die for the Revolution but Don't Ask Me Not to Diet." In *Unbearable Weight*, Susan Bordo admitted that she went on a diet while she was writing the book and lost twenty-five pounds.[47] In *Fat Talk*, Mimi Nichter described her fixation on her own body weight, despite always being a thin person.[48] In her study of commercial weight loss groups, the feminist sociologist Kandi Stinson explained her own reasons for dieting, despite "knowing better":

> By the time I joined the weight loss program in July 1994, I was nearly seventy pounds overweight. I didn't feel very well, had recurrent knee problems, was chronically tired, and found it increasingly hard to buy clothes in regular sizes—all compelling personal reasons for wanting to lose weight. At the same time, I felt ambivalent and conflicted. As a sociologist and a feminist scholar I was all too conscious of the deeply embedded cultural prejudice against obesity, the unrelenting pressure on women to meet a rigid ideal of thinness, and the lowered self-esteem, endless dieting, and eating disorders that result. As naïve as it seems now, I wasn't sure whether I could be a feminist and still want to lose weight.[49]

In her poignant discussion of her decision to enroll in a weight loss program, Stinson described a number of very understandable reasons for wanting to lose weight—a desire to feel more energy and less pain, and a desire to fit into clothes in "regular sizes." She also points out the contradictions between being a "dieter" and a "feminist," suggesting that perhaps were she a better feminist she wouldn't have succumbed to the desire for a thin body.

What I would argue, however, is that Stinson's dream of a thinner body can be perceived as very feminist. And although Stinson refers to health issues in her defense of weight loss, I would suggest that feminist desires for weight loss also stem from inherent cultural ideologies regarding the civilized body. That is, to the extent that feminism means claiming a place of equality and resisting the position of "other," it is no wonder that feminists have had a peculiar relationship to weight—both recognizing the way ideas about weight get wielded against women but also wanting to resist the stigma of "weak willed" and "primitive" that fatness connotes. For some women, a thin body has served as a strategy—and a temptation, as the "confessions" of the activists above suggest—to mitigate against the identity of "female," which poses so many risks of discrimination and inferior status. Indeed, for those women wanting to move into what had been charted as a "man's world," to assert their rightful place in territories previously marked "masculine," a thin body has often been seen as a necessity. The legacy of this focus on body size and fatness, and its inherent connections to fundamental beliefs about race, class, and the evolutionary "fitness" for citizenship, helps to explain contemporary feminist ambiguity over fatness as more than an interest in health or an individual idiosyncrasy.

The articulation of *fat* as prima facie evidence of one's uncivilized status, and thus incapability for the full rights of public citizenship, has had lasting and powerful effects that continue to reverberate today. The following chapter, "Narrating Fat Shame," moves us forward in time to popular culture narratives of the 1990s and the first decade of the 21st century. These narratives illuminate the ways that the 19th- and early 20th-century ideology of the fat, degenerative body persists. Indeed, fatness continues to be such a powerful, easily understood marker of the "fallen body" that it can be drawn on effortlessly to portray the upward and downward mobility of a large cast of characters. And just as the history of first-wave feminists demonstrated, this ideology of fat denigration works in complicated ways to enforce other forms of body typing by race, by class, and by gender. The notion of a "civilized body" is alive, well, and dangerous.

5

Narrating Fat Shame

At one point in Pixar's computer-animated 2008 blockbuster film *WALL-E*, the white captain of the spaceship looks forlornly at the series of "captain" portraits hanging in his quarters. The ones on the left all show robust, virile former captains, standing erectly and looking quite formidable. As the portraits move toward the right, the captains become increasingly bloated and fat, and in the final ones the captains are no longer even standing or sitting but are lying nearly prone in lounger chairs so loaded with electronic options that they have obviated the need for actual bodily movement. The message is clear: as this satellite community relied increasingly on technological advancements, the body, the mind, and human resolve deteriorated. The portrait series illustrates a kind of devolution, in which robust, independent, masculine white men have degenerated into bloated masses. From the pinnacle of civilization they have declined into an infantile state, dependent on technology to move, think, and even feel for them. The creators of *WALL-E* could have chosen to represent the colony's inhabitants in any number of ways to illuminate the tragic effects of overreliance on technology. Perhaps the people could have lost their hands (the robots did the grasping), mutated into snakelike bodies without bones (no need to stand), or developed tiny heads with no eyes, mouth, or ears (the robots had taken over the need for sight, speaking, hearing, and even thinking). But the creators chose a powerful, easily understandable shorthand to designate the downward evolution of these people: fat. I would suggest it is not just because we are in an "obesity epidemic" that the creators could rely so easily on this shorthand, but also precisely because the 19th- and early 20th-century meanings of fat as designating an uncivilized body are alive and well today.

Viewers of *WALL-E* knew that it is OK to laugh at and ridicule these people who suck down milkshakes and wobble on lounger chairs. Viewers also knew to cheer (at least silently) when the captain decides to get off his lounger and rouse the spaceship's inhabitants with a commanding, boot camp–like speech. These people needed to be shaken up, to change their ways. If they are humiliated in the process, it will perhaps provide more incentive to avoid such a debased state in the future. With the exception of fat activists who vociferously challenged the film's depiction of fat people, and one writer from the *New York Daily News* who suggested it might not be in Disney's best interest to insult its fat viewers, for the most part reviewers responded quite positively to the film.[1] They didn't worry that fat kids might lose courage and esteem by watching the film. Rather, they suggested the film sent a good message about the dangers of an overreliance on technology, encouraging kids to turn off the computer and go outside and play. The reviewers' blindness regarding the depiction of fat people and the humiliation they face can be explained within a cultural context that normalizes the idea that fat is a "discredited attribute," and the fat person a "debased being," one deserving of little respect or dignity. As the captains' portraits illuminated, the fat person is seen as the degenerate, the one who has moved furthest from the pinnacle of a civilized state, the one who requires a "shake-up" to return to the normal progress of human evolution.

Like the series of captains' portraits in *WALL-E*, an exploration of contemporary narratives about popular American figures—from Britney Spears to Barack Obama—suggests that *fatness* is often used as a motif to tell the story of one's upward, or downward, mobility. The use of fat as a powerful moral sign makes sense considering its cultural history. As "Fat and the Un-Civilized Body" explained, by the late 19th century fatness became a sign of a deficient body, one linked to the primitive, to the female, to the African, to the Hottentot. The thin body, in contrast, was one that was superior in quality: European-American, white, closest to the divine. The most civilized body was the thin body. Indeed, for those who sought a better place within society, one from which they had been barred because of physical traits, a thin body served as a way to mitigate the effects of their other stigmatized physical characteristics. We saw this most clearly in the tactics of white suffragists, who exploited the idea of the white thin body to make a case for their right to vote, to participate fully as American or British citizens. Within contemporary narratives, weight gain designates a loss of position, a figurative and literal move down in the social and economic hierarchy. In contrast, the loss of weight marks upward mobility, a gain of stature, a sign of one's moral, physical, and psychological improvement. "Thin" means one has a more civilized body, "fat" a less civilized one. Significantly, many of these contemporary narratives may not be explicitly *about* the person's body. That is, the meaning of fatness is so *normalized* as a "discrediting attribute," to use Erving Goffman's term, that it can be quickly tapped to convey something about the larger improvement or decline in a person's life.

The Fat as Inferior

WALL-E exists within a cultural context that not only abhors fatness and the fat person as a sign of degeneracy, but also one that has made the degradation of fat people a media ritual. Television shows like *Bulging Brides, Celebrity Fit Club, Honey, We're Killing the Kids*, and *The Biggest Loser* encourage viewers to peer and gawk at the contestants, taking pleasure in the ways they are goaded with tempting snacks and punished with arduous exercise routines. As Alessandra Stanley writes in her piece on weight loss shows, "There isn't much punch or visual payoff to a loss of 20 or 30 pounds; viewers have come to expect 100– and 200–pound miracles. Contestants who weigh 300 and 400 pounds are stripped down physically and emotionally, put in form-fitting bike shorts and forced to get on a scale, as clumsy and vulnerable as the human blobs of the future in *WALL-E*."[2] Indeed, the rituals of humiliation that these contestants face certainly evoke the memory of the spectacle of Sara Baartman, displayed for the pleasure of British and French audiences, antagonized with food, drink, chains, and ridicule; in the same way, these contestants are paraded in front of international audiences and prodded with tasty, fattening meals, insults, and exercise paraphernalia.

Of course, the analogy only goes so far. Baartman was a slave. These contestants are presumably acting of their own free will. Nevertheless, the idea that a person is degraded enough to deserve such treatment is an idea that has persisted from one century to the next. Moreover, the very justification given for the treatment has remained the same. Georges Cuvier defended his unethical autopsy of Baartman, and the French Musée de l'Homme defended its exhibition of her genitals and all-body cast relief, in the name of scientific discovery and human progress. The producers and viewers of the contemporary shows likewise defend the shows as "helping" contestants and humanity fight the "obesity epidemic." The idea of human progress and the "civilized body," then, undergird the rationale for both spectacles of humiliation.

The Fallen Woman

Georges Cuvier and his fellow scientists commented not just on the fatness of Baartman's buttocks, breasts, and stomach, but also on her genitalia, to "uncover" the presumably distinctive attributes of her labia and of the renowned "licentious" sexuality of Hottentot women in general. Fat, African, and overly sexual were all traits assigned to the lower levels of the evolutionary scale, a triage of characteristics that continued throughout the 19th and

20th centuries. Cesare Lombroso's 19th-century work on the "natural" criminal, which I discussed in "Fat and the Un-Civilized Body," certainly reiterated these connections. His work defined the typical characteristic of prostitutes as fatness, an atavistic tendency found, according to him, in some deviant white women and in all "native" and African women. And these ideas continue to resonate, whether in the novels of writers like Toni Morrison who challenge their authority, or their endless rehearsal in popular culture narratives about figures like Britney Spears, Monica Lewinsky, and Oprah Winfrey.

Toni Morrison's 1970 debut novel, *The Bluest Eye*, poignantly touches on these cultural connections among fatness, color, and female sexuality. The novel itself is about the relationship of two young African American girls, Frieda and Claudia, to Pecola, another young African American girl who in the end descends into madness, hating her own black body and worshipping the blue eyes of white people. In the Ohio town where these girls grew up, Morrison says, "the line between colored and nigger was not always clear: subtle and telltale signs threatened to erode it, and the watch had to be constant." Fatness is one of those signs. Indeed, when Frieda is sexually molested by their boarder, her sister finds her crying in her room, neither because she is in any pain (he only touched her breasts, she explains) nor because her father almost murdered the man, but because she fears that she might be, in the words of one of the neighbor women, "ruined." "What's ruined?" her sister Claudia asks. The dialogue between the two, in which neither understands the nature of sexual violence, the concept of physical virginity, or the lives of prostitutes, is both touching in its innocence and telling in terms of the stigma surrounding fatness:

> "You know. Like the Maginot Line [one of the town prostitutes]. She's ruined. Mama said so." The big tears come back.
> An image of Frieda, big and fat, came to mind. Her thin legs swollen, her face surrounded by layers of rouged skin. I too begin to feel tears.
> "But, Frieda, you could exercise and not eat."
> She shrugged.
> "Besides, what about China and Poland? [the other prostitutes in town] They're ruined too, aren't they? And they ain't fat."
> "That's because they drink whiskey. Mama says whiskey ate them up."
> "You could drink whiskey."[3]

The childish logic of Frieda and Claudia—that the boarder touched Frieda's breasts, so now she is "ruined," so that must mean she is going to become fat—as well as their solution (get whiskey so she'll stay thin) is certainly amusing, one of the only funny scenes in a very painful novel. But it's also revealing of the way that fatness serves as that powerful signifier of that line between the civilized and the primitive, or, to repeat Morrison's words, between "colored and nigger." The children in Morrison's novel knew this "reality" of fat stigma, and how it was connected to female sexuality and blackness, long before they could articulate other cultural truths.

Far from the world of innocence that Morrison portrays in *The Bluest Eye* are the 2007 depictions of Britney Spears, one of the best-selling music stars in history. Beginning her career as a young teen on the Disney Channel's *New Mickey Mouse Club* in 1993, Spears's first four albums earned the position of number one on the *Billboard* charts. As with any media star of her stature, the tabloids and entertainment media have followed Spears's career and personal life in excruciating detail, from her life as a teen star, to her marriages, to her decision to have children. Their coverage gained an additional boost in 2007 with news of Spears's alcoholism, shaky marriage, child custody battles, possible mental illness, and rocky performances. As the title of the 2007 *Us Weekly* article, "Anatomy of a Breakdown," suggests, however, the story of her downfall—which includes questionable parenting techniques, violent behavior, and drug and alcohol binges—is largely told through a narrative about her fat body. "Anatomy of a Breakdown" focuses primarily on the debacle of her performance at the MTV Video Music Awards. It begins with a close-up shot of Spears angled so that her thigh looks oversized. "As if things couldn't get worse, a pantiless Spears inadvertently flashed her privates while slumped in a car after the show," the caption reads. These two details—the fat thighs and the pantiless crotch—set the tone for the national coverage of Spears and the VMA performance. The *New York Daily Post* said that Spears was "stuffed into a spangled bra and hot pants and jiggled like Jell-O," while *E! Online* described the horror of the "bulging belly she was flaunting." The *Us Weekly* story recounts the weeks prior to the performance, describing her partying and relaxing in the hotel suite, her erratic decision to fire staff, and the many missed rehearsals. Moreover, this story, as well as others in the *New York Times* and on *Yahoo! News*, fixate on her dancing, eating, and drinking with P. Diddy and other African American male rappers. All the articles inform us that she did not return home from her evening of partying with Diddy and his friends until 6 a.m. the day of her performance. It all added up, *Us Weekly* tells us, to a "perfect storm." Seeing a video of herself during the disastrous performance, Spears apparently "flipped out" and ran backstage, yelling, "Oh my God, I looked like a fat pig! I looked like a fat pig." She was, the magazine tells us, inconsolable.[4] We have a story here that the anthropologist Cesare Lombroso could have told, complete with all the signs of atavistic traits and behaviors. She is overly sexed (flashing her crotch), identifying with the primitive (hanging out with black men), and fat (though she is still only a size 10, the articles focus relentlessly on her oversized body and suggest she sprayed on an "ab-defining" product to create the illusion that she had stomach muscles). She is the fallen white girl—and fat is the key to portraying her as such.

Just as fatness narrates her downfall, a newly thin body is what later becomes the motif for her comeback. "Revealing her new tanned and toned figure, it seems Britney Spears has finally put her troubles behind her," the *London Daily Mail* reported in May 2009. "It was a stark contrast to this time last year, where she was seen on holiday in Costa Rica looking bloated and out of shape."[5] After showing pictures of her "bloated" body compared to her newly sleek body, the article went on to report that Spears was on break from a successful concert tour, vacationing with her two young sons, her father and brother, and a new (white) beau, her manager. Her spending still seemed outrageous, but perhaps that was simply the diva-like lifestyle of the superrich, the article suggested. The insinuations of mental illness, out-of-control sexuality, and primitive behavior had all been forgotten with the newly slender body.

Just as the Spears story recounts her downfall and comeback through a narrative of her fatness, the story of another "fallen white girl"—Monica Lewinsky—reveals the way that the narrative of weight loss can be used to reclaim an identity as a civilized person. A 1999 ad campaign by the commercial diet group Jenny Craig, featuring Monica Lewinsky as their guest star, illuminates in a powerful way a "dieting narrative" that moves the primitive, impulsive fat woman into a new status of civilized and controlled. (Monica Lewinsky is, of course, the infamous White House intern who had an affair with President Bill Clinton, which apparently began when Lewinsky bent down, revealing her thong underwear.) In *The Obesity Myth*, Paul Campos argues that the U.S. public was fixated on the "guilt" of the Lewinsky/Clinton pair not just because of the evidence of "kinky sex" but because their mutual fatness marked them as already culpable. That is, Clinton's known struggles with his "excess" weight and Lewinsky's rotund body provided solid verification that these were two people who were impulsive, whose bodily cravings were out of control. Moreover, Campos argues, Lewinsky's identity as a *Jewish* woman evoked stereotypes of the oversexed "Jewess," whose sensuality and desire for power knew no bounds.[6]

Jenny Craig's choice to feature Monica Lewinsky was fascinating. In the fall of 1999 newspapers began to report that Lewinsky had already lost thirty-one pounds on the Jenny Craig weight loss program, at which point the company approached her about starring in a commercial. Supposedly she signed a contract offering her one million dollars for her appearance in the ad, as well as her promise that she would lose another thirty pounds. Their company spokesperson reported that they were "not concerned" that Lewinsky was the notorious "other woman" who brought down the president; rather, he suggested that she had great name recognition and that her "success" would be valuable to share with potential customers.

In contrast to the spokesperson's repeated denials that Lewinsky's "other woman" status was important, it seems likely that this identity was key to Jenny Craig's choice to highlight her weight loss. Lewinsky's notorious "excesses"—excess appetites for food and sex, even excess underwear, with her thong peeking over her trousers—made her a compelling star for the struggling weight loss corporation. And, indeed, the commercial definitely raised these issues of excess. Toward the beginning of the spot, Lewinsky referred to all her other failed diets: "I mean, if it was stand on your head, I tried it. If it was eat only grapefruits, I tried it. Magic diet pills, I tried it." Jenny Craig, however, has tamed her. She no longer has to do it (here meaning dieting, though certainly most people are thinking of something else) on her head. She is seen watering flowers and cutting out a dress pattern—thoroughly domesticated activities. The camera then switches to a scene that looks like a bedroom—all in pinks and pastels. "One of the most amazing things about Jenny Craig for me," Lewinsky states, "is that I haven't felt deprived on this program at all." We know, of course, that in the past Lewinsky has had "trouble" depriving herself (and if we didn't get the allusion, Jenny Craig put her in the bedroom for us to be able to "see" it); Jenny Craig helps to stem the appetite, to get the body back "under control."

And, finally, we know that Lewinsky is a person who has sinned—against her country, certainly, and against civilization with her bodily desires. Jenny Craig helps to put Lewinsky back into a rightful place within society, allowing Lewinsky to purge herself of her wrongdoing. In fact, Lewinsky concludes the commercial, set against a plain background, "I think Jenny Craig is a great program for someone who not only wants to lose weight but who's looking to change their life."

Jenny Craig made a calculated gamble here, putting its finger right on the pulse of the issues about excess, desire, control, and sin that are associated with fatness. Interestingly, however, the gamble did not pay off. A number of franchises refused to run the ad, arguing that Lewinsky was not an appropriate "role model." "As a person who has been successful on our program, she's done great," said one franchise owner. "But as a person to look up to, there certainly are some issues there. I wouldn't be pleased if my daughter came home and said I want to be just like Monica Lewinsky."[7]

After a short run with the ads, the Lewinsky campaign was indeed cancelled, but Jenny Craig would not confirm why. I would suspect, however, that it was because of her excess "excesses" in all senses of the terms—her weight, her sexuality, and her ethnicity. For one thing, Lewinsky supposedly failed to lose the final "excess" thirty pounds she had promised. That tenacious fat, as well as Lewinsky's history as a Jewish woman who did indeed have sexual urges, were details that prevented her from being "pushed" up that scale of civilization. The Jenny Craig company had gambled that with weight loss Monica Lewinsky would be able to shed the stigma of her notorious past. It was a reasonable—if ultimately miscalculated—guess. Despite Jenny Craig's efforts, she remained the fallen, ethnic, fat woman.

In contrast to Britney Spears or Monica Lewinsky, it's difficult to connect the words "fallen woman" with the media mogul and television entertainer Oprah Winfrey. Listed by magazines like *Forbes* and *Life* as one of the "most influential" figures of the 20th century, Oprah is also extraordinarily wealthy, earning a spot on the *Forbes* 400 list for decades. Her television show alone, which has perfected the art of talk show conversations and confessions, attracts millions of viewers each week. Her ability to change and influence American fads and interests is so powerful that it has been dubbed the "Oprah Effect."[8] Yet, despite this extraordinary level of achievement, Winfrey's life story has been characterized by a tremendous focus on her struggles with her body weight. Indeed, some of her most popular shows have focused on her dieting struggles and successes, such as the 1988 episode when Winfrey, wearing her new skintight size 10 jeans, wheeled onto the stage a wagon carrying sixty-seven pounds of fat, the amount of weight she had lost. This was just one of the first weight loss "successes," as each weight loss has been followed by an eventual weight gain. In 2009, for instance, she embarked on yet another weight loss attempt to deal with what she called the "brown elephant in the room," her latest forty-pound gain.[9]

In thinking about this fixation on Winfrey's weight, one could see it as a calculated ploy by Winfrey herself to focus on something that humanizes her, that "brings her down" to the level of the people whose support she relies on for her popularity and success. One could see this as an "everywoman" strategy, an attempt to provide a source of connection between herself and her viewers. If this is the case, however, I would suggest it likely is an appropriation "after the fact," meaning that Winfrey is making the best use of a situation that she genuinely makes her unhappy. Winfrey's personal story is a carefully crafted narrative of an African American woman who began life so poor that she had to wear potato sack dresses to school, who endured sexual abuse as a child and young teenager, and who lifted herself out of this morass through hard work, a sharp mind, and an ability to connect with people, especially over issues of self-improvement. As an African American, self-made, female star, weight gain poses a threat, not necessarily of being seen as a promiscuous woman (as it was for Spears or Lewinsky), but definitely as a woman who has lost her "civilized" body, who has, to bring back that haunting line from *The Bluest Eye*, moved from "colored to nigger."

The best-selling book and video that Winfrey produced with her personal trainer, Bob Greene, in 1996 and 1997 illuminate the powerful meanings that Winfrey attaches to fatness and weight gain. In the book *Make the Connection: Ten Steps to a Better Body—and a Better Life* and the video *Make the Connection . . . It's About Changing Your Life*, Winfrey explained that despite all her successes, her weight made her feel like an out-of-control failure. (Note the similarity to the original "dieter's story" of William Banting, who in the 19th century felt himself a failure despite his significant success as a businessman.) Even when she won the Emmy for best talk show host, she couldn't enjoy herself, and instead fretted that her "too-fat knees" would show when she sat down, and that the TV cameras would catch her at an awkward angle as she exited the limo. She describes herself as having "hit bottom," out of control, depressed, angry. According to her narrative, the very next day she met up with Bob Greene, the personal trainer who worked with her on a daily basis to lose weight, and who then became her coauthor for both the book and video.

What is so remarkable about the video and the book is the way it emphasizes Winfrey's "failure" as a dieter, contrasting it with the success she achieves once, as she explains, she puts "forth the effort to take care of myself." The video box even includes a free "personal wallet-sized card with Oprah's Daily Routine!" suggesting that viewers could also achieve her weight loss success if only they followed such a schedule. The video does provide glimpses of the work of her full-time staff, including an exercise physiologist, who designs and accompanies her on her exercise routine; a chef, who provides her with low-calorie, nutritious, and tasty meals; and a valet, who takes care of all the details of her life so that she might have time to "take care of myself." By emphasizing Winfrey's encouragement of Louise, the African American valet, who herself goes on a fitness and weight loss program, the video suggests that the full-time staff members are unnecessary: *anyone* could accomplish what she has accomplished.

As the scholar Connie Razza suggests, Winfrey's book and video are all about individual responsibility and the American dream. Her story suggests that her move from poverty and obscurity to wealth and fame are due to the same level of self-determination and powerful willpower as her move from fat to fitness. Her success provides "evidence" that anyone can accomplish the American dream, which Razza argues now means not just economic success, but also a level of "fitness" and health: "Her new approach to weight loss and her new vision of the American dream isolate individuals from her social context, producing the illusion of success by distracting women from external contributors to their weight problems (i.e., regional, professional, sociological pressures) and systemic limitations on their economic success (i.e., sexism, racism, prejudice against overweight women)."[10]

Razza further argues that "her identification as a model for women's fitness generally, rather than for black women's fitness in particular, suggests a project of deracination that is a common part of her public persona."[11] What Razza means by this is *not* that Winfrey denies that she is black, but rather that Winfrey wants to deny that blackness—and race in general—matters. What is essential to note here, however, is the way that Razza's argument needs to be expanded once one has thought through the cultural stigma of fatness. That is, in order to deracinate herself, to prove that "anyone" can make it, Winfrey *must* lose weight. Otherwise, the weight of all that fat will always, de facto, mark her as a "black woman," with all the accompanying connotations of inferior, primitive, bodily, and out of control. It is no wonder that Winfrey felt a "failure" when she was fat, and was compelled to "prove" that her weight loss was a matter of her triumphant will, rather than that of a skilled staff that provided her with the training, the support, and the delicious meals to make it happen.

In "Weight Loss Confession," the 2009 story about her most recent weight gain, Winfrey said, "It [referring to money, fame, success] doesn't mean anything if you can't fit into your clothes. It means the fat won. It means you didn't win. . . . I am mad at myself. I am embarrassed."[12] Since the end of the 19th century, fatness has, as I argued in the first chapters of this book, served as a potent signifier of the line between the primitive and the civilized, feminine and masculine, ethnicity and whiteness, poverty and wealth, homosexuality and heterosexuality, past and future. Within weight loss narratives, the past is often represented as a yoke, which is lifted as the person enters a new, thin life, crossing that symbolic borderline described above. When a person sheds the fat, she or he supposedly also sheds everything else that was on that side of the "line." Fatness is what Winfrey calls the "brown elephant in the room," threatening to pull her back into that past of African American oppression, of extreme poverty, and of sexism. No wonder the striving for thinness has such a powerful hold on her, no matter her financial and professional success.

Masculinity and the Fat Body

In *Fat Land: How Americans Became the Fattest People in the World*, Greg Critser describes the humiliation he felt when "some guy called me fatso": "In upwardly mobile, professional America, being fat—and having someone actually notice it and say something about it—is almost as bad as getting caught reading *Playboy* in your parents' bedroom when you're ten. Shame, shame, shame."[13] Being called "fatso," to Critser, was like having his budding masculinity exposed and teased. It was also particularly disgraceful, Critser says, within an "upwardly mobile," that is, upper middle class, environment. Strikingly, Critser recounts this anecdote not as evidence of the unfairness and meanness of fat stigma, but as a legitimate form of ridicule. Internalizing the ideology of the *thin*, civilized, masculine body, Critser believes he has failed as a upwardly mobile man. Like the contestants on the weight loss shows, he thinks he deserves to be mocked and taunted, for he has lost his position on that Great Chain of Being. The fatness threatens his status as a man and as a person of distinction and wealth.

Critser is able to climb back up that ladder of civilization by first losing weight and then writing a best-selling book that exposes the American "obesity epidemic." (Whether he has maintained that weight loss or regained it, as 95 percent of dieters do, is a another question.) Other men who believe that their fatness threatens their masculinity, and who accept the legitimacy of this narrative, however, have not found such a lucrative or relatively safe way to climb back up that ladder of civilization. Indeed, one AP story about an American soldier is particularly noteworthy—and tragic—for the way it unproblematically connects weight loss to masculine heroism.

In 2004, the Associated Press reported on Justin Hunt from California, who, at 390 pounds, was too heavy to join the Marines. He wouldn't listen to the rejection of the recruiting officers, however, and he began an exercise and dieting routine that brought him down to 207 pounds, low enough to be allowed to enlist. During boot camp he lost even more weight, getting down to 177 pounds. Eventually he was sent to Iraq. There, after all his efforts to join the Marines, he died in an explosion.[14]

What is noteworthy about this story is that it merited a full-length Associated Press article. Since March 2003 thousands of American citizens have died in Iraq, and while their individual stories often are reported in their local press, they do not usually gain national attention. In the context of a country that is fixated on fatness as a matter of national shame and as a security threat, as Frank Deford's words attested to in the introduction, Justin Hunt was indeed a national hero, one deserving of particular attention. Although unspoken, the article, in recounting his weight loss and his persistence, suggests Hunt was quite embarrassed by his size. His fatness prevented him from meeting the standards of the military, that bastion of masculine responsibility and privilege. Through his persistence and determination, however, he finally was able to meet the military's standards and to serve the nation. What is particularly salient about the story is that in reality, Hunt's fatness had *protected* him, by preventing him from joining the armed forces. But the article reinforces the idea that Hunt chose thinness—and by implication manhood—over safety. He had achieved manhood even if it meant sacrificing his own life.

Neither the Critser book nor the articles about Hunt recount their racial backgrounds. Photos, however, suggest that Critser is white and that Hunt was African American.[15] This adds another twist to the comparison between these two stories. Critser's story is largely an ideological one, in which he excoriates fat in order to regain his manhood. Hunt's quest to join the military may have been less ideological than a practical economic decision, considering the comparatively fewer work options open to a young, African American man with only a high school education. Yet the stories of both men emphasized the ways that fatness represented a loss of strength and virility, a threat to their masculinity. And although Hunt's decisions may indeed have been economically motivated, the stories of two other African American men, both celebrities, suggest that there may indeed have been ideological factors at play. For African American men, fatness evokes the memory of earlier stigmatized figures, from those of childlike characters lampooned in minstrel shows and television sitcoms to those of primitive brutes, unsafe to be around women and certainly uncivilized.

In 2002, *People* magazine celebrated the weight loss victory of Al Roker, the African American NBC *Today* show host and weatherman. The article described the formerly 320-pound man as a "passionate foodie who once ate Quarter Pounders in pairs and Krispy Kreme doughnuts by the half dozen." They quoted Roker as describing himself during one particular binge episode as a "whale with plankton—just open your mouth and inhale." Roker explains that he always bristled at the Fat Albert jokes, and with each year of professional success, those jokes became more and more unbearable. Roker did not want to be seen as Fat Albert, the comic, very fat, cartoon character created by Bill Cosby in 1969. Fat Albert, while loveable and funny, is also childlike and uncouth, never growing up, always the member of a gang in North Philadelphia. Roker transforms himself, risking his life through weight loss surgery, eating smaller meals, and working out regularly. "He was always a cuddly hug," said his wife, Deborah Roberts. "Now he's this strong, sexy hug."[16]

The *People* story on Roker's weight loss suggests that as the fat disappears, he moves across that transitional line, from the primitive to the civilized. With a thin physique, his body will presumably no longer "say" Fat Albert, will no longer suggest he is childlike, loveable, a member of a poor, African American community. Moreover, his weight loss moves him symbolically not only from the realm of primitive to civilized, but also from that of childhood into adulthood, heterosexual manhood, from a "cuddly hug" to a "strong, sexy hug." His success at weight loss seems to verify the reality of the American dream: anyone can make it, regardless of economic, social, ethnic, or educational background or context, into the moneyed arenas traditionally dominated by white men. To cross that line, however, it was important for him to move from "fat" to "thin."

The weight loss "success" story of Al Roker contrasts sharply to the story of Kirby Puckett, the baseball Hall of Famer, made famous both by his tremendous hitting for the Minnesota Twins in the 1980s and early 1990s, and by his good natured, home team spirit. The 2003 *Sports Illustrated* cover story on Puckett recounted his fall from fame, fortune, and Minnesota whiteness into the world of scandal, sexual crimes, and fat women on welfare. This is not a story of weight gain, per se, but rather a story in which *fatness* narrates his downfall.

Frank Deford's 2003 story recounts the upward and downward slope of Puckett's life, from his early days in the projects of Chicago, to his famed playing and philanthropy in Minneapolis, to the loss of eyesight that cost him his playing ability. Finally, it discusses the accusations of philandering, violence, and even sexual assault levied by his ex-wife, his mistress, and a woman whom he supposedly attacked in a local bar. The cover, a 1980s picture of him, smiling and trim in his blue Twins uniform, contrasts sharply with the inset picture of his bloated, unsmiling, spectacled face. The inside illustration, by artist Thomas Reis, emphasizes Puckett's double chin and fat lips. Flesh hangs over his collar. A teardrop falls below the eye glasses, which reflect an earlier image of the smiling, young, and presumably "good" Kirby Puckett. Chronicling his rise to fame, and his subsequent moral downfall, the story uses fatness as the consistent theme of his ruin.

All who followed Puckett in the 1980s and 1990s know that Kirby was never a thin man. As a phenomenal hitter, however, there was a certain allowance given for his size and shape, described as a "cantaloupe with legs." Those athletic—and social—skills as a ballplayer and as a happily married philanthropist guaranteed his status as a masculine, civilized man. His corpulence simply tempered those qualities so that he was perceived as a "nice guy," as Deford said in his article, "adorable, chubby and bald, Everymanish."[17] The scholar Jerry Mosher argues that such a notion has been common to representations of fat men, such as Norm on the 1980s sitcom *Cheers*.[18] Once the accusations of sexual infidelity and violence emerged, however, the older vestiges of ideas about black men appeared; not quite the harmless black minstrel figure, in Deford's article Puckett appears as a dangerous criminal figure, unable to control any bodily impulses. Stories about public urination, violence, and sexual assault certainly challenged his status as a civilized, masculine citizen.

What is significant for my purposes is not whether Puckett was actually guilty of these accusations, but rather the way that his fatness served as the *tangible* representation of a body *out of control*. The tear sliding down the Puckett's fat cheek in Reis's illustration certainly gives us a sense of this, and the words in the article do as well. In describing the end of Puckett's playing days, for instance, Deford writes, "Then he wasn't a ballplayer anymore, let alone a whale of one. Then he was just back to being fat little Kirby Puckett." No longer a virile player, no longer a masculine hero, he was just "fat and little." One might add flabby, impotent, and no longer a man. The story contrasts him to his ex-wife, who clearly has the "will" that her ex-husband lost—or perhaps never even had, the article suggests:

> She is her own woman now, grown up and come to grips. . . . None of the terrible stress of the last year is visible upon her face, and she looks far younger than her 37 years. Maybe it is because she is a resilient Minnesotan, imbued with the belief, which she often expresses, that no matter what has happened, three things can make life whole again: hard work, love and God. . . . She has brown saucer eyes, long curly hair and a few cute freckles on her nose and cheeks. *Unlike her roly-poly ex-husband, she has a trim figure.* She is, in fact, beautiful, so that it is human nature for everyone who sees Tonya to pause and ponder how her husband could ever have strayed from a woman so gorgeous. (emphasis added)

The depths to which Kirby had fallen were highlighted in his ex-mistress's comment about his love choices. He pursued women, she said, who had "low self-esteem, were overweight, on welfare and had kids." In other words, he pursued fat, poor, black women—powerful signifiers of the derogatory "other" that had been culturally established by the early part of the 20th century. The caption for the final photograph of Puckett, apparently going in for a hearing regarding his trial on charges of sexual assault, read, "Grounded: Puckett, who weighs at least 60 pounds more than he did as a player, seldom ventures out as he awaits trial."[19] Becoming fat—and pursuing fat—was both a sign of his downward mobility and perhaps the greatest sin of them all. Unlike Critser, Hunt, and Roker, Puckett experienced a backward evolution, a move into degeneracy and atavism. The story read so much like an obituary that Puckett's actual death in 2006, from a stroke, came as no surprise.

"Not Ralph Kramden": The Obamas, Nationalism, and Fat Stigma

Contemporary stories of fat shame, such as those of Monica Lewinsky and Oprah Winfrey to those of Al Roker and Kirby Puckett, suggest the level of danger that fatness poses, especially for those seeking to shed other stigmatized identities of race, sex, and class. A fat body can threaten to unravel all the best efforts at upward mobility, conjuring up historical and cultural memories of that Great Chain of Being in which fatness was considered to be a characteristic of the most primitive, the most "ethnic," the most sexually loose females, the most *inferior* people. A thin body, in contrast, promises to hoist a person into the realm of the "most civilized body" and to erase the cultural meaning of other stigmatized physical characteristics. For those seeking the highest positions in our nation, I would argue that it is especially important to be thin, to demonstrate physically that they are *fit* for those levels of responsibility and privilege. It came as no surprise to me, then, when Paul Campos pointed out the extent to which political commentators ridiculed and dismissed some of the female candidates for the Supreme Court nomination in 2009 based on their body size.[20] Just as with the suffrage battle in the early 20th century, fat denigration was being deployed to undermine, and to delegitimize, the efforts of those seeking the full rights and privileges of our citizenry, in this case a position on the Supreme Court. Some of the critics framed their fat-disparaging comments as concerns about "health," but considering the powerful, easily understood negative connotations surrounding fatness, one has to be skeptical. To bring attention to the candidates' fatness is to mark them as inferior and unfit, certainly not suited to a position on the highest court in the nation.

No one knows the significance of a thin body more powerfully than those seeking presidential office. Indeed, a *New York Times* article during the Democratic presidential primaries in 2007 noted in detail the candidates' focus on maintaining a thin body: "Candidates—and even their spouses—must keep the pounds off, or risk the sort of ridicule that Bill Clinton and Al Gore endured. Elizabeth Edwards once landed at an airport in the 2004 election campaign to find a sign that said 'fatso' waiting for her. This time around, she has whittled herself by several dress sizes while campaigning, a change she attributes not to her breast cancer or treatment, but to the Special K protein bars, bananas, hundred-calorie snack packs and rice cakes she totes along." Mike Huckabee, who had lost significant weight prior to the campaign, noted, "If you're really overweight, some people just look at you and immediately sort of write you off. They just assume you're undisciplined."[21] Dismissing a candidate because of body weight may seem odd, considering the extensive range of attributes one might want to consider, including a candidates' voting record, political views, and work history, none of which has to do with body size. But the historical and cultural weight of fat stigma, begun in the 19th century, suggests that body size provides a quick means for voters to assess a candidate's inner fitness for office. Indeed, the newspaper editorials mocking President Grover Cleveland for his body size, and the articles detailing his attempts to lose weight, suggest that this has been true at least since the 1880s.[22] Thus it makes sense that Barack and Michelle Obama should focus so extensively on fitness, even when critics charge the first family as being elitist in their attention to body size, food, and exercise.[23]

Details about the Obamas' fitness routines and eating habits proliferated in the media throughout the campaign and into the presidency. Presumably the Obamas were fine with this attention, considering they responded at length to journalists' fitness and food questions and that Michelle brought increased attention to the issue through the planting of the White House organic vegetable garden. Numerous media sources have reported on Barack Obama's physical development, noting he had been a "chubby teen" who slimmed down by the time he played high school basketball. His regular exercise routine, his continuing love for playing basketball, and his reluctance to eat junk food fill the pages of popular magazines. "Most of my workouts have to come before my day starts. There's always a tradeoff between sleep and working out. Usually I get in about 45 minutes, 6 days a week. I'll lift one day and do cardio the next," Obama was reported as saying in *Men's Health* soon before the November 2008 election.[24] Earlier that year, a *U.S. News and World Report* article noted that Obama recoiled in horror when a political commentator suggested he was like Ralph Kramden from the 1950s television sitcom *The Honeymooners*:

A regular gym rat, [Obama] takes pride in his slim and trim good looks. So you can imagine his shock when *USA Today* political scribe Kathy Kiely recently told the candidate that his bickering with foe Senator Hillary Clinton reminded her of the quarrels between Ralph and Alice Kramden of *The Honeymooners.* "And I'm Ralph?" quizzed Obama, somewhat horrified to be compared to beefy Jackie Gleason's character. "It's not my body type!" Kiely says he protested. "It's just a metaphor, Senator," she assured him as campaign aide Robert Gibbs offered: "Oh no, now he's going to double his workout."

That would be some task. His campaign cochairman Senator Dick Durbin tells us that Obama's a devotee of the Senate gym and that campaign insiders set aside an hour each day for the 46-year-old to run on the treadmill and lift free weights or even play basketball. Another reporter, *Chicago Sun-Times* Washington Bureau Chief Lynn Sweet, has worked out beside the candidate and describes him as "studious and serious, thorough and businesslike." Wife Michelle is also a fitness fan, doing 90 minutes of cardio, weight training, and calisthenics.[25]

This anecdote about Obama "recoiling in horror" at the suggestion that he was like Ralph Kramden suggests what is at stake ideologically in the maintenance of a "trim and slim body." Played by Jackie Gleason, *The Honeymooners* Ralph Kramden was a loudmouthed, poorly educated, white bus driver who lived with his wife in a run-down apartment in Brooklyn. Instead of saving money or working hard to get ahead, Ralph relied on get-rich-quick schemes, one crazier than the next, which all inevitably failed. His fat body was the source of much of the show's humor, such as the time his mother-in-law announced he was arriving long before she could see him. "How did you know it was me?" Ralph asked. "I could feel the floor sag," she replied.[26] No wonder Obama chafed at this joke: Ralph's fat body is linked to his low status, to his poor work habits, to his childlike reasoning and outrageously bad temper. Moreover, his thin, penny-pinching wife, Alice, is much smarter than he is, which must have made this analogy especially irritating to Obama, since he was supposed to be Ralph and Hillary Clinton, Alice. Obama's rejection of that analogy ("not my body type") is also a rejection of all that our culture associates with fatness: primitive behaviors, atavistic impulses, low class position. At the time of this story Obama was locked in a tight battle for the Democratic nomination, the first African American who looked like he might have a real shot at the presidency. As a consequence, it was especially important that he steer far away from all the negative, racist associations white America made about African Americans. When he good naturedly told the reporters, "I'm no Ralph Kramden," he was also telling them not to pull him down that ladder, not to connect him to all the "low-class" behaviors and beliefs that had been attributed to nonwhites, to immigrants, and to ethnic Americans.

The press repeatedly has focused not just on Barack Obama's fitness, but also on that of his wife. A *New York Times* article in March 2009 detailed Michelle Obama's concern over her body:

> The first lady said she was not naturally thin and, like most other people, had to exercise and watch what she eats. "I have hips, and I have them covered up with these pleats," she said, pointing to her Maria Pinto skirt. To keep those hips from spreading, she said, she follows an exercise regimen of light weights, calisthenics, jump-rope and a cardiovascular routine that includes interval running. "This is work," she said. Regular exercise allows for dessert, French fries and a burger—every now and then. But she would eat the fries every day if she could. "They are my favorite food in the whole wide world," she said. "I could live on French fries."[27]

This exchange with the *New York Times* reporter reveals the Michelle Obama that many Americans have grown to love: a woman of candor and humor, who knows how to poke fun at herself and her family, and who genuinely cares about her own health and that of her family. Inviting local schoolchildren over to dig up the White House lawn for the much-anticipated organic vegetable garden provided more evidence of her concern for the environment, for healthy, local eating, and for improving the lives of children and the well-being of her community. To read these details—of her interest in healthy eating, exercising regularly, growing a vegetable garden—as having an additional ideological level is not to take away from this praise, but rather to point out the complex meanings evoked by this much-beloved public figure. As the first African American first lady, Michelle Obama has been the object of intense scrutiny. Indeed, many political commentators pointed out that even more pathbreaking than electing the first African American president is having the first African American family in residence at the White House—not as slaves, servants, or staff, but as *the first family*. In a *Newsweek* editorial soon after the election, Allison Samuels reflected on what it meant to her as an African American woman to have a black first lady, one who could challenge all the horrific stereotypes of African American women as drug addicts, welfare queens, or unfit single mothers.[28] Indeed, the negative stereotypes of African American women are powerful and numerous;

Samuels did not even mention that other derogatory image, of the fat black mammy, a figure likely to be seen working at the White House, caring for a white family rather than her own. And, of course, the "welfare queen" is simply a more recent version of the Venus Hottentot, a fat woman whose appetites for sex and food know no bounds. Michelle Obama, Samuels reminds us, has the power to contest all those images, to present to the world an African American woman who is well educated, hardworking, a good mother, and married. No wonder, considering the historical burden of all those derogatory representations, that it is important for her to keep her body in check, to keep those hips from spreading. It is important to erase any signs that might suggest a link to those denigrating cultural figures.

In a March 2009 editorial, Maureen Dowd wrote that the political commentator David Brooks told her Michelle Obama should quit wearing those sleeveless dresses. "She's made her point. Now she should put away Thunder and Lightning," he apparently said, later adding, "She should not be known for her physical presence."[29] That Brooks should make such comments suggests that no matter what efforts Michelle Obama exerts to shape the image she projects, and to deflect any negative associations, her body nevertheless may evoke historical and cultural meanings over which she has no control. A toned and fit body should have moved Obama up that symbolic ladder, far from the negative associations of primitive, ethnic, uneducated, and low class that fat has historically "meant" for the last century. That Brooks would scrutinize her body for signs of primitivism, suggesting she was too physical, too strong, too much like the brute environmental elements of thunder and lightning to be successful among the brainy "policy wonks" (Brook's words) of Washington DC underscores the powerful and slippery ways that racism, sexism, and body typing continue to work. Brook's comments also suggest why both Obamas might also be concerned about the body size of their children. In a November 2008 issue of *Parents* magazine, Barack explained, "A few years back—you'd never know it by looking at her now—Malia was getting a little chubby." Michelle then added, "And her doctor—he really monitors this type of thing—suggested we look at her diet. So we cut out juice boxes, sweets, and processed foods." Certainly on one level this focus on cutting out junk food from their daughters' diet can simply be read as good parenting, especially as Barack then added, "But we're not hyper about it."[30] On another level, however, this is also an ideological lesson, teaching the girls how to survive in a world that will scrutinize their bodies unmercifully for signs of inferiority and primitivism. Fatness is one of those signs, this lesson teaches, one too dangerous to evoke.

The Continuing Power of Body Typing

For early 21st-century readers, the presumption that physical, psychological, and moral traits are closely linked may be perceived as either quaintly outmoded or obviously wrong. We don't "read" people's earlobes for signs of their criminal tendencies, as 18th- and 19th-century phrenologists did, nor do we see mental illness as a sign that one's soul is wrestling with the devil, as the Puritans did. Nevertheless, the idea that one's physical *body* can be read for signs of personal worthiness and quality persists, despite laws that challenge discrimination and educational forums that unpack the insidious ways that these ideas thread their way through cultural practices and beliefs. The powerful 19th-century thinking about the evolution of human beings into stages of civilization has not disappeared, but it has, I would argue, woven itself cleverly and tightly into the fabric of everyday life and popular culture. Certain body types continue to be seen as superior, signs of one's more advanced placement on the scale of humanity. While some bodily signs have lost their power (think here of the earlobe), other physical signs have maintained or even grown in meaning. *Fatness* is certainly one of these. Moreover, fat denigration works in complicated ways to reinforce the existence of racism, sexism, homophobia, and all other processes by which our culture categorizes and oppresses people through bodily hierarchies and stigmatization. Like any other form of oppression, however, those affected do resist. The following chapter takes up the voices of those who, in the words of Marilyn Wann, "refuse to apologize" for their fat bodies. Their organized resistance is only decades old, but the roots of the stigma they are countering go back, of course, to the 19th century. In rejecting fat denigration, not only do they seek freedom from the endless cultural and personal criticism about the inadequacy of their bodies, they also challenge the very notion of a civilized body.

6

Refusing to Apologize

In *FAT!SO? Because You Don't Have to Apologize for Your Size!* Marilyn Wann writes that the words "large, big-boned, overweight, chubby, zaftig, voluptuous, Rubenesque, plump, and obese are all synonyms for fear." She urges readers to "practice saying the word *fat* until it is the same as *short, tall, thin, young,* or *old.* Chat with your fat. Give it pet names. Doodle *fat* on your notepad during meetings. . . . Use the word *fat* with your parents, with your partner. Let friends in on your secret. Say, 'By the way, I'm fat.'"[1] In her 1998 book, Wann urges fat people to come "out" as fat, to quit hiding themselves within layers of cultural degradation and self-hate, to stop battling their bodies with dangerous and useless dieting practices. She urges readers to speak up for themselves and other fat people and to see the physician's scale for what it is, a tool of intimidation and humiliation rather than a source of healing or treatment. Clever sayings to encourage readers to feel "flabulous" edge the bottom of each page, including "Don't worry if you wiggle," "Wear horizontal stripes," "Just Say No to Diet Drugs," and "chunky-dunking," a fat activist way to say "skinny-dipping." Interspersed throughout the text are four "anatomy lessons," pictures of fat bodies, butts, upper arms, stomachs, and chins, that she calls "visual counterpropaganda" to the constant stream of ultra-thin images that saturate our mass media. For Wann, the answer to fat shame is to lose the stigma, not the fat.

Including contributions by other fat activists as well as her own written pieces, *FAT!SO?* includes articles on the connection between fatness and health, medical and insurance discrimination, the diet industries, fashion issues, sexuality, and teenage suicide and depression. In other words, Wann's book is a condensed version of all the forms of fat activism that are taking place in the United States. Resisting a sixty-billion-dollar-a-year diet industry and the ideology of fat denigration that sustains it, fat activists "refuse to apologize" for their size.[2] They challenge medical connections between illness and fatness, barriers to full access in both the public and private spheres, and ideological constructions of fatness as ugly, dangerous, and lazy. As the

National Association to Advance Fat Acceptance information guide explains, in response to the question, "Why do we use the word 'fat' so freely?" "'Fat' is not a four-letter word. It is an adjective, like short, tall, thin, or blonde. While society has given it a derogatory meaning, we find that identifying ourselves as 'fat' is an important step in casting off the shame we have been taught to feel about ourselves."[3]

Most fat activists have come to "cast off the shame," however, only after many years of trying to lose weight—through dieting, medications, counseling, hypnosis, or even surgery. Most (although not Wann, who says she has had only two small forays into weight loss attempts) could fill pages with the diet groups they have joined, the doctors they have seen, the pills they have taken, the therapists they have worked with, the acupuncturists, herbalists, surgeons, and personal trainers they have paid to help them lose weight. Many of them have indeed lost weight, only to have gained it back many times over. For some these are stories of money thrown out the window at useless "cures" or the inevitable frustration as the weight is regained; for others, these are stories of painful medical procedures, dangerous drug combinations, humiliation in the doctors' offices, or weight loss surgery that have left them living with serious health problems. As one writer, Deborah Gregory, describes it, the pain of "living large" manifests itself in a number of ways.[4] Facing extreme hostility—from cruel childhood taunts and catcalls on the street, to insults from their own family doctors and laughing dismissal of their issues by lawyers, journalists, and academics—fat activists have nonetheless persevered in their quest both to change the powerful ideas about the dangers and ugliness of fat and to find full acceptance in a society that has for the last hundred years fully stigmatized and rejected fat people.

This chapter takes a turn from the construction of fat stigma, which has its origins in late 19th-century culture and has persisted and threaded its way into contemporary culture, to the social movement of fat activism. As a social movement, fat activism challenges the very roots of fat stigma, the way that fat serves, in Goffman's terms, as a visual and physical "discrediting attribute," one that fundamentally decreases a person's life chances. If ridicule and derision have worked as some of the main tools for creating and sustaining fat denigration (consider the *Life* magazine cartoons, the fat women postcards, the pro- and anti-suffrage propaganda, the Britney Spears exposé), fat activists draw extensively from humor and satire, just as Wann does, to counter fat stigma and to encourage a fat-positive point of view. Indeed, much of the work of fat activists depends on just that, the creation of a new point of view, an alternative way of thinking about fat, about beauty, and about health.

Just as feminists in the 1970s relied on "consciousness-raising" sessions to encourage women to *see* the unequal lives led by men and women, fat activists also must encourage others to *recognize* fat denigration and to see it as unjust. And just as second-wave feminists created groups and networks to support one another as they developed strategies for dealing with everyday, personal oppression as well as systemic, cultural, and economic inequities, fat activists have formed social communities and advocacy organizations to provide friendship, solidarity, and strategies for fighting discrimination.

In *Stigma*, Goffman explained that people will often deal with their "spoiled identities" by "admitting guilt" and going to "extreme measures" to try to purge that identity. For fat people, this means an endless litany of self-deprecating remarks, a constant acknowledgment of fat as a problem, and a continued foray into costly, demoralizing, and often dangerous weight loss methods—diet plans, fasting, over-the-counter and prescription drugs, and, increasingly, weight loss surgery. Fat activists reject these "managing techniques," instead opting for fat positive communities and a new way of *seeing* fat. They argue they have rights to pleasure, to friends, to romantic partners, to good health care, to fair treatment in jobs, and to a built environment that allows them access—*no matter what their body size*. Particularly within the contemporary context of increasing national and international concern over the "obesity epidemic," their ideas are radical and often seem incomprehensible to those who have fully embraced the idea that fat is dangerous, unseemly, and contagious. For many fat activists, their work seems not radical but rather a matter of survival. For them, the war on fat is really a war on fat people.

The myriad routes that fat activism has taken within the last decades are many, from a flourishing of fat positive literature, websites, and blogs, to a complex set of legal battles and antidiscrimination suits, to a host of fat-positive local groups and a national organization, the National Association to Advance Fat Acceptance, which acts as a clearinghouse, hosts a national conference, and helps local chapters to coordinate fat-only social events and workshops. The Health at Every Size movement, which I discussed briefly in the first chapter, is one of the most important, tangible aspects of fat activism, helping fat people, their health providers, and everyone for whom "weight loss" takes precedence over other treatment plans. All of these strands of fat activism deserve their own, detailed studies, which scholars in the new field of fat studies will hopefully address. This chapter, in contrast, considers, in a very broad sense, the ways that fat "revolting bodies," to borrow the title of Kathleen LeBesco's book, have chosen to revolt against the idea of the thin, civilized body.[5] From an exploration of its historical roots in the 1960s, to its connection with early second-wave feminism, to the articulation of a fat-positive perspective in its literature and a fat-person advocacy in its legal battles, this chapter addresses in a very broad sense the world of fat revolution and its rejection of the stigma that has percolated so powerfully since the end of the 19th century.

Origins of Fat Activism

Fat activism as a movement emerged in the late 1960s, at the same cultural moment as the gay liberation movement, the second wave of feminism, the welfare rights movement, the student and antiwar movements, and the black power, Chicano, and Native American movements. In the same ways that each of these groups—women, gays and lesbians, African Americans, college students, and so forth—identified and challenged the oppressions they faced, fat people began to examine the ways that society discriminated against them. Participants in all these social movements often had a particular, singular identity, as a student, or a black person, or a woman, or a peace activist—that mobilized their activism. Fat activists were no different. As one of the members of the Fat Underground, a radical fat activist group in the 1970s, explained, "Fat was the crisis area, the area where our identification ran highest and where we felt most strongly persecuted."[6] Of course, no matter what the "motivating" identity was, social movement participants also had other intersecting identities, some of which were masked sources of privilege, while others were explicit sources of oppression. The strategies, approaches, and theories of early fat activists all reflect this diversity of identities. Indeed, many early fat activists were also involved in a range of other movements, such as welfare rights, radical psychological therapy, leftist politics, civil rights, and black power.

By far the most likely movement to which fat activists were connected was feminism. While fat denigration was a mainstay of first-wave feminism, within second-wave feminism fat women found a place that encouraged new bodily perspectives by challenging the valorization of the thin body. As the writer Susan Stinson explained, "There was a lot of pushing the boundaries about what women should look like [in second-wave feminism], and fat was included in that."[7] In particular, the intersections between fat activism and lesbian feminism created a dynamic combination in which activists articulated a new, queer vision of the fat female body, rejected dominant psychological and physiological understandings of both fatness and gender, and claimed full rights as citizens. What is particularly fascinating is the way that this more radical approach both was supported by and came into conflict with what one might call "mainstream" feminism.

Bill Fabrey, the husband of a fat woman, began the first national fat organization in 1969, the National Association to Aid Fat Americans. "When I began NAAFA, all the fat people I knew had bought into the prevailing myth that said they are inferior because of the size of their bodies. It took me—a thin man, someone not in their oppressed group—to have enough self-confidence to fight for size acceptance," he recalled in an interview for the fat-positive magazine *Radiance*. After a year, the association had more than one hundred members. Rather cautious and conservative, the original NAAFA sought to raise fat people's self-esteem and to fight the derogatory and damaging ideas mainstream society had about fat people; like the first groups that emerge in many social movements, it sought to integrate their members into society, not to radically disrupt the entire culture. Indeed, Fabrey recalls that when he started NAAFA he was a "middle-of-the-road, middle-class guy, someone who was unaware of the many social and minority issues that were emerging."[8]

A thin, heterosexual white man sympathetic to the situation of his fat wife, Fabrey was relatively uninformed about the ways that fat oppression intertwined with other forms of cultural oppression. Others, however, immediately saw the connections. In the 1972 first full issue of *Ms.* magazine, the welfare rights organizer Johnnie Tillmon wrote, "I'm a woman. I'm a black woman. I'm a poor woman. I'm a fat woman. I'm a middle-aged woman. And I'm on welfare. If you're any one of those things, you count less as a person. If you're *all* of those things, you just don't count, except as a statistic."[9] Connecting her identities as a woman, an African American, a poor person, and an aged person to being fat, Tillmon put her finger on the ways that these cultural stigmas and oppressions interlock. Indeed, Tillmon recognized all those factors—age, race, class, and body size—that had by the turn of the century been used as markers of status on the "evolutionary" scale. Any one of those identities, she pointed out, made one count "less as a person"—as a lesser person, one lower on that scale of civilization. Multiplying those identities, she continued, placed one off the scale entirely: "You don't count, except as a statistic." In other words, as a fat, poor, African American woman, she might be the *object* of scientific or sociological inquiry, as Sara Baartman was, but she wouldn't count, she wouldn't matter as a member of society, as a person within her own right.

Fabrey wrote a letter to *Ms.* that was published in the following issue, thanking the magazine for pointing out the connections between fat and discrimination. As a whole, however, NAAFA was much more cautious about making the links that Tillmon pointed out. Indeed, political disagreements among members of NAAFA led to the formation of the California-based Fat Underground by the early 1970s. Chapter officers and members of the Los Angeles NAAFA, Summer-Vivian Mayer (known by her radical name of Aldebaran), Judy Freespirit, Gudrun Fonfa, and Sara Golda Bracha Fishman drew from the then-popular ideas of "radical therapy" to confront doctors, psychologists, and public health officials with their ideas about fat oppression. They argued that fat people experienced what they called "mystified oppression," which made it difficult for them to speak up for themselves and claim their own rights as human beings. What they meant by this was that a clever oppressor does not say, "We will torture you until you submit to our will." Instead, the oppressor says to the victim, "This treatment may seem painful or unfair, but it is for your own good." Weight loss treatments, they argued forcefully and as publicly as they could, were a form of mystified oppression. The Fat Underground challenged the medical profession by doing their own health research on obesity and health; they documented countless cases of discrimination against fat people; they pointed out the ways that culturally induced self-hatred and discriminatory practices caused health and psychiatric problems in fat people; they publicized the failure rates and health risks of diet programs and the disordered eating patterns that dieting causes; they urged fat women to reclaim and rediscover their sexuality and sensuality. They passed out pamphlets in public bathrooms, hospitals, and doctor's offices with the bold headline "BEFORE YOU GO ON A DIET," which discussed both the stigma fat people faced but also the failure rates and dangers of various diet strategies. They gave talks on radio shows and visited women's centers. One of their most clever public interventions was "harassing local weight-loss institutions," showing up at diet centers and clubs for the "free" introductory lecture. When it came time for questions, "we would attack the program's medical theory and success rate. Our goal was to shake the lecturer's confidence and turn away customers," explained Sara Fishman. At one point the Fat Underground also interrupted a meeting of psychologists and other professionals on weight loss. As Lynn McAfee, then known as Lynn Mabel-Lois (she took the first names of her mother and grandmother), remembers, "We marched out onto the podium and all stood in a line. I physically pushed the guy at the podium [laughing] and I gave a short speech that I had written on the bus earlier, about how they are committing genocide. And then we marched out. Actually, we RAN to our cars so we didn't get arrested."[10]

According to the founders of the Fat Underground, national NAAFA officers asked the LA chapter to tone down both its rhetoric and its feminist
orientation. "Our confrontational stance eventually drew the attention of
NAAFA's main office. Although some of the leadership privately applauded
us, officially we were told to tone down our delivery, and also to be more
circumspect about our feminist Ideology, [*sic*] which most NAAFA members were not ready for," Fishman remembered. The point of NAAFA, officials argued, was to integrate fat people into society, not to alienate the mainstream. In response, the LA activists quit NAAFA and formed their own
group, the Fat Underground. Fishman explained that "the name of our new
group, the Fat Underground, was suggested by Judy Freespirit; its initials
expressed our sentiments. We numbered one man (who soon left) and four
women. Judy and I wrote the Fat Liberation Manifesto late in 1973. In it, we
expressed the Fat Underground's alliance with the radical left and our inten-
tion to battle the diet industry."[11]

The "Fat Liberation Manifesto," written in November 1973, argued that
fat people were entitled to full rights as human beings, that sexism and fat
oppression worked together in the objectification of women's bodies, that fat
oppression was linked to other forms of oppression, and that the U.S. Constitution protected the rights of fat people. It further singled out as "special
enemies" the "reducing" industries, and argued that the institution of science
colluded with financial and medical interests to continue the oppression of
fat people. Cleverly revising Marx's "Working men of all countries, unite!"
the "Manifesto" concluded with, "FAT PEOPLE OF THE WORLD, UNITE!
YOU HAVE *NOTHING* TO LOSE . . . "

The use of Marx's slogan underscores the ways that the founders of the
Fat Underground saw the explicit connections between fat oppression and
capitalism. In particular, they understood how corporations hurt them as
fat *women*: "We are angry at mistreatment by commercial and sexist interests. These have exploited our bodies as objects of ridicule, thereby creating an immensely profitable market selling the false promise of avoidance
of, or relief from, that ridicule." Despite their explanation that they saw their
"struggle as allied with the struggles of other oppressed groups against classism, racism, sexism, ageism, financial exploitation, imperialism and the
like," however, the Fat Underground paid little attention to the ways that
racial oppression also linked with body size and corporate oppression.[12]

The contrast between NAAFA's careful approach and the Fat Underground's explicit, in-your-face approach is typical of the range found in early
fat activism, from tentative and halting, to articulate, angry, and forceful. As

with many other movements, some of the earliest attempts at activism were marked by worry that members themselves were bringing on trouble. Just as the first writings of the lesbian group Daughters of Bilitis cautioned members in their periodical the *Ladder* to dress conservatively and avoid bars (indeed, its statement of purpose included in each issue explained that the organization advocated "a mode of behavior and dress acceptable to society"), much early fat activism prodded participants to wear appropriate clothing and speak reasonably.[13] And just as these early, careful approaches within social movements generally gave way to more audacious and widespread demands (the *Ladder*, for instance, was taken over by a young group of lesbian feminists who were angry with the conservatism of their elders), early fat acceptance groups gave way to fat activist groups who spoke of fat pride—and fat anger—not just freedom from discrimination.

As Lynn McAfee, one of the first members of the Fat Underground, remembers, the group often used its initials, "FU," in order to demonstrate the "group's contempt for thin society." As mentioned above, the FU picketed, marched, and disrupted diet group meetings with questions designed both to rattle the instructors and educate the other fat people.[14] One of their first public demonstrations took place in August 1974 at the Women's Equality Day festival in Los Angeles, in order to honor the popular—and fat—singer Mama Cass. Cass Elliot, of the Mamas and the Papas, had just died in England after one of her concerts. Rumors began to spread internationally that she had died from choking on a ham sandwich, or that she died from choking on her vomit after stuffing herself with food. Ironically, Elliot had just lost eighty pounds after fasting four days a week during the previous eight months. The fatal heart attack that Elliot experienced was likely precipitated by this extreme weight loss measure. One of the founders of the Fat Underground, Aldebaran, remembers that Mabel-Lois went on stage at the Women's Equality Festival and "gave a speech eulogizing Cass and indicting the medical profession for her murder . . . at least twenty fat women walked up on stage with Lynn, carrying candles and raising clenched fists. Some of them were strangers who joined the march on the spot." Another participant, Sara Fishman, described the demonstration as a "symbolic funeral procession," and remembers that Mabel-Lois spoke of the inspiration Elliot had been as a "fat woman who refused to hide her beauty." She also remembers that Mabel-Lois accused the medical profession of committing "genocide against fat women," since doctors knew the dangers of weight loss yet still recommended it.[15] Alternative feminist periodicals in the area also picked up on the story of the unfair treatment the mainstream press was giving Mama

Cass. An article by Sharon Bas Hannah, published in a 1974 issue of *Sister*, a Los Angeles, feminist underground paper, read, "One of the earliest reports about her death said that she choked on a ham sandwich. That's not how she died though: Naomi Cohen [Cass Elliot's original name] choked on the culture, on the stale empty air and worthless standards of our conditioning. But Fat Power/Pride and love of sensuality is being reborn and is here to stay!"[16]

Years later, when asked about her mother, Owen Elliot, who was seven when Cass died, said, "The National Association for Fat Awareness [*sic*] made my mom their diva. I don't totally agree with that. She accepted who she was, a sexy woman who was never short of boyfriends, but I think if she could have been thinner, she would have. I'm overweight right now and I'm still beautiful. But God, it would be nice to be thin and I think that's where she was at, too."[17] In contrast to Owen's perspective that "it would be nice to be thin," fat activists said that Cass was a victim of "mystified oppression"; that it was the weight loss industry, not fatness, that killed her; and that Cass was beautiful *as* a fat woman, not despite the fact that she was fat.

Shadow on a Tightrope

By the mid-1970s there were fat liberation organizations like the Fat Underground in cities across the nation, in places like Minneapolis, New Haven, Boston, San Francisco, and Washington DC. Fat feminist groups often sprang up within women's centers as fat women began to see their body size experiences as critical to their own identities and politics. One of the founders of the Feminist Caucus of NAAFA, Carrie Hemenway, described at some length the centrality of the women's center in Northampton, Massachusetts, in her development as a fat activist.[18] Involved in leftist politics in the 1970s, Hemenway began to meet some of the feminist leaders in her community. She started going regularly to women's center meetings, where she took part in consciousness-raising groups, developing confidence to leave an abusive marriage and to think critically about gender and identity. She forged a friendship with another fat woman; after attending a concert together one evening, she tentatively broached the subject of their fat bodies. There, in the car, they spoke for hours, basically "forming the premises of fat feminism" that others throughout the country, unbeknownst to them, were also doing. She sees this now as part of a "collective consciousness," one that emerged quite naturally from a feminist politics that connected the personal and the political, and that encouraged women to believe in the truthfulness of their own experiences. "So," Hemenway remembers, "we decided to form fat consciousness-raising groups. We were going to take back the word 'fat.' Because we realized at that time, to put this very bluntly, that we hated ourselves." At their first meeting Hemenway and the other women "talked about our premise, and had people share their stories, and the whole thing was, we're smart, we're good, we can believe in ourselves, and that it's OK to accept your body as it is. You may change at different times in your life, but it's not good or bad to be fat. And, we can't wait until that magic day when we're thin, we need to get on with our lives."[19]

Susan Stinson was still a teenager in Colorado when Hemenway was forming her first fat consciousness-raising group in Northampton in the 1970s. When Stinson arrived in Cambridge, Massachusetts, after she graduated from college in 1983, a women's center was as important to her as it was to Hemenway. At the University of Colorado, Stinson had found herself moved by many of the readings in her women's studies classes, ones that said "women shouldn't be defined by their looks." Even though Stinson thought that many of these feminist writings implicitly included a phrase "except if you're fat," she nevertheless found the rhetoric liberating. Once she arrived in Cambridge, she located a fat lesbian group at the Cambridge women's center. These women, she remembers, gave her the confidence to become a writer. They also allowed her to recognize the "soft, sensual resource" of her own body, her own flesh.

While the Fat Underground disappeared from the cultural scene just as many of the other fat feminist groups did by the early 1980s, their writings and ideas remained central to the fat acceptance movement. Indeed, a feminist publisher, Aunt Lute Press, put out the position papers of the Fat Underground in 1983 under the title *Shadow on a Tightrope*. Stinson remembers seeing the call for submissions to *Shadow* when she was a college student in the early 1980s. At the time, she couldn't imagine actually submitting something. Once she arrived in Cambridge the book had been published, and she started meeting some of the contributors within her fat activist, lesbian circles. Connecting with these women was a profound experience, as, for Stinson, *Shadow* was a life-changing text, one that pointed to an entirely new way of thinking about and experiencing her body.

Although Stinson did not see the call for submissions until the early 1980s, the authors had actually been trying to get their book published since the mid-1970s. In 1976, Fat Underground member Vivian Mayer tried to find a feminist publisher for the book. None of the presses expressed interest, Mayer explained in the introduction to the 1983 volume, because they thought the "book would appeal only to a very small readership, namely, women who 'liked' to be fat." Convinced of the significance of fat oppression and of the ways it linked to feminist politics, Mayer began Fat Liberator Publications, which photocopied and mailed out copies of key fat liberation pieces. In 1980, Lisa Schoenfielder and Barb Wieser edited the collection of fat liberator pieces, called for additional submissions, and eventually founded a press that would publish this germinal work in fat activism.[20] Indeed, even years later fat activists often refer to this book as key to their body size politics. Marilyn Wann, for instance, remembers that she saw the book at a book fair in San Francisco when she was straight out of college in the late 1980s. It fairly "sparkled" at her, she jokingly recalls, enticing her to buy it. The book allowed her to articulate what she already "knew" inside, and it still holds a place of honor on her bookshelf, as well as in the list of resources in her own book *FAT!SO?*

The reluctance of feminist presses to publish *Shadow on a Tightrope* suggests that the fraught relationship activists had with fatness did not stop with the first wave of feminism. That is, first-wave feminists clearly saw some of the problematic ways that body politics were used to control and oppress women, but at the same time they also engaged in fat denigration to further their own agenda. During the 1970s and 1980s, thin feminists often did not see the connections between fat oppression and gender oppression. Wann remembers reading Julia Kristeva, Toril Moi, and even Kim Chernin while at Stanford, thinking that they "obviously did not have fat women in mind." Hemenway remembers hosting a women's meeting at her house, when a "very evolved, feminist faculty member, and activist" pointed to a Sara Lee cake and said, "Do you know if you didn't buy things like that, you wouldn't have a weight problem?" At the same time, however, the underlying philosophy of second-wave feminism, connecting the personal and the political, allowed fat women to speak the truth of their own experiences, to articulate the connections between fat oppression and women's liberation, and to gain the courage to stand up for themselves. As Karen Jones wrote in "Fat Women and Feminism," which was published in a 1974 Connecticut NOW newsletter, "Stripped of the benefits of male chivalry, the condition of fat women reflects the true position of women in our society. We must not be silent any longer; for as long as fat women are oppressed, no woman can be liberated!"[21]

Even if feminist presses were not always embracing of fat activism, they nevertheless provided the most regular outlets for women writing about fat liberation. Periodicals like *off our backs*, the *Women's Review of Books*, *Ms.*, and *Sinister Wisdom* all published fat liberation pieces, wrote exposés of the diet industries, and reviewed fat activist literature.[22] When Susie Orbach published *Fat Is a Feminist Issue: A Self-Help Guide for Compulsive Eaters* in 1978, and then her second version, *Fat Is a Feminist Issue II: A Program to Conquer Compulsive Eating* in 1982, feminist periodicals also provided the key outlet for fat activists to articulate their concerns about Orbach's insistence on weight loss and her idea that fatness was itself a pathological response to a patriarchal world.[23]

Fat feminist activists also found allies in the Boston Women's Health Book Collective, which published its first edition of *Our Bodies, Ourselves* in 1970. The first editions said little about fat per se; the 1974 edition, for instance, simply said, "We feel tremendous pressures from our society to stay 'thin and beautiful' and to diet, if need be, to maintain these thin standards. Such standards usually have little to do with our physical and emotional well being, so we often find ourselves trying to look attractive at the expense of our overall health. Some of us have found it helpful to discuss issues of women and weight with other women, who almost invariably share the same problem." By the early 1980s, the book included an excerpt from the Boston Area Fat Liberation Group, including the following suggestions: "No matter what anyone says to you . . . you have the *right* to go anywhere and do anything you like. . . . You have the right to respond angrily to the nasty things people say to you or about you. . . . Take up all of the space your body occupies—no more hunching or slumping to try to look smaller." It explained to readers that "much of our ill health as fat women results from the *stress* of living with fat-hatred—social ridicule and hostility, isolation, financial pressures resulting from job discrimination, lack of exercise due to harassment, and, perhaps most important, the hazards of repeated dieting." Hemenway remembers going to a women's rights march in the early 1980s in Washington DC. Wearing their "Women of Substance, Women of Power" T-shirts, her group saw members from the Boston Women's Health Book Collective on the sidelines. She remembers, "They had written some good stuff about bodies, and so we yelled our thanks to them, as we walked by. And they got it."[24]

NAAFA and NOW

Even as the smaller fat liberation groups were flourishing and then waning, the National Association to Aid Fat Americans continued to grow stronger; indeed, within a few years it had changed its name to the National Association to Advance Fat Acceptance, rather than the much more tentative—and ambiguous—"to aid fat Americans." The shift in name also indicated a shift in perspective, from what Goffman termed a "normal" helping those with stigmatized identities, to a new approach in which fat people spoke up for and acted on their own behalf. (Nevertheless, thin people were—and are—still welcome as members of NAAFA, as advocates, allies, lovers, and friends of fat people.) While the women-only environments of early women's centers and feminist consciousness-raising groups allowed many fat activists the freedom and confidence to articulate a fat-positive identity, NAAFA from its origins explicitly provided space for men and for women, and was predominantly a heterosexual community. Indeed, along with the educational and legal goals, much of NAAFA's emphasis was on the social, creating a fat-friendly environment in which fat people could enjoy themselves, find romantic partners, and forge friendships without apology or shame. NAAFA events—both nationally and regionally—included workshops on everything from finding appropriate medical care and building self esteem to fighting discrimination through legal channels. They included plus-size fashion shows and provided space for vendors to sell products appropriate for fat people—everything from clothing and swimwear to adequately sized furniture and toilet seats. And, importantly, the conventions all included a dance or ball, in which members "dressed to the nines," as member Carrie Hemenway remembers, baring arms and legs in revealing, ornate gowns. As a fat activist in Northampton, she remembers seeing the photographs of NAAFA parties in their newsletters, thinking to herself, "If all else fails, I could go and join the Wonderful World of NAAFA." In a fat-denigrating society, the overall cultural message is "these bodies don't belong." NAAFA conventions provided an antidote to that point of view: safe spaces, with appropriately sized furniture and accessible spaces, in which fat people could seek practical and legal advice, friendship, romance, pleasure, and, above all, a sense of belonging.

Although most members of NAAFA from the beginning were women, the leadership was predominantly male and, as the tensions with the Fat Underground revealed, decidedly not feminist. In the early 1980s, Hemenway had become a member of NAAFA and started attending conferences regularly. Along with some other women she decided to form a Feminist Caucus, which held regular Fat Women Conferences, meetings that included workshops, talent shows, clothing exchanges, and confidence-building sessions. Part of their goal was also to challenge the sexism they saw in the organization. "What happened is that as the Feminist Caucus grew, so did women's voices at NAAFA," Hemenway recalled. "And, so, the Feminist Caucus started interrupting sexism when it would happen. You know, the men who were leaders were like Hugh Hefner and it was OK for them to comment on someone's buttocks or curves or whatever, and it was acceptable by the group culture, the group ethos. . . . We did it in different ways, good-natured boos or hisses or whatever. So that stopped a whole way of communicating. And they would say, 'Ah, it's that Feminist Caucus again!' And it was. But it took on a more respectful tone."

Tension between the NAAFA officials and the Feminist Caucus erupted again in 1987 when caucus members wanted to acknowledge both the Fat Lips Readers Theater and *Matrix*, a lesbian feminist journal that had published a special issue on the "Voices of Fat Liberation," by giving them NAAFA's Distinguished Achievement Award. According to Karen Stimson, the NAAFA board refused to give the awards, objecting to the nude imagery and explicit lesbian sexuality in both the theater and the journal. At this point, however, fat radicals did not simply leave but rather resisted, organizing a letter-writing campaign. As a result, a new award was created and given to these organizations, NAAFA officially acknowledged the centrality of feminist perspectives, and many of the Feminist Caucus members gained seats on the board.[25]

Not only did feminist members of NAAFA work to influence their organization to see the significance of gender and sexuality oppression, they also worked to influence mainstream feminist organizations to see the relevance of fat oppression. After taking part in a national women's rights march, in which they wore their "Women of Substance, Women of Power" T-shirts, Feminist Caucus members decided that they should work to get the National Organization for Women to adopt a fat-positive perspective. Begun in 1966, NOW was by far the largest national feminist organization, so the decision of the Feminist Caucus to lobby this organization meant that they were eyeing the most well-known, well-established feminist entity in the country. Although local chapters often took a more radical approach to their politics, as the 1974 Connecticut article on fat liberation suggested, the national organization focused primarily on challenging legal discrimination against women.[26] Hemenway and other NAAFA Feminist Caucus members joined NOW and began staffing a fat-positive table at regional and national conferences, handing out leaflets, selling "Women of Substance, Women of Power" T-shirts, and providing a full range of fat activist reading materials. For years, their attempts to bring an anti-fat-discrimination resolution to the floor of the national conference failed. In 1988, however, Hemenway and her cohort finally convinced the regional conference of NOW to pass the resolution regarding size acceptance. At the next national conference, NOW adopted the following antidiscrimination resolution:

WHEREAS fat people face daily discrimination in the areas of employment, insurance, medical treatment, education, adoption, access, and social interaction,

WHEREAS women are the main victims of discrimination based on size,

THEREFORE BE IT RESOLVED that National NOW shall be officially on record as opposing all size discrimination, and

BE IT FURTHER RESOLVED that NOW, its chapters, and officers shall not discriminate against anyone based on size, and

BE IT FURTHER RESOLVED that National NOW shall make a public statement condemning size discrimination, especially in the areas of employment, insurance, medical treatment, education, adoption, and access, and

BE IT FURTHER RESOLVED that National NOW shall be in favor of adding "SIZE" or "HEIGHT AND WEIGHT" to the protected categories under existing equal opportunity laws and regulations, and

BE IT FURTHER RESOLVED that NOW shall endorse future local, state, or federal laws which ban size discrimination.[27]

Passing this resolution was significant both symbolically, as it indicated NOW's solidarity with fat activism, and also literally, as local and regional chapters considered ways to support the resolution and to educate their members. Hemenway recalls that for years after the resolution passed, NAAFA's Feminist Caucus would receive phone calls, letters, and other inquiries from NOW members who were trying to support the resolution. The crux of NOW support for the resolution rested on the premise that "women are the main victims of discrimination based on size," and the focus of their support was legal, to add "size" to the already-considered categories of protection. For other fat activists, however, the question was more philosophical, and returned, in a poignant way, to that hierarchy of bodily beauty first articulated by Aristotle and then by Havelock Ellis and the other social scientists of the late 19th and early 20th centuries. They wanted to reclaim the fat body as beautiful.

Queer Beauty

NAAFA and groups like the Fat Underground differed on many issues, from the root causes of fat denigration to the best strategies to combat it. They also differed in terms of their primary sexual orientation—Fabrey's group being largely heterosexual, the Fat Underground and other fat liberation groups being largely, though not entirely, lesbian. Many of the most outspoken fat activists, such as the original members of the Los Angeles Fat Underground, perceived some of NAAFA's activities as reinforcing compulsory hetero-sexuality and the power of the male prerogative to "gaze" at women. Why, for instance, should we endorse beauty pageants for fat women, members of the Fat Underground asked, considering that they were offensive for *all* women? Despite these differences, the emphasis on fat women reclaiming their beauty, their sensuality, and their sexuality was quite similar between the two "wings" of the movement. Indeed, I would argue that lesbian femi-nism and a "queering" of dominant ideologies of gendered beauty shaped the entire fat empowerment movement, from the most heterosexually oriented fat acceptance to the most radical lesbian fat activism.

In remembering the early years of the Fat Underground, Sara Fishman described their awakening into their own sexual beauty. As fat women, each had been taught to be a "'sexless fat girl': everyone's best friend, no one's lover." She described hanging out with a group of other women in a secluded setting, enjoying their naked bodies and their all-women community:

> Ariana had access to a cabin in a secluded mountain forest, about an hour's drive from Los Angeles. There we went for occasional weekend retreats. We sunbathed in the clearing in front of the cabin. We talked or slept or read all day. We cooked the meals that we had fantasized about while on diets and ate double and triple portions, and then dessert, without shame.
>
> The seclusion, the absence of men, and the abundance of simple physical comfort brought into focus our shared habit of seeing ourselves only "from the neck up." We'd all been told that we had a "a pretty face." We decided that from then on, we were also beautiful from the neck down. But such a change required a new aesthetic. We learned about the ancient goddess image, such as the round little Venus of Willendorf, whose long, oval breast draped over a perfectly spherical belly. We talked about learn-ing to belly dance. We redefined flab in terms that could have come from the biblical "Song of Songs." In Lynn's words, "Your belly is like marble. Your arms are like the ocean." We replaced the Amazon warriors of femi-nism with our own image of enormous, soft earth mothers.[28]

Fishman's story indicates a transformative shift in perspective—from seeing herself as a "sexless fat girl" to an "enormous, soft earth mother," someone who was beautiful *and* desirable. In Goffman's terms, she had cast off both a tremendous shame as well as a sense that she was only entitled to condi-tional acceptance as a "sexless fat girl," never deserving to be anyone's lover or romantic partner. This transformation came up again and again in the stories of fat activists. Hemenway moves from being someone who says, "Quite bluntly, we hated ourselves," to a person who enjoys seeing the women in their sleeveless, revealing dresses at NAAFA events. She particularly remembers the second meeting of her fat consciousness raising group, when "people started taking their coats off. And we could see the beauty of each person, and remarked on it. It was a really good experience."

For African American fat women, claiming beauty was a two-step process, of challenging both a white aesthetic and a thin-valorizing culture. As Andrea Shaw put it in her recent study, fat black women "embody disobedience" by the very fact of their existence. The Guyanese-British poet Grace Nichols articulated one of the most powerful expressions of black fat beauty in the early 1980s. In *The Fat Black Woman's Poems*, Nichols conveys the story of a witty, perceptive fat black woman who asks questions about politics, sexuality, family, and culture. Significantly, however, the first poem in the collection claims "Beauty" for black women, suggesting that this aesthetic judgment is as important for survival and vitality as institutional and political power. "Beauty / is a black fat woman," the poem reads, "walking the fields / pressing a breezed / hibiscus / to her cheek / while the sun lights up / her feet. Beauty / is a black fat woman / riding the waves / drifting in happy oblivion / while the sea turns back/ to hug her shape."[29] And, indeed, it seems that once she has claimed her own beauty, she can reject those cultural images that have so haunted black women. As she later writes, "This black fat woman ain't no Jemima." Not surprisingly, this powerful collection of poetry has maintained its influence, most recently being turned into a play, *Fat Black Woman Sings*, by the South African playwright Napo Masheane. As one reviewer wrote of the play, "the vexing issue of female beauty is laid bare by five fabulously figured women," four of whom are fat, and all of whom are black.[30]

Susan Stinson dedicated her 1993 book of poetry *Belly Songs: In Celebration of Fat Women* to "every fat woman who has ever caught a glimpse of her own power and beauty." For Stinson, fat activists encouraged her to see her body not just as something that experienced fat oppression, but also as a "soft, sensual resource." "I have a physical knowledge of what my body is that is profoundly different from what the culture tells me," she said. Her poetry makes this very clear. In *Belly Songs*, for instance, Stinson describes going to the hospital to lose weight. The medical personnel described her body as made of "cubes of butter": "They said each quarter pound I lost was like cutting a cube of butter off a big block." She returns home, and feels her body: "I feel the pulse in my thumbs, then find the pulse in the place of my thickest fat. It's delicate and regular, there, yes, there, yes, there. It comes from the underside where my palms are resting, from the left half and the right half, from veins that curve out with the rest of me. This is not dead lard. It's my body. It's my living fat." Rejecting the common sense of fat as "dead," as "leech," Stinson claims her fat as integral to her own body, to her own self. Cutting the fat is cutting herself.

In a series of poems, "Kitchen," "Passing," and "Ways a Whale Gets Hungry," Stinson describes eating with a friend and lover in the kitchen, turning into a whale, living as a whale, and eating as a whale: "Leaving the tradition of a woman in the body of a cat, we become whales, all mouths, all surface, all grace." The poems celebrate the beauty and sensuality of the whale slipping through the water. The series provides a provocative counterpoint to a postcard I found in Cape Cod one summer, "Having a Whale of a Time," mocking two fat white women who look out on the ocean. It is no surprise that Stinson draws on the idea and image of the whale, simultaneously rejecting the common insult and reclaiming the creature's beauty, finesse, and strength.[31] In a different poem, Stinson describes a conversation between the narrator, a fat woman, and her thin, feminist friend. The thin friend, drinking a diet soda, describes a nightmare where huge globules of fat are "melting off her like slabs of warm wax." The fat narrator responds, "My fat does not detach. It has a motion like liquid. It moves in waves, it ripples. It is not a virtue, not a sin, it's a bodily element with its own purpose and beauty. /I'm an admirer of liquids. Water is a regular blessing, goes in pouring, keeps all human motions possible. Milk in the mouth is something with substance. It brings sleepiness. Warms. Fills. But you're drinking hate in that can."[32] When Stinson's narrator says, "You're drinking hate in that can" of diet soda, she might be referring to the known physical risks of artificial sweeteners, as opposed to milk and water. But, more fundamentally, that "hate" is the cultural imperative that sees the fat body as a "nightmare." For Stinson, it is important to rewrite that fatness as a "bodily element with its own purpose and beauty."

The transformation in perspective that Fishman, Hemenway, and McAfee described taking place in the early 1970s, and the claiming of beauty that Nichols and Stinson convey, was repeated time and again in the memories of fat activists, even decades later. Marilyn Wann remembers feeling like "not quite a person" throughout her teens and early twenties, someone for whom a "career, sex life, marriage" would not be possible. Her shift in consciousness allowed her to see fat bodies in new, positive ways. As a result she decided to begin each chapter of *FAT!SO?* with a "study" in fat parts of the body—butts, double chins, bellies, upper arms—all conveyed in a way that simultaneously mocks the objectification of the fat body in medical exposés,

Performing since 1997, the Padded Lilies, in their own words, get "out the message that fat women in bathing suits are hot, and can get out there and do whatever they like!" Deflecting the derision fat women face, they both encourage fat women to take pleasure in their own bodies and challenge aesthetic standards that denigrate fat women. (Courtesy of Sharon Sheffield; credit: Pete Stern.)

and celebrates their size and diversity. As one of the founding members of the Padded Lilies, a synchronized swimming group in the San Francisco Bay Area, she explained her advice to "fat people everywhere . . . Get mad! Then get a bathing suit!" The Padded Lilies formed as an offshoot of a "women of size–only" weekly swim group; they now perform publicly (including on the *Tonight Show*), and see their work as a "political act"—"fat women in bathing suits are hot, and can get out there and do whatever they like!"[33]

The symbol for *FaT GiRL*, the 'zine for "fat dykes and the women who love them," is a fat woman in a bikini, giving a power salute. This quite clearly is a queer image of beauty, a fat woman, rolls of flesh revealed on her arms and belly, arms thrust in the air in a decidedly unfeminine manner. In a culture where fat women continue to be seen as an "repulsive sights, degrading alike to their sex and civilization," to remind us of Dr. Williams words in the early 20th century, *all* fat women who claim their own beauty are queer, challeng-

From 1994 to 1997, the San Francisco *FaT GiRL* collective published their 'zine, whose symbol, a fat woman in a bikini giving a power salute, challenged dominant representations of both gender and fatness. (Courtesy of Max Airborne; credit: Fish.)

ing the notion of the properly gendered and embodied "civilized" woman. As Wann says, "My gender performance [as a fat woman] was not really getting me anywhere." That is, even though Wann identifies her sexual orientation as heterosexual, it was impossible for Wann to be a properly coded heterosexual woman as long as she was fat. Whether the fat women "dress to the nines" at the NAAFA balls, expecting and receiving pleasurable looks from their male partners, or whether women enjoy their fleshy bodies at a wooded retreat as Fishman did in the early 1970s, they are "queering" and "claiming" beauty.

Access Issues

In 1994, Max Airborne published the comic "Chainsaw" in the first issue of *FaT GiRL*. The comic asked readers if they were "tired of living in a world where you don't fit?!! Try using a CHAINSAW!! Dinner booth too narrow? Take out a piece of the table! Stall too small? Take out the wall! And that seat you've always wanted on the bus? . . . " The cartoon shows folks running for their lives as the chainsaw-wielding fat person gleefully claims the full-length backbench.[34]

Like all of Airborne's humor, this piece is biting and forceful. It certainly conveys one of the key problems for fat people in the United States: access. As Goffman reminds us, stigma is exacerbated depending on the context.

In contrast to NAAFA's careful articulation of environmental discrimination against fat people, Max Airborne's comic "Chainsaw" much more bluntly exposes and challenges the ways the built environment limits and determines the lives of fat people. (Courtesy of Max Airborne.)

A world that is not physically designed for fat people supports stigma and shame and literally prevents people from living fully in the world. Even if they work to shift their ideas about beauty and fatness, their lives are profoundly limited when they *literally do not fit in*. For fat activists, then, "not fitting in" is more than a figurative term. It is the reality of spaces that are too tight, barring one from access to a world beyond one's own apartment or house. For some people, lack of access can mean no job, no social life, no public entertainment. Fat acceptance communities encourage members to take part in various forms of activism to encourage public spaces to be accessible to fat people. This might mean speaking with doctors about larger chairs for the waiting and examining rooms. This might mean boycotting an airline, such as Southwest, that charges fat passengers for two tickets rather than simply providing adequately sized seating. This might also mean providing emotional support to others after humiliating or difficult situations arise. Hemenway, for instance, remembers one very fat woman coming to a fat women's meeting for the first time. She told the story of breaking someone's toilet when she was visiting their home, an event that discouraged her from trying to go out again. The group rallied around this woman, shared their own stories, and gave her the confidence to once again seek out friendships and outings.

In the last decade, one fat activist, Elizabeth Fisher, has focused her attention on the car industry by lobbying for new laws regarding seat belts in automobiles. What motivated Elizabeth Fisher to become an activist regarding seat belts for fat people was the purchase of her Honda Odyssey minivan. She chose the Honda precisely because it best fit her body. Stunned to find out that Honda didn't provide any type of extender for the seat belt, which was far too small, she spearheaded a movement to require that automobile makers provide a way for larger people to use a seatbelt. Federal regulations only require automobile makers to provide seatbelts that fit passengers up to 6 feet tall and 215 pounds. Fisher points out that this kind of regulation literally presumes that larger people do not deserve or have the right to the protection afforded smaller people. Using as her motto "Seat Belts Should Fit Every Body!" Fisher began a nationwide petition and pushed for legislation to ensure that every car manufacturer be required to provide customers with the opportunity to purchase an extender.[35] Considering that forty-nine states require passengers to wear seat belts and that seat belts have clearly been demonstrated to save lives, the fact that auto manufacturers are allowed to avoid making extenders suggest that fat people are in some way considered noncitizens, people for whom breaking the law is irrelevant, and for whom normal protective devices aren't deemed necessary.

Indeed, one of the health risks of being fat is that one is more likely to die in a car accident, simply because it's impossible to wear a seat belt. This is a problem of access and discrimination, not one of the inherent dangers of fatness itself, fat activists point out. In a memorial to one of their members who died in a car crash in 1999, the Seattle-based fat activist group Sea-FATtle explained, "We do not know for sure if Carolyn's size contributed to her death. We do know, however, that she was larger than standard seat belts are designed for and she did not have one secured. Her driving companion, wearing a seat belt, survived the crash. The chances of having Carolyn with us today would certainly be greater if her van had been fitted with seat belts of a size to accommodate those of us larger than a Barbie doll model."[36] Don't fat people deserve the same protection as nonfat people? the activists ask.

Legal Fat Activism

For many in the fat acceptance movement, fighting employment discrimination is as important as challenging access barriers. Much of this discrimination relates to jobs for which a "professional appearance is required." Sondra Solovay, in her pathbreaking book *Tipping the Scales of Justice: Fighting Weight-Based Discrimination*, explains that fat people often find themselves rejected for jobs for which they know they are well qualified. Many even stop trying for jobs that require a "professional appearance," because they know that potential employers will see their fatness as, de facto, unprofessional. Solovay argues that employers see fat people as inherently morally defective, lazy, and out of control, certainly not qualities associated with "professionalism." Moreover, to "look professional" means to exhibit the signs of upwardly mobile class status; as the literature and cartoons analyzed earlier in the book demonstrate, however, from the end of the 19th century onward, fatness has been seen as existing on the "other side" of the upwardly mobile, with the working class, the primitive, the nonwhite.[37]

For fat people in the United States, there is very little legal protection against employment discrimination. Unlike federal legislation that bars discrimination on the basis of sex, race, national origin, and religion, there is no such national law that prohibits discrimination on the basis of body size. Antagonism toward the development of legislation barring fat discrimination resides on a number of fronts. Unlike sex, race, and national origin, fatness is seen by most as a mutable condition that one chooses, despite the fact that dieting and other weight loss measures have been shown over and again to fail. Unlike religion, which presumably one should not *have* to change though one can, at least in the United States, fatness is seen as something that one would be crazy to want to hold on to. In other words, one can't expect a Catholic or Jew to want to, or be required to, convert, but one of course would expect a fat person to *want* to become thin and to be *working toward* that end.

Using a mixture of petitions, public hearings, and clever demonstrations, fat activists have pushed a number of municipalities—including Santa Cruz, San Francisco, and Washington DC—to pass legislation that prohibits discrimination against fat people. Jennifer Portnick, a thirty-eight-year-old woman in San Francisco, was one of the first to use this legislation to fight the discrimination she faced as a fat woman. A regular aerobics participant at a Jazzercise class, Portnick's instructor thought she should train to be an instructor herself, as she so obviously enjoyed and excelled at the class. Jazzercise rejected her application, however, saying she would need to delay becoming an instructor until she developed "a more fit appearance." The corporation further encouraged her to "quit eating carbs" in order to facilitate her weight loss. Outraged, Portnick's former instructor and friends engaged in a letter-writing campaign on her behalf, particularly noting the way that she encouraged other plus-size women to take part in exercise. Despite the letter-writing campaign, Jazzercise still did not relent. Instead, Maureen Brown, director of Jazzercise franchise programs and services, wrote, "Jazzercise sells fitness. Consequently, a Jazzercise applicant must have a higher muscle-to-fat ratio and look leaner than the public. People must believe Jazzercise will help them improve, not just maintain their level of fitness. Instructors must set the example and be the role models for Jazzercise enthusiasts."[38]

What is particularly striking in Brown's statement is the way that she confuses "fitness" with "not fat." That is, no one measured Portnick's metabolic fitness—her heart rate, her glucose levels, her cholesterol levels—or her strength, agility, or stamina. Indeed, no one at Jazzercise challenged her actual ability to teach back-to-back Jazzercise classes on a daily basis. They simply judged her as "unfit" because she was still fat.

Portnick replied to Jazzercise that this was the body she had had all her life and that it was not going to change. She then asked the San Francisco Human Rights Commission to consider her case of weight-based discrimination. The commission ruled in her favor, and as a result Jazzercise has dropped all its weight restrictions for instructors. After her case was successfully mediated, the International Size Acceptance Association publicized Portnick's response: "A lot people are like me. I'm eating a healthy diet, I'm working out, I should be able to do anything I want to do. And sometimes doors are closed. But the good news is, if we stand up for ourselves, there can be positive social change."[39]

Much contemporary legal fat activism focuses on children, who in many ways cannot "stand up" for themselves. In *Tipping the Scales of Justice*, Sondra Solovay writes of a number of cases where parents lost custody of their child precisely because the child was fat. As she quips, "If the child is fat, is the parent unfit?" Unlike adults, for whom the cultural assumption is that fat people lack self-control and sufficient willpower, and thus are responsible for their own body size, children are seen as innocent and not responsible for their own fatness. As the National Coalition for Child Protection Reform explains, when children are fat, the culture turns to the "all purpose diagnosis: Somehow it must be the parents' fault."⁴⁰ One of the most publicized instances of parents being accused of reckless endangerment regarding their fat child was the case of Anamarie Martinez-Regino, a three-year-old from New Mexico. Not only did organizations like the NAAFA and the International Size Acceptance Association take up Anamarie's case, but the *New York Times Magazine* did a long story on her in 2001, after she had been returned to her parents.

Fat from the time she was an infant, Anamarie had been taken to numerous pediatricians and specialists by her American-born mother and Mexican-born father. Hospitalized a number of times and put on ultra-low-calorie diets (five hundred calories a day at one point), Ana often lost weight initially, only to regain it when she returned home. By the time she was three, she weighed 120 pounds and was 50 percent taller than an average child her age. In addition, she was slow to walk, slow to speak, yet had early tooth and hair development. According to the *New York Times*, doctors became alarmed for Ana's health when they heard reports that she had been given solid food, instead of the liquid diet they had finally prescribed to try to control her weight. They reported her case to the New Mexico Children, Youth, and Families Department, arguing that Ana was being abused because her parents failed to follow through on treatment plans for Ana's weight loss. The state of New Mexico soon thereafter gained custody. Unlike other parents involved in similar court decisions, however, Ana's parents immediately sought media coverage, contacting NAAFA and ISAA, and sharing their story on *Good Morning America*.⁴¹

After a number of months in foster care, and under the treatment of yet another physician, Ana lost about ten pounds, but by no means was "cured" of her obesity or other developmental problems. Once her case went to court, however, the judge could find no evidence either that her parents had a psychological problem called Munchausen syndrome by proxy, which causes parents to ill treat their children in order to gain attention for themselves, or that they were otherwise unfit to take care of Ana. The court first returned physical custody to Ana's parents, and then, after caseworkers had sat for months in the Regino-Martinez household observing her care, legal custody as well.

Interestingly, the physician who was able to mediate between Ana's family and the court, and seek her release from foster care, sees no blatant discrimination in this case. Instead, he sees it as a case of good intentions gone awry. Ana's situation, he argues, is probably at the "intersection of genetics and environment." That is, he thinks that she probably has some syndrome yet to be medically identified *and* that Ana's parents, perhaps unconsciously, fed her too much and too often.[42]

In contrast, the parents' lawyers and the fat activists see Anamarie's case not as the "intersection between genetics and environment" but as the intersection between ethnic and fat discrimination. As the lawyers for Anamarie's case argue, "What made them think they had the right to take her? Can obesity really be called a form of abuse? And if this were a wealthy, white, professional family, would their child have been taken away?" Moreover, the lawyers say, "There were so many veiled comments which added up to 'You know those Mexican people, all they eat is fried junk, of course they're slipping her food.'"[43] Organizations like the National Association to Advance Fat Acceptance, the International Size Acceptance Organization, and the National Coalition for Child Protection Reform also see Anamarie's case as blatant fat discrimination. They pointed out that many of the treatments Anamarie had been forced to endure—such as the liquid diets and the ultra-low-calorie diets—are known to fail and are suspected of wreaking havoc on metabolisms, causing participants to gain more weight than they would have otherwise. The fat activist Laurie Avocado, who created a website devoted to Anamarie's case, argued that it would have been very unlikely for Anamarie to be removed from her own family had we not been amid this "national hysteria about weight." "The parents haven't been charged with a crime," she continued, "but the state accused them of feeding the girl solid food after a doctor recommended a liquid diet. How many children with other conditions are monitored that closely? Does the government step in every time a sick child misses a dose of medicine? How often are children with asthma removed from homes where parents smoke? Or don't vacuum often enough?"[44]

Moreover, fat activists argue that parents of all fat children are affected by this national hysteria, not just the parents of extraordinarily fat children. As the NAAFA chairperson Leslie DiMaggio, warned, "Parents of fat children are ashamed, they feel like it's something they have done. Now, there is the fear on top of it that their children can be taken away."[45] Sondra Solovay, in her defense of fat children and their parents, argues that we must learn to distinguish between the fact that fat children are often abused (e.g., being teased and bullied) and the idea that fatness itself is abuse:

> Many children are physically and emotionally abused because they are fat. Yet, being fat is not the same thing as being abused. For a court to equate fat with abuse is unconscionable. It does a disservice to actual cases of child abuse and makes a mockery of the few rights children have. It is important not to let the extreme cases of weight based court intervention eclipse the myriad subtle injustices that happen on a daily basis. Small changes in behavior proliferate in such a hostile legal environment—a mother accepts a less favorable divorce settlement, a father is afraid to ask the government for help with his child, a parent fears letting a child attend school—all worried that, if the courts become aware of their fat children, they will take them away."

In other words, Solovay argues that blaming parents for their child's body size simply exacerbates the problems that fat children already face. To identify parents as "unfit" simply because their children are fat is one of the most dangerous aspects of what fat activists see as the "national hysteria about weight."[46]

A Shift in Consciousness

The problems created by fat stigma and bodily discrimination are so far-reaching that it is surprising that some fat people are indeed able to come to an acceptance of—indeed pleasure in—their own bodies. At this point, I turn to the narrative of one fat woman whose story clearly illuminates the myriad ways that a fat activist community can facilitate a shift in consciousness. Moreover, her story brings together some of the tensions and difficulties inherent in fat acceptance communities, which many of the other narrators and writers also suggest in their fat activist work.

I spoke with Deborah Harper in the summer of 2003 for nearly three hours, in order to explore how she came to reject the endless rounds of dieting, surgeries, and medications that most fat people engage in.[47] Harper is a white woman in her early thirties, living in the Washington DC metro area. A speech therapist, Harper is extremely heavy, carrying most of her weight in her thighs and legs. I had connected with her by e-mailing and calling the DC-area NAAFA chapter, and asking if anyone would be available for an interview. None of the officers was available, but Deborah, a self-described "inner core" of the chapter, e-mailed me to say she would be happy to meet.

I drove to her apartment late on a summer afternoon, after she had gotten home from work. She had with her a male friend, a thirtyish African American man, strongly built and svelte, who described himself later in the interview as both a "fat admirer" and a "military man." It seemed that Deborah had chosen a companion for the interview who would both challenge any preconceptions that I might have of fat women as romantically unattractive, and protect her in case I turned out to be a dangerous psychopath rather than the scholarly interviewer I presented myself as. After a lifetime of being very fat, in addition to being savvy about meeting people online, Deborah knew to be cautious.

Deborah had been a member of the DC chapter of NAAFA for about three years when I met her; she explained that she went to about 90 percent of the events, and often traveled to other cities to meet with the big and beautiful communities there. She described herself as happy both with herself and with the community she was part of. But this had not always been the case. She described how her ex-husband had called her "repulsive" and her family had pressured her, unsuccessfully, to lose weight. Her father had even promised her a dollar for every pound she would lose.

Deborah said that her world changed around 1996, when she started surfing the Internet. As she explained, "It was through the Internet in January of '96. I decided what is that information superhighway and so I decided to go online and find out and like within a week or two I did a search on *BBW* [*Big Beautiful Woman*] 'cause I had been getting the magazine and found like a kazillion of links." She continued, "[I] found the chat rooms on AOL, and started talking to people and you know just sort of went, 'Oh my gosh. There are men who like fat women. Cool.'"

When I asked her if it was the dating possibilities that propelled her into the online world of "big and beautiful," she said the dating part didn't initially take off, but the "online knowledge" and the "camaraderie" were extraordinarily important. She described the "true friendships" she made, the importance of "hearing the things that they are going through; when you can share stories and you can experience things and you hear about the husbands who tell their wives everyday that they need to lose weight or you hear about the families, both positive and negative." Indeed, Deborah was describing moments of consciousness-raising, of breaking silences, of connecting with other people. Hearing her speak so eloquently about the Internet, I asked her what people did before its arrival. Deborah responded passionately: "Stayed at home. Feel like no one would ever like them; feel like they were alone. You know. I think it takes a lot of strength to get beyond what society tells you about yourself and it is much easier when you have some kind of a support system. And the Internet is providing that for a lot of people." Interestingly, in the same year that Deborah started to use the Internet—1996—Seal Press published *Wired Women: Gender and New Realities in Cyberspace*, a collection of stories of women using the web. The editors of the collection, Lynn Cherny and Elizabeth Reba Weise, looked for the ways that cyberspace and computer-mediated communication provided new spaces for women, many of whom identified with "oppositional" or "alternative communities." Clearly, by 1996 the Internet was not just for "computer geeks" but could provide a space and a form of communication for those who had never connected previously.

After a number of months, Deborah found out that one of her online groups, "BBW Regulars," were going to have a "bash" in Miami. She explained that since the bash was only four hours away (she lived in Tampa at the time), it was an easy decision to go. A distance of four hours, however, could also be used as an excuse to miss the event; clearly the online communities made her feel extraordinarily comfortable, welcomed, and desirable. She says that the first moment she went into the hotel, "You walk in and people see that you're fat. 'Oh, you must be with us!' they said."

For people who are not fat, finding a community that *recognizes* and *welcomes* one may seem like an ordinary event. For Deborah, however, this was not the case. As Max Airborne humorously depicted in her cartoon, nothing is easy if one is fat: the built environment does not fit (from chairs to aisles to bathroom stalls), and the possibility of embarrassing oneself (a chair breaking, getting stuck, stepping on someone's toe) or being humiliated by someone else (from outright insults on the street to guarded snickers or "helpful advice") often lead fat people to avoid the public world as much as possible. And, as the work of Sondra Solovay highlighted, fat people face not only cultural and environmental problems but also outright discrimination—from not being served in stores to being refused jobs. Being part of a "BBW" bash, however, meant that the built environment had been checked out (chairs big and strong enough, bathroom facilities adequate), that the hotel or ballroom was explicitly welcoming of fat people, and that there were people there who would not only avoid insults, but would actually welcome the fat person unconditionally. (At least in terms of her body size, that is. Certainly these groups, as with all groups, had their own dynamics that may have made some people more welcome than others. Deborah, for instance, spoke of the difference between certain organizations and their expectations for "proper" behavior, or in other cases, their tolerance and encouragement of "wild" behavior.) No wonder Deborah began seeking out more and more events.

Both the online and the in-person fat communities that Deborah was part of began to encourage the fat activism she had already begun on her own. Deborah spoke of her many attempts to break the taboos limiting fat women. At a church retreat, for instance, during the hottest days of summer, Deborah refused to wear pants despite the cultural prohibition against showing off fat legs. She spoke with pride about the ways that other fat women started to wear shorts when they realized she had begun doing so.

Deborah's childhood activism moved to yet another level as she became part of fat acceptance communities. In particular, she started to challenge the medical establishment. She spoke with passion about the mistreatment that fat people get at physicians' offices; in particular, she pointed out the ways that doctors mocked fat people, blamed all their health problems on their weight, and often overlooked other medical issues. She discussed at length the problems she had had with her own knee. One of the doctors just glanced at the X-ray, took a look at Deborah, and told her that she had severe arthritis and should lose weight. That physician didn't even lift her pant leg to look at or examine her knee. (She finally found a doctor who actually examined her knee, diagnosed it correctly, and offered a treatment plan that has worked well.) No wonder, she said, that fat people often avoided going to doctors.

As a result, Deborah said that she has begun her own one-woman campaign, which began with her brother who is a doctor. She now leaflets her own doctors with fat activist literature, and scribbles notes and questions on any medical literature she finds in their offices that supports what she sees as size discrimination. When I asked her what she thought about the alarming—and widespread—statistic that obesity caused three hundred thousand deaths a year, she replied:

> I would believe that if I knew that they [the researchers] were accounting for all the confounding and competing factors. For instance, does this account for the fact that so many obese people will defer care for very long periods of time, because of the difficulty of going to the doctor? The fact that there is no fat-friendly seating, the humiliation they face, et cetera. Of course, those who don't get medical care will have undiagnosed diabetes, cholesterol problems, heart problems, arthritis, cancer. What if all these folks could get treated as quickly as their thin counterparts?

Part of her dream is to encourage everyone—including all medical professionals—to take part in fat simulation, not as a kind of joke like in the film *Shallow Hal*, but as a form of education about the experiences and limitations that fat people face and the way that fat stigma continues to serve as a publicly acceptable form of discrimination. She makes a point to tell me how impressed she is with the way many do make quiet and polite accommodations for her. For instance, at the beauty parlor where she goes, they unscrew the arms of the chairs, without saying a word, before she even arrives.

Deborah describes both her participation in fat acceptance parties and dances and her attempts to educate family members, doctors, and coworkers as a form of feminist activism. Like Hemenway, Stinson, and Wann, she has used the tools of a feminist perspective to allow herself to see the ways that the life of a fat woman is especially "painful and dangerous, compared to either thin women or even fat men," who experience, she argues, a level of tolerance not given to fat women. Indeed, the fat acceptance world that Deborah inhabits is one largely made up of women. Ironically, then, women are in the majority both at the weight loss centers *and* at the fat acceptance bashes. It is probable that the extraordinary stigma U.S. culture attaches to female fat propels women either to be adamant about taking off the weight *or* to challenge that stigma that so oppresses them. Any particular fat woman might likely have inhabited first the world of weight loss and then, when it became clear that the weight was never going to disappear, the world of fat acceptance.

Deborah's story is a fascinating example of a woman moving from silence to voice, from isolation to community. Both a new form of technology—the Internet—as well as the *embodied* experiences of the bashes and the dances facilitated Deborah's movement through these processes. My interview with Deborah underscored the importance of her newly found social community, which sustained her within a fat-denigrating culture that has stigmatized fatness for over a century and increasingly frames "obesity" as a crisis and the obese person as the culprit. Moreover, the interview revealed the centrality of new technology—particularly the Internet—to create the conditions for the emergence of that community. Deborah's narrative serves as an exemplar of a person fighting stigma and moving into both personal awareness and cultural activism. This certainly does not mean, however, that there is closure to Deborah's narrative. She spoke at length about the complexities of the world of fat admirers, for instance, as well as the perplexing questions that new surgical options raise.

As Deborah pointed out, fat admirers—those who prefer fat partners, the larger the better—pose a dilemma within the fat acceptance movement. A central part of the fat acceptance movement is celebrating fat and countering the shame and derision usually accompanying fatness. Fat admirers, usually men who generally are thin themselves, are condemned in the larger culture for actually finding sexually appealing that which is loathed by the mainstream—fat women. E. Smith, the African American man who sat with Deborah and me during our conversation, described himself as an "FA" (fat admirer). He said that when he served in the military, he began to read *Dimensions* magazine, which is filled with both fat accepting articles and nude and seminude photos of fat women. While many who served with him teased him about reading *Dimensions*, he also said that there were a lot of FAs, they just weren't "out" with their desires. In the last few years, Smith had also begun going to NAAFA events and dances, meeting and dating fat women. While both Deborah and her friend seemed quite satisfied with the presence of FAs at the fat acceptance events, they also spoke about the problems FAs pose for many fat women. In particular, they spoke about the ways that some FAs prey on fat women who "feel bad about themselves" and whose lack of self esteem and confidence allow them to be easy victims of abuse. Some FAs, they said, make fat women feel like they should be "grateful" for any attention they get. Deborah said that there are now a number of lists posted on fat acceptance Internet sites of FA "jerks" who emotionally or physically abuse fat women.

In speaking about what Carrie Hemenway had called the "shadow side" of NAAFA, the world of abusive fat admirers, neither Deborah nor her friend raised the different and less tangible problem: the ways that FA publications like *Dimensions* encourage a kind of fetishism that reflects the opposite of mainstream society's fascination with but hatred of the fat body. Indeed, the existence of "gainers" and "encouragers" (women and men who purposefully work to become fatter and fatter in order to please their, usually male, encourager) was a controversial area that neither Deborah nor her friend discussed. Neither did they raise the specter of compulsory heterosexuality—the way that the presence of male FAs reinforces the objectification of women's bodies and the idea that the primary purpose of women is to be attractive to men. In contrast, both Deborah and E. see the presence of FAs as a pleasurable aspect of fat acceptance communities—fat women have access to men who find them attractive as they are, and men have access to women whose bodies please them.

Certainly, however, many fat activists are lesbians, women who articulate their rejection both of compulsory heterosexuality and of having a thin body that is desired by most men. Indeed, many of the most outspoken fat activists, such as the original members of the Los Angeles Fat Underground, identify themselves as lesbians. Interestingly, within fat acceptance groups like NAAFA and ISAA there are few fat men, either heterosexual or gay. As Deborah argued, fat men have a greater measure of acceptance within the larger society; indeed, their attractiveness to both men and women may have as much to do with their loyalty, their personality, or their moneymaking ability as with their body shape. Or, as the number of "bear" websites attests, their attractiveness to some gay men may indeed rest on their very fatness.[48]

In her interview, Deborah also raised one of the most complex issues facing fat acceptance communities today: the increasing popularity of weight loss surgery. The official point of view of most fat activist members and organizations is explicitly against these procedures. Citing the severe health complications and risk of death associated with the surgery, as well as the lack of follow-up studies indicating either continued weight loss or long-term improved health, NAAFA "condemns gastrointestinal surgery for weight loss under any circumstances." The organization argues that treating "co-morbidities" of obesity serves as insufficient justification for the extraordinary measure of mutilating the digestive tract, considering that alternative treatments exist. In other words, fat patients with high blood pressure, heart disease, diabetes, or arthritis, all of which are linked to obesity, can be treated without resorting to weight loss surgery. Moreover, NAAFA argues that the "psychosocial suffering that fat people face is more appropriately relieved by social and political reform than by surgery."[49] In other words, the problems of fat discrimination and stigma are best challenged through political activism and cultural change than by forcing fat people to mutilate their bodies, fat activists argue. Just as it would be insufficient and offensive to fight racism by encouraging black people to bleach their skin white, or to challenge anti-Semitism by converting Jews to Christianity, fat activists argue that fat people should not be forced to become thin in order to expect fair and decent treatment within society. Social problems, in other words, should not be solved by inflicting medical "solutions" on those who are experiencing the problems. Indeed, some fat activists see weight loss surgery as a form of genocide against fat people, the ultimate example of how the "war on fat" is indeed taken out on fat people.

That said, weight loss surgery is increasingly popular even among members of fat acceptance organizations. Deborah spoke about the intense advertising that fat people face—in doctors' offices, in magazines, on television talk shows—that encourages them to undergo the surgery. That propaganda, coupled with the severe and unrelenting stigma that fat people experience on a daily basis, helps to explain why so many fat people are choosing weight loss surgery, despite its known risks and its unknown outcomes. One physician, writing for the *New Yorker*, argued that in the future it will take increasing fortitude for fat people to resist the pressure to go under the knife.[50] For members of the fat acceptance communities who do choose gastroplasty, and whose surgery is successful, the social issues are complex. Is one still a member of the community if one has rejected the fat body? That said, many in the fat acceptance community are quick to return, weight regained and health compromised. As many in those communities point out, there are far too many "weight loss survivors," those who have undergone the surgery only to experience severe health complications. Unfortunately, as activists like Susan Mason point out, those who are considering weight loss surgery often don't want to hear from the "survivors," as they desire so desperately to believe in this last-ditch and extraordinary measure to become thin.[51]

Conclusion

Fat activists like Deborah Harper speak of the joyous psychological relief they experienced when they came to accept themselves as fat people, shedding not pounds but layers of culturally induced self-loathing with the help of their newly found fat accepting communities. In her best-selling memoir *Wake Up, I'm Fat!* Camryn Manheim (who won an Emmy for her role on the TV drama *The Practice*) remembers rejoicing when she found the fat acceptance movement: "In *Dimensions* I found articles about fat positivism and self-love, poetry praising big beautiful women, and items on the dangers of dieting. I felt like I had discovered a parallel universe, a world in which fat was accepted, lauded, and desired. In the back of *Dimensions*, I found a list of other fat-positive magazines and newsletters: *Radiance, Fat!So?, Rump Parliament* (love that title), *Large Encounters, National Association to Advance Fat Acceptance* (NAAFA), *Metabolism, Belly Busters, BBW, and Super Women.* I spent $400 subscribing to these magazines."[52] The roots of fat stigma run deep, however, and have also been given a new dose of fertilizer with concerns about the "obesity epidemic." Even Manheim, who has been a stalwart supporter of fat acceptance, recently recanted her position. In an advertising spread within *Newsweek*, which promoted "heart-healthy" products like the cholesterol-lowering drug Crestor and Quaker Oatmeal, Manheim wrote, "Yes, I want to be very clear about this. People remember me accepting an Emmy and saying, 'This is for the fat girls.' I am a proponent of self-acceptance, but I am not a proponent of fat acceptance."[53]

Despite the loss of such supporters, fat activists continue to fight the stigma attached to fatness in a myriad of ways—whether as the members of SeaFATtle who "raise consciousness by raising hell," as the conservatively dressed members of NAAFA who engage in public speaking events, or as the legal scholars who go to court on behalf of fat adults and children. Originating in the same cultural moment as other post–World War II social movements, fat activism drew extensively from feminist resources (like women's centers) and feminist theories (particularly the idea that the personal is the political) as it developed and grew. Today, many of NAAFA's approaches and perspectives seem very similar to those of the Fat Underground and other organizations like it: it has numerous policy statements on everything from dieting to weight loss surgery to size acceptance legislation, and it encourages specific activist endeavors, from letter-writing campaigns to infiltrating audiences and posing difficult questions to weight loss gurus. (NAAFA still, however, encourages members to be "well-groomed and appropriately dressed, especially when publicly representing NAAFA.")[54] And, as further evidence of the ways that the tactics and ideas of NAAFA and the Fat Underground influenced each other, the founder of NAAFA, Bill Fabrey, and one of the founders of the Fat Underground, Lynn McAfee, now both serve on the Council on Size and Weight Discrimination.[55]

Some of the most powerful fat activism merges fat and queer activism, from the 1970s lesbian Fat Underground to NoLose, a contemporary group dedicated to "ending the oppression of fat people and creating vibrant fat queer culture."[56] These groups fundamentally undercut the notion of a "normal" body, challenging at its core the idea that fat women are "degrading to their sex and to civilization." Whatever attempts groups like NAAFA have made to be "respectable," however, have not necessarily protected it from abuse from a fat-hating culture, however. An automatic message warning about the illegality of hate mail pops up on the computer screen when e-mailing the organization ("Please note that any e-mail deemed as hate mail and containing abusive or inappropriate language may be deleted or forwarded on to relevant authorities at the discretion of the NAAFA Board of Directors and may not receive a response."). Just as every stigmatized group in the United States knows, it is dangerous to challenge the idea—to queer the idea—of the "civilized body." Refusing to apologize is a bold step.

Conclusion

"The horror! The horror!"

In 2006, I came across an "Over the Hedge" cartoon strip that pointed to the crux of my argument about fatness. Written and drawn by Michael Fry and T. Lewis, "Over the Hedge" recounts the observations and experiences of three animals—a raccoon, a turtle, and a squirrel—whose habitat has been taken over by suburbia. In this particular strip, we see R. J., the raccoon, and Verne, the turtle, observing something in the distance. R. J. begins by saying, "Oh, Lord." Verne, the turtle, then chimes in, "The horror . . . the horror . . . " "We shouldn't be subjected to this," he continues. "You're right," says R. J. who proceeds to make a call on his cell phone. "Who're you calling?" asks Verne. "Society for the Prevention of Embarrassment to Animals," answers R. J. What is it that has these two animals so riled up? It is the sight of a very fat man, belly hanging over a too tight Speedo suit, walking down the sidewalk.

On the one hand, this comic strip is relatively easy to read. The animals are grossed out and embarrassed to see this barely clad fat man clutching an oversized drink. It's the kind of stigma, as described by Goffman, in which the person with the spoiled identity is only allowed in circumscribed spaces. And clearly this fat man has overstepped those boundaries, to the point of embarrassing even the resident suburban animals. Verne's choice of words to describe what he is seeing, "The horror . . . the horror . . . ," takes us out of 21st-century suburbia, however, and back to the late 19th century. These words refer to Joseph Conrad's novella *Heart of Darkness*, first published in serial format in 1899. This book recounts the story of an Englishman, Charles Marlow, who is sent on an expedition down the Congo, into the "heart of darkness," to locate another Englishman, Kurtz, and return him to "civilization." Marlow eventually does find the ivory trader Kurtz, and brings him onto the Belgian cargo ship. Before they can return to England, however, Kurtz dies, with Marlow next to him. As he lies dying, Conrad tells us that

Kurtz "cried in a whisper at some image, at some vision—he cried out twice, a cry that was no more than a breath—'The horror! The horror!'"[1]

For Marlow, the narrator of the story, Kurtz's dying vision that evokes these words is the barbarism that he has witnessed, in Africa, and in himself, as he became a maniacal tyrant willing to engage in whatever oppression and torture was necessary to secure his fortune in ivory. The "heart of darkness," thus, is both the continent of Africa, clearly juxtaposed to the civilized nation of England, and the inner depravity that lurks within the soul of every human being. All that keeps this sordidness in check are the controls and mores of civilized culture. Conrad's novel, then, clearly reflects dominant thinking at the time, which posited a scale of civilization whose pinnacle was England (and by extension all of Western culture) and whose nadir was Africa. Likewise, each person had within him the possibility of degeneracy, unless buoyed and controlled by civilization. In his dying moments, Kurtz envisioned the primitive, evil impulses that created a barbaric culture, one exemplified by the African continent and by Kurtz's own actions. When Verne yells out, "The horror . . . the horror . . . ," then, he is saying that, like Kurtz, he is witnessing the "heart of darkness," in this case the fat, unleashed body, uncontrolled by civilized clothing or checks on appetite. The cartoon takes us from the 21st-century denigration of fatness back to its roots in the 19th-century concept of a civilized (and uncivilized) body, for which fatness was a key sign of the barbarism and primitivism of an inferior people.

When fat activists speak of their attempts to make the word "fat" neutral, as along the lines of descriptions of hair or eye color, it sounds relatively straightforward and easy. Reclaiming the word "fat," however, is anything but simple, for it is to challenge the layers of connotation that have their origin in the 19th century. In the 21st century, fatness continues to conjure all the meanings that have been attributed to inferior peoples for over a hundred years: lazy, gluttonous, lacking willpower, primitive. The connotations are so powerful, and so firmly rooted, that cartoonists can write, "The horror . . . the horror . . . ," and readers can quickly *know* what the writers mean. The associations are also so prevailing that contemporary writers casually link the fat body to the African and to the homosexual, just as the "obesity" writers did in the early 20th century. In a 2005 memoir, for instance, the author of *Fat Girl*, Judith Moore, imagines how her father felt growing up as a fat boy:

> In 1928, my father was fourteen, an inch short of six feet, and weighed two-hundred-plus pounds. . . . When he caught sight of himself in downtown plate-glass windows he could not believe this was who he was. His belly

rode before him and his buttocks stood high, like Africans', and his buttocks ground, up and down, giant turbines propelling his flesh. He wore his trousers pulled up to mid-belly; the trousers pulled against his fat.

Naked, before he stepped into the shower, he saw that his stomach hung down over his penis and his breasts were pendulous as women's.[2]

Her father's fatness, then, pulled him down the scale of civilization, from a white person to an "African," from a young adolescent boy to an emasculated creature with pendulous breasts and a hidden penis. Moore's description of her father bears an uncanny resemblance to Cuvier's description of Sara Baartman, if one simply replaces the fat covering the penis with the fat that he describes covering her female genitals. Moore did not have to read the original documents by Cuvier to arrive at this description, however. The connections between fatness, Africanness, and a grotesque, "queer" femininity have been passed down in cartoons, literature, political satire, and even medical documents for more than a century. The association of fatness with inferior, primitive qualities is so persistent that it is no surprise that Moore, in recounting her life as a fat woman, concludes, "I am ashamed and I am resigned to my shame."[3]

This ideological connection between fatness and inherent inferiority also helps us to understand the 2009 controversy at Lincoln University, the first historically black college in the United States, over its "Fit for Life" physical education class. "Fit for Life" was a graduation requirement only for those students with a body mass index over thirty. James DeBoy, the chair of the school's Department of Health and Physical Education, explained that it was important to be "honest" with students: "We, as educators, must tell students when we believe, in our heart of hearts, when certain factors, certain behaviors, attitudes, whatever, are going to hinder that student from achieving and maximizing their life goals." National interest turned to Lincoln as the first students for whom the graduation requirement applied began to complain. "I didn't come to Lincoln to be told that my weight is not in an acceptable range," argued Tiana Lawson, who wrote a school editorial challenging the requirement. "I don't know why they would want some people to be more healthy than others," she continued. Alumni wrote to the college outraged that a "Euro-American" standard of beauty was being applied to these students. Others were concerned about the legality of singling out some students for particular requirements. By the beginning of December, Lincoln's Faculty Senate voted to terminate the requirement, instead opting for an "optional" course in which "obese" students would be encouraged to enroll.[4]

Having traced the powerful ways that fatness continues to be linked to a lower status on the evolutionary scale, it should come as no surprise that the Lincoln administration would be concerned about their students' weight. Certainly their rationale of students' health should not be entirely dismissed; indeed, universities and colleges have since their inception in the United States focused on the "entire" student, including physical, spiritual, social, and intellectual fitness. But even more powerful is the particular context of historically black colleges, for whom it has been key to demonstrate the inherent *worthiness* of their students within a nation that denigrated and, until relatively recently, legally discriminated against people of African heritage. Just as the Obama family articulated a concern with their daughter's weight, knowing that it could lessen her "life chances," to return to Goffman's term, Lincoln paid particular attention to its students' body size and the threat that fatness posed to their chances for upward mobility and a respectable social status. It should come as no surprise, then, that this historically black college would be the first university in the United States to try to institute a policy demonstrating its commitment to the civilized, "healthy" standards of a slim body.

Since the turn of the last century, fatness has served as a sign that one is inherently incapable of withstanding the pressures and pleasures of modern life, including the responsibilities and privileges of citizenship. The "modern" woman was mocked for her enjoyment of travel and shopping, the ethnic immigrant for his desire to take part in the political process, the suffragist for her aspiration to vote alongside men—all by portraying those who sought more power and privileges as *fat*. It makes sense, then, that those who sought to shed stigmatized backgrounds, whether of gender, race, or class, often took part in weight reduction schemes and in fat mockery of their own in order to validate themselves as "civilized." This was the case for the white suffragists of the early 20th century, who portrayed themselves as thin, wispy, and good-looking, and the anti-suffragists as fat, ugly, and old. This focus on a thin body has also been true for contemporary public figures, from Oprah Winfrey to the Obama family, who have moved into positions of power and authority previously closed to African Americans.

Some readers, I imagine, will wonder why it matters if some people continue to engage in weight loss strategies simply for cultural reasons, if indeed that body helps to validate oneself as well equipped for the pressures and privileges of modern life. As Jean Renfro Anspaugh bluntly concludes, discussing her decision to enroll in the internationally recognized Duke University Diet and Fitness Center, "Thin is just better, no matter how much

I try to challenge that stereotype. The world really does love you thin and hate you fat."[5] The consequences of fat denigration, however, are quite significant. As the stories of fat activists suggest, the stigma that fat people experience within a thin valorizing culture are formidable and dangerous, from the bullying children face to extraordinary loss of self-esteem to discrimination suffered in employment, housing, legal institutions, and medical care.[6] Further, the shame of fatness fuels our extraordinarily large weight loss industries, estimated to reach sixty billion dollars by 2010.[7] These numbers are not expected to go down, despite the significant economic downturn. Indeed, one might imagine that during an economic crisis, people will feel even more compelled to invest whatever money they have in dangerous, extreme measures to lose weight if that will give them an the edge in the job hunt.

Fat stigma is a problem, then, most obviously because it leads to discrimination against fat people. This should be enough reason for us to consider seriously—and to excavate—the cultural roots of our fat-denigrating ideas. On an even broader level, however, we should be concerned about fat stigma because it allows the idea of a "civilized body" to continue unabated. Just as the travel writers' hierarchies of people and countries were overlaid with the late 19th-century sociologists' and anthropologists' hierarchies of evolution and civilization, today those theories have been overlaid with hierarchies of "health" and "fitness." Remarkably, they all look surprisingly similar. Today's "healthy" body is one that is thin, stripped of any vestiges of fatness, just as Cuvier's and then Lombroso's most civilized bodies had no signs of fat. And, significantly, just as those 19th-century theories of civilization were frequently used to justify discrimination and inequities based on "science," today's theories of the "fit" body justify unfair treatment, such as the recent decisions making adoption harder and sometimes impossible for fat people, and brutal "cures," such as the increasing prevalence of weight loss surgery, even among children and adolescents. Reinforcing the dangerous idea of the "civilized body," fat denigration intersects with and exacerbates racism, sexism, classism, and homophobia, and all the other means by which our culture classifies and oppresses people based on bodily attributes and social standing. Indeed, if we want to think clearly about health issues within this national and international anxiety regarding the "obesity epidemic," we had better work to strip away the cultural baggage that has fueled a fat-hating perspective. Otherwise, we are simply "treating" people for the horror of a stigmatized identity, one that has little to do with real, physical health risks.

Notes

NOTES TO CHAPTER 1

1. Dillon, "Evictions"; Dillon, "DePauw Cuts Ties"; "National Short Takes—Indiana," 20; Hewitt, "Kicked Out!" 197–198; Delta Zeta Sorority, "Delta Zeta Files Federal Lawsuit"; Adler, "Great Sorority Purge," 47; Depauw University, "Delta Zeta Sorority Files Lawsuit."

2. Schwartz, *Never Satisfied*, 178, 198.

3. Open NY, "The Measure of a Man."

4. Goffman, *Stigma*. More recent work by psychologists and sociologists like Esther Rothblum, Jeffery Sobal, and Donna Maurer provide excellent studies of the specific stigma fat people face and the negative consequences of that treatment, as well as the various coping mechanisms they use. See Sobal and Maurer, *Weighty Issues*.

5. LaBute, *Fat Pig*.

6. Brillat-Savarin, *The Physiology of Taste*, 261.

7. Harter, "Mauritania's 'Wife-Fattening' Farm"; letters from high school students in Namibia to Mooreland Elementary School students, Carlisle, Pennsylvania, August 2006, in author's possession.

8. Becker, *Body, Self, and Society*.

9. More recent scholarship in *The Social Psychology of Stigma* explains, "Rather than assuming that the experience of being stigmatized inevitably results in deep-seated, negative, and even pathological consequences for the personality of a stigmatized individual, researchers in this area now assume that people who are stigmatized experience a set of psychological predicaments, which they cope with using the same coping strategies as those used by nonstigmatized people when they are confronted with psychological challenges such as threats to self-esteem." Dovidio, Major, and Crocker, "Stigma," 2.

10. Edut, *Body Outlaws*.

11. "Epidemic" is a technical term from the field of epidemiology that refers to a disease found at levels higher than expected. In common usage, however, it refers to an *infectious* disease. See "Obesity Epidemic" in Gilman, *Diets and Dieting*, 202. See also National Institutes of Health, "Prevalence Statistics Related to Overweight and Obesity."

12. Deford, "Commentary."

13. Neergaard, "Child Obesity."

14. Clinton Foundation, "Alliance for a Healthier Generation."

15. See, for instance, Long, *AIDS and American Apocalypticism*.

16. Koop, "In Spite of Diet Drug Withdrawal."

17. Sontag, *Illness as Metaphor*, 3.

18. For instance, in 2008, the Obesity Society published a paper defining obesity as a disease. At the end of the paper, the authors acknowledged that "the Obesity Society and members of the writing group have accepted funds from multiple food, pharmaceutical, and other companies with interests in obesity." Allison and the TOS Obesity as a Disease Writing Group, "Obesity as a Disease," 1172. As investigators for the *New York Times* noted in 2009, however, many articles in medical journals do not even acknowledge their ghostwriters or financial ties. See Wilson and Singer, "Ghostwriting Is Called Rife"; Singer and Wilson, "Medical Editors Push for Ghostwriting Crackdown"; Oliver, *Fat Politics*.

19. HAES advocates refer to the research of such scholars as Bacon, *Health at Every Size*; Campos, *The Obesity Myth*; and Gaesser, *Big Fat Lies*. For a general discussion of the HAES movement, see Henig, "Losing the Weight Stigma." In addition to Gaesser's *Big Fat Lies*, for research that challenges the obesity and disease link see Cogan and Ernsberger, "Dying to Be Thin in the Name of Health."

20. Bacon and others, "Size Acceptance and Intuitive Eating."

21. For statistics on weight loss surgery, see American Society for Bariatric Surgery, "Bariatric Surgical Society Takes on New Name"; and American Obesity Association, "Obesity Surgery." For information on surgical costs, see Gawande, "The Man Who Couldn't Stop Eating."

22. Koop, "In Spite of Drug Withdrawal."

23. Ezzell, "Fat Chances," 94.

24. See Mark, "Deaths Attributable to Obesity," 1918; Centers for Disease Control, "Telebriefing Transcript"; and Centers for Disease Control, "CDC's National Leadership Role in Addressing Obesity."

25. Eisenhower, *Public Papers of the President*, 1038.

26. PETA ad available online at http://www.peta.org/mc/ads/obeseusabb_LO%20REZ.pdf (accessed September 7, 2010).

27. Freedman and Barnouin, *Skinny Bitch*, 186; Freedman and Barnouin, *Skinny Bitch: Bun in the Oven*, 24.

28. Freedman and Barnouin, *Skinny Bitch*, 145, 10, 44.

29. Kingsolver, *Animal, Vegetable, Miracle*, 130; Pollan, *Omnivore's Dilemma*, 100; Critser, *Fat Land*.

30. Schlosser, *Fast Food Nation*, 239–243.

31. Interestingly, one of the first contemporary food activists, Frances Moore Lappé, makes only one small reference to "losing pounds." *Diet for a Small Planet*, 142. See also Sinclair, *The Jungle*.

32. For a discussion of these statistics regarding dieting and women, and for a further exploration of her own dieting experiences, see Stinson, *Women and Dieting Culture*, 212.

33. Schwartz, *Never Satisfied*. See also Stearns, *Fat History*; and Klein, *Eat Fat*.

34. Indeed, within the field of women's studies as a whole, the body has played such a fundamental role as a point of inquiry that there is far too much research for me to record here. Nevertheless, it's important to point out that some of the earliest well-known "second wave" feminist texts, from Betty Friedan's 1963 *Feminine Mystique* to Toni Morrison's first novel, *The Bluest Eye*, which came out in 1970, to Barbara Ehrenreich and Deirdre English's 1978 *For Her Own Good: Two Centuries of the Experts' Advice to Women*, explored the damaging effects of dominant beauty and body standards on girls and women. Scholars produced a tremendous amount of research on dieting practices and the cultural

valorization of thinness, including books like Susie Orbach's *Fat Is a Feminist Issue* (which, ironically, was both a study of thin ideals and a diet book itself), Joan Jacobs Brumberg's *Fasting Girls* and her later book *The Body Project*, Naomi Wolf's best-selling *Beauty Myth*, and Mimi Nichter's *Fat Talk: What Girls and Their Parents Say About Dieting*. For the most part, studies like these focused on the ways the cultural imperative for thinness affected white girls and women, though Nichter supplemented her study with an additional group of African American girls to explore their feelings about body size, and studies like Becky Thompson's *A Hunger So Wide and So Deep* explored disordered eating among women of color, both lesbian and heterosexual. Susan Bordo's 1993 *Unbearable Weight: Feminism, Western Culture, and the Body* remains one of the most important theoretical and conceptual explorations of how the connections between gender and body/mind dualism infiltrates and affects contemporary culture.

35. See also Gard and Wright, *Obesity Epidemic*; and Tomrley and Kaloski-Naylor, *Fat Studies in the UK*.

NOTES TO CHAPTER 2

1. "Cure of Obesity," *San Francisco Daily Evening Bulletin*, June 29, 1869; "How to Reduce Obesity," *San Francisco Daily Evening Bulletin*, July 17, 1869.

2. *Life*, January 20, 1887, 43; *Life*, June 30, 1887, 373.

3. "To Reduce Obesity New Gymnasium Devices to Make Graceful Forms," *Emporia (KS) Daily Gazette*, January 15, 1891.

4. *Life*, July 23, 1914, 156.

5. *Life*, October 22, 1915, 737.

6. *Life*, December 3, 1914, 1042.

7. *Life*, July 9, 1914, 81.

8. Cramp, *Nostrums and Quackery*, 460–461.

9. Schwartz, *Never Satisfied*, 191, 197; American Medical Association, *Nostrums and Quackery*, 459.

10. *Harper's Weekly*, February 19, 1881, 127.

11. *Life*, March 12, 1908, 51.

12. "The Old Sow in Distress, or the Country Parsons Return from Tithing," approx. 1780–1820, Library of Congress, Prints and Photographs Division.

13. *Harper's Weekly*, February 26, 1881, 132; *Harper's Weekly*, February 5, 1881, front cover; *Life*, February 3, 1887, 71.

14. John T. McCutcheon, "A Swell Gent," originally published in the *Chicago Tribune*, December 1, 1916, Library of Congress, Prints and Photographs Division.

15. "Not a Homeopathic Dose," *Life*, January 11, 1883, 15.

16. Anne Wilmot, "The Happy Expression," *Godey's Lady's Book*, February 1849, 102–103.

17. *Harper's Weekly*, April 9, 1881, front cover; *Harper's Weekly*, May 19, 1988, 363; J. S. Pughe, "Pride Goeth Before Destruction," 1900, Library of Congress, Cartoon Drawings Collection; Ryan Walker, "Our Flesh and Blood Fattened Him," originally published in the *Daily World* between 1890 and 1940, Library of Congress Prints and Photographs Division; Rollin Kirby, "Yours of Recent Date Received and Contents Noted," December 30, 1937, Library of Congress, Prints and Photographs Division.

18. Herbert Johnson, "I've Got the Engine Started But . . . ," originally published in the *Saturday Evening Post* between 1912 and 1941, Library of Congress, Prints and Photographs Division.

19. Thompson and Murphy, "No Pay Raise."

20. Holmes, *African Queen*, 38.

21. Letter from American Medical Association Program Chair Dr. Irving Wolman to Dr. Stuart S. Stevenson, School of Public Health, Harvard University, March 23, 1949, American Medical Association Archives, Chicago, Illinois.

22. Stearns, *Fat History*, 11.

23. Banting, *Letter on Corpulence*, 11, 5, 20.

24. Densmore, *How to Reduce Fat*, 1, 4, 5.

25. Ibid.

26. Brillat-Savarin, *Physiology of Taste*, 243.

27. Brumberg, *Body Project*.

28. Harvey, *Corpulence*, 10, 13, 27, 11.

29. Smith, *How to Get Fat*.

30. Gilman, "Yellow Wallpaper"; Mitchell, *Fat and Blood*, 18.

31. Adipo-Malene advertisement, *Godey's Lady's Book*, August 1890, vi; "Vigoral," *Life*, November 11, 1897, 401; "Neave's Food," *Godey's Lady's Book*, August 1890, vii; Scott's Emulsion advertisement, *Life*, November 24, 1892, 317; Aerated Oxygen Compound Company advertisement, November 17, 1892, *Life*, 292.

32. "Are Fat People Healthy," *Christian Recorder* (Philadelphia), December 12, 1878.

33. *Life*, April 7, 1887, 202.

34. *Harper's Weekly*, June 30, 1888, 475.

35. Herbert Johnson, Associated Newspapers, 1921 or 1922, Library of Congress, Cartoon Drawings Collection.

36. *Harper's Weekly*, January 22, 1881, 63.

37. *Life*, August 19, 1897, 147.

38. *Life*, August 6, 1914, 242.

39. Ibid., 241.

40. *Life*, October 1, 1914, 590.

41. *Life*, April 16, 1908, 412.

42. *Life*, March 12, 1908, 281.

43. Stearns, *Fat History*; Schwartz, *Never Satisfied*.

44. Schwartz, *Never Satisfied*, 27–37.

45. Ibid., 127.

46. Ibid., 186.

47. Griffith, *Born Again Bodies*, 18.

48. Bederman, *Manliness and Civilization*, 14–15.

49. "Obesity Unhandsome and Unsafe," *Atchison (KS) Daily Champion*, September 19, 1888.

50. Gorn and Goldstein, *Brief History of American Sports*, 92.

51. Finck, *Girth Control*, xi, 16.

52. Williams, *Obesity*, 69.

53. Ibid., 69, 70.

54. Ibid., 70.

55. Ibid., 73. Emphasis added.

56. Bordo, *Unbearable Weight*.

57. Lovart, *Too Fat*.

58. Bordo, *Unbearable Weight*, 117.

59. Lovart, *Too Fat*, 2, 4.

60. Ibid., 16, 17.

61. Ibid., 23.

62. Ibid., 26.

63. Ibid., 124.

64. "Obesity v. Matrimony: Instructive Story of a Stout Young Lady," *Raleigh (NC) Register*, July 9, 1884.

65. "Obesity No Cause for Divorce, Jury in Switzerland Decides," *New York Times*, May 1, 1927.

66. Johnson, *Why Be Fat?* 157, 37.

67. Alice Marshall Women's History Collection, Penn State Harrisburg, Middletown, Pennsylvania.

68. Scharff, *Taking the Wheel*; Shaffer, *See America First*; Seiler, *Repulic of Drivers*.

69. Library of Congress Cartoon Drawings Collection; Alice Marshall Women's History Collection.

70. Thompson, *Eat and Grow Thin*, 14, 15.

NOTES TO CHAPTER 3

1. Bradshaw, *On Corpulence*, 6.

2. Williams, *Obesity*, 4.

3. Ibid., 77, 67.

4. Finck, *Girth Control*, 2, 3, 9.

5. Schiebinger, *Nature's Body*.

6. Bederman, *Manliness and Civilization*, 31–41; Bancroft, *Book of the Fair*, 62, 63.

7. Rafter and Gibson, "Introduction," 18.

8. For more information on Havelock Ellis, see Hallam and Street, *Cultural Encounters*.

9. Qureshi, "Displaying Sara Baartman." Qureshi's description of Baartman on display (p. 236) is from Chambers, *The Book of Days*, 621.

10. Cuvier, "Extrait d'observations."

11. Qureshi, "Displaying Sara Baartman," 233.

12. Cuvier, "Extrait d'observations," 263, 264, 265, 269.

13. Hobson, *Venus in the Dark*, 3.

14. Hall, "The Spectacle of the Other," 269.

15. Rafter and Gibson, "Introduction," 7.

16. Lombroso, *Criminal Woman*, 126, 122, 123.

17. Ibid., 100, 103, 53, 57.

18. Finck, *Girth Control*, 289.

19. Williams, *Obesity*, 77, 67.

20. Hall, "The Spectacle of the Other," 264.

21. Kipling, "White Man's Burden," 290–291.

22. "There Will Be a Reaction Against the Big Waist When Women Begin to Mourn Lost Figures," *New York Times*, May 25, 1913.

23. Today one can also find these complex standards of bodily beauty that evoke both attraction and repulsion. Jennifer Lopez's highly pronounced buttocks receive favorable comment, for instance, and Sir Mix-a-Lot's "Baby Got Back," more popularly known as "I Love Big Butts," propelled him to stardom. This fat-celebrating popular culture, coupled with the popular cosmetic surgery for buttock enhancement, might make one think that fat is now perceived as good. But cosmetic surgeons describe the enhancements as "shapely and round," not at all the "trembling mass of fatty tissue" that Cuvier describes. Patients get the allusion/illusion of the sexually charged backside, but not the negative connotations of a fat body. At the same time, it's essential to note that these "positive" representations are also highly racialized. See Cosmetic Surgery Directory, "Buttock Augmentation."

24. Collins, *Black Feminist Thought*, 78.

25. Christian, as quoted in ibid., 72.

26. "William H. West's Big Minstrel Jubilee," New York, 1900, Library of Congress, Cartoon Drawings Collection.

27. *Harper's Weekly*, October 16, 1880, 667.

28. *Life*, July 22, 1897, 63.

29. *Harper's Weekly*, July 3, 1880, 423.

30. *Harper's Weekly*, November 5, 1881, 752.

31. *Harper's Weekly*, July 2, 1881, 435.

32. Alice Marshall Women's History Collection, Penn State Harrisburg, Middletown, Pennsylvania.

33. Ibid.

34. Preble, "Obesity and Malnutrition," 741.

35. "Sense and Nonsense About Obesity," 1946; "Psychiatric Aspects of Obesity in Children," 1942; "Obesity in Childhood and Personality Development," 1941; "Study of Illness Among Children of Different Cultural Backgrounds," January 11, 1944, all from the Papers of Hilde Bruch, John P. McGovern Historical Collections and Research Center, Texas Medical Center Library, Houston, Texas.

36. Collens, *Collens System of Diet Writing*, 28.

37. Williams, *Obesity*, 1.

38. Saukko, "Fat Boys and Goody Girls," 33. She quotes from Angel, "Constitution in Female Obesity."

39. Gard and Wright, *Obesity Epidemic*, 108–112.

40. Gard and Wright wisely point out the fallacy of presuming that science is ever ideologically neutral, especially when it comes to fat: "Our conclusion . . . is that not only does the state of scientific knowledge not ameliorate social stigma, but it may also even set the scene for more sophisticated and supposedly well-informed personal and institutional forms of stigmatization" (14). For further discussion of the use of gene theory and its connections to eugenics, see LeBesco, "Quest for a Cause."

41. "About Fat Men: Ancient Greeks and Romans Ostracized for Their Obesity," *St. Paul Daily News*, April 18, 1891.

NOTES TO CHAPTER 4

1. *Judge*, June 4, 1910, cover image.

2. "Fe'he males" cartoon found in Sheppard, *Cartooning for Suffrage*, 73.

3. Susan B. Anthony to Gerrit Smith, December 25, 1855, in Stanton and Anthony, *Selected Papers of Elizabeth Cady Stanton and Susan B. Anthony*, 312.

4. Stanton in Parton, *From Eminent Women of the Age*, 400.

5. Postcards-Suffrage Collection, Fawcett Library of Women's History, London Guildhall University.

6. Postcards-Suffrage Collection, Fawcett Library of Women's History, London Guildhall University. This poster was also located, as a postcard, at Alice Marshall Collection, Penn State Harrisburg. In *The Spectacle of Women*, Lisa Tickner discusses the extensive use of British propaganda, both pro- and anti-suffrage, in the United States (pp. 266–267).

7. *Life*, April 23, 1908, 426.

8. In *These Days of Large Things*, Michael Clarke discusses the phenomenon of "growing women" and "shrinking men" in the popular literature of the time period. Significantly, however, the trend he identified, and the largely positive way in which popular literature portrayed it, was of women growing in height. The women lampooned in these anti-suffrage cartoons are not only taller than their husbands, but also much thicker in girth. Clarke notes no positive associations with women who are tall and *fat*.

9. Postcard from the Suffrage Collection, Sophia Smith Archives, Smith College, Northampton, Massachusetts.

10. Women of the West Museum, Suffrage Collection, Boulder, Colorado, http://theautry.org/explore/exhibits/suffrage/ (accessed July 27, 2010).

11. "The Suffragette Face: New Type Evolved by Militancy," *Daily Mirror*, May 25, 1914, found in Tickner, *Spectacle of Women*, 171.

12. One might read this image as a commentary *on* black women in the suffrage movement, rather than a caricature of white suffragists turning *into* fat black women. The historical context makes this unlikely, however. While there certainly were African American women who were very active in the fight for women's suffrage, historians have not located much visual propaganda from the campaign that deals with African American as protagonists in the long battle. That is, the cartoons, posters, and postcards from the movement—both pro- and anti-suffrage—generally dealt with white women. (The Kansas cartoon is one of the exceptions I located.) Moreover, the sign shown in the hall, "Women's Suffrage Convention," suggests that this refers to one of the mainstream, white suffragists conventions. If it were a convention organized by African American women, the title would have likely denoted this, such as "National Association of Colored Women's Clubs Suffrage Convention." Even if one were to maintain the possibility that this is *about* black women as suffragists, a similar reading occurs. Suffrage, in this case, becomes linked to fat black women, in much the same way that the Kansas cartoon mocked the "equality" of black women being on equal footing with the white gentlemen in the voting line.

13. "The Only Way" cartoon, n.d., found at the Alice Marshall Women's History Collection, Penn State Harrisburg; L. M. Glackens, "The Steadfast Suffragette: There Was Method in Her Starvation," first published in *Puck*, May 7, 1913, 4, found at the Library of Congress, Prints and Photographs Division.

14. Finnegan, *Selling Suffrage*, 46, 81.

15. "The Anti-suffrage Society as Portrait-Painter," Postcards-Suffrage Collection, Fawcett Library of Women's History, London Guildhall University.

16. J. A. Waldron, "Even Santa Clause," *Judge*, 1913, "Suffrage-Graphics" at the Alice Marshall Collection, Penn State Harrisburg.

17. Seitler, "Unnatural Selection."

18. "The Anti-suffrage Society as Dressmaker," published by the Suffrage Atelier, Postcards-Suffrage Collection, Fawcett Library of Women's History, London Guildhall University; "Do You Use a Sewing Machine," New York Woman's Suffrage Association, Suffrage Collection, Sophia Smith Archives, Smith College.

19. "Ye Anti-Suffrage League," Anti-suffrage Collection, Fawcett Library of Women's History, London Guildhall University.

20. N.d., Suffrage Collection, Sophia Smith Archives, Smith College.

21. Marshall, *Splintered Sisterhood*.

22. "The Vote," Suffrage Atelier, May 18, 1912, Fawcett Library of Women's History, London Guildhall University.

23. Schwartz, *Never Satisfied*, 122–23; Pollack, *One Woman, One Vote*.

24. Andolsen, *Daughters of Jefferson, Daughters of Bootblacks*, 80.

25. Collier-Thomas, "Frances Ellen Watkins Harper," 50.

26. Details from her life as a mother are drawn from Baker, *Sisters*, 93–135. Quotation on the power of the mind is drawn from Stanton's "Address on Woman's Rights," September 1848, in Stanton and Anthony, *Selected Papers of Elizabeth Cady Stanton and Susan B. Anthony*, 102.

27. Baker, *Sisters*, 133.

28. Stanton, *Eighty Years and More*, 34, 35.

29. Stanton, "Address on Woman's Rights," in Stanton and Anthony, *Selected Papers of Elizabeth Cady Stanton and Susan B. Anthony*, 102.

30. Theodore Tilton in Parton, *From Eminent Women of the Age*, 343, 358.

31. Stanton and Blatch, "Foreword," in Stanton, *Elizabeth Cady Stanton as Revealed in Her Letters, Diary, and Reminiscences*, xvi.

32. Stanton, *Eighty Years and More*, 419; Baker, *Sisters*, 131.

33. Stanton, *Elizabeth Cady Stanton As Revealed in Her Letters, Diary, and Reminiscences*, 322.

34. "You—As Others See You," *Independent Woman*, May 1927, 13.

35. Ida B. Cole, "Health and Your Job," *Independent Woman*, March 1922; Margaret H. Speer, "Live and Learn—But Eat and Earn," *Independent Woman*, January 1927, 24.

36. "She Found a Pleasant Way to Reduce Her Fat," *Independent Woman*, February 1924, 30; Marguerite Agniel, "The Gentle Art of Reducing," *Independent Woman*, February 1929, 64.

37. Reducex advertisement, *Independent Woman*, July 1928, 288.

38. Elizabeth MacDonald Osborne, "What Support?" *Independent Woman*, February 1928, 73.

39. "Women of discrimination" advertisement, *Independent Woman*, April 1929, 192.

40. National Association of Colored Girls, *Girl's Guide*, 1933, in Williams and Boehm, *Records of the National Association of Colored Women's Clubs*.

41. Lowe, *Looking Good*, 40–41.

42. Cramp, *Nostrums and Quackery*, 459. Emphasis added.

43. Documents dated June 17, 1913, and February 28, 1914, "Obesity Cures" collection, American Medical Association Archives, Chicago, Illinois.

44. Chesser, *Slimming for the Million*, 19.

45. Ibid., 99.

46. Advertisement, n.d., "Obesity Cures" collection, American Medical Association Archives, Chicago, Illinois.

47. Bordo, *Unbearable Weight*, 30.

48. Nichter, *Fat Talk*, x.

49. Stinson, *Women and Dieting Culture*, 3.

NOTES TO CHAPTER 5

1. Smith, "Disney's 'WALL-E.'"

2. Stanley, "Plus-Size Sideshow," 19.

3. Morrison, *The Bluest Eye*, 87, 101.

4. O'Leary, "Anatomy of a Breakdown"; Aquilante, "Britney a Bust"; Noveck, "Harshest Words Saved for Britney's Body."

5. "Britney Spears Unveils Bikini Body as She Shows Off 'New Man.'"

6. Campos, *The Obesity Myth*, 185–198.

7. Biddle, "Drugs"; "Some Jenny Craigs Reject Lewinsky Ads"; "Scandal Hurts Jenny Craig Ad Campaign."

8. Wyatt, "Tolstoy's Translators Experience Oprah Effect."

9. "Oprah's Weight Loss Confession."

10. Razza, "Running With Her Head Down," 265, 275.

11. Ibid., 265.

12. "Oprah's Weight Loss Confession."

13. Critser, *Fat Land*, 1, 2.

14. Fox, "Marine Shed Weight to Fight, Dies in Iraq."

15. Military City, "Marine Lance Corporal Justin T. Hunt."

16. Tauber and Dagostino, "100 and Counting."

17. Deford, " Secret Life of Kirby Puckett," 58.

18. Mosher, "Setting Free the Bears."

19. Deford, "Secret Life of Kirby Puckett," 60, 63, 64, 68.

20. Campos, "Fat Judges Need Not Apply."

21. Kantor, "Where the Votes Are, So, Unfortunately, Are All Those Calories."

22. "Cleveland's Growing Girth: He Tries the Massage Treatment to Reduce His Increasing Obesity," *The North American* (Philadelphia), October 30, 1886; "Movement Cure for Obesity: How the President Is Said to Be Getting His Flesh Reduced," *Bismarck (ND) Daily Tribune*, December 15, 1886; "President Cleveland's Physical Condition: He Weighs 300 Pounds," *Irish World and American Industrial Liberator* (New York), July 15, 1893.

23. Moore, "The Challenger."

24. Ibid.

25. Bedard et al., "Washington Whispers," 8.

26. "The Great Jewelry Robbery," a "Honeymooners" sketch aired during *The Jackie Gleason Show*, February 26, 1955, CBS.

27. Burros, "In Her Own Fun-Poking Words."

28. Samuels, "What Michelle Means to Us."

29. Dowd, "Should Michelle Cover Up?"

30. Hickey and Lawler, "A Conversation with the Obamas," 144.

1. Wann, *FAT!SO?* 28–29.

2. Cooper. *Fat and Proud*; Bovey, *The Forbidden Body*; Solovay, *Tipping the Scales of Justice*; Miley, "New Year, New Round of Diet Programs."

3. National Association to Advance Fat Acceptance website, http://www.naafa.org/, in author's possession.

4. Gregory, "Heavy Judgment."

5. LeBesco, *Revolting Bodies*.

6. Wilson, "Fat Underground Throws Weight Into Obesity War."

7. Stinson, personal interview, Northampton, Massachusetts, February 24, 2009.

8. Fabrey, "All Set to Fight Discrimination."

9. Tillmon, "Welfare As a Woman's Issue," 111.

10. Fishman, "Life in the Fat Underground," 7; McAfee, personal interview, Birdsboro, Pennsylvania, June 7, 2010.

11. Ibid., 4, 5.

12. Freespirit and Aldebaran, "Fat Liberation Manifesto."

13. Daughters of Bilitis, "Purpose of the Daughters of Bilitis," 2.

14. Shanewood, "An Interview with Medical Rights Champion Lynn McAfee," 4.

15. Fishman, "Life in the Fat Underground," 6.

16. Hannah, "Naomi Cohen Choked on the Culture."

17. Marshall, "No One's Getting Fat Except Mama Cass."

18. For a further discussion of the significance of place in the creation of feminist consciousness, please see Enke, *Finding the Movement*.

19. Hemenway, personal interview, Northampton, Massachusetts, February 26, 2009.

20. Mayer, "Foreword," in Schoenfielder and Wieser, *Shadow on a Tightrope*, xvi; McBride, "Fat Survivors in Thin Society."

21. Jones, "Fat Women and Feminism."

22. See, for instance, "Bodies and Fat," *Ms.*, September 1977; "Spoiled Identity," *Sinister Wisdom*, Spring 1982, 10; "More on Fat Liberation," *off our backs*, December 31, 1979, 31.

23. Orbach, *Fat Is a Feminist Issue*; Orbach, *Fat Is a Feminist Issue II*; Tabor, "Fat Is a Feminist Issue," 18; House, "Fat Is a Feminist Issue," 18.

24. Boston Women's Health Book Collective, *Our Bodies, Ourselves*, 80–81; Boston Women's Health Book Collective, *The New Our Bodies, Ourselves*, 8; Boston Women's Health Book Collective, *Our Bodies, Ourselves: A New Edition for a New Era*.

25. Stimson, "Fat Feminist Herstory, 1969–1993: A Personal Memoir," Fat Liberation Archives.

26. For a discussion of the ways that the history of local NOW chapters suggests that legal and cultural, radical and liberal activism often merged, see Gilmore, *Feminist Coalitions*.

27. NAAFA, "All Set to Fight Discrimination"; "Anti-Size Discrimination Resolution," National Organization for Women Collection, Schlesinger Library, Radcliffe Institute, Harvard University, carton 26, no. 5.

28. Fishman, "Life in the Fat Underground," 5.

29. Nichols, "Beauty," 7; and "The Fat Black Woman Remembers," 9, *The Fat Black Woman's Poems*.

30. Dlamini, "Fat Black Women Sing It Like It Is."

31. Stinson, "Belly Song," 3-5; "Kitchen," 18; "Passing," 19-20; and "Ways A Whale Gets Hungry," 20, *Belly Songs*.

32. Stinson, "For the Taste of It," ibid., 32-33.

33. Marilyn Wann, personal phone interview, May 29, 2009; Sheffield and Bailey, "Spotlight on the Padded Lillies."

34. Available at http://maxairborne.com/comics/comic2.html (accessed August 10, 2010). Airborne's story is quite profound. At the age of thirteen, she was forcibly committed to a psychiatric hospital, against her will, in order to lose weight. For a year and a half she lived on a five-hundred-calorie-a-day diet. For years after her release, she had to return for "weigh-ins" in order to avoid future institutionalization. Sondra Solovay has pointed out that developmentally disabled adults are sometimes institutionalized against their will for weight loss purposes, just as was Max Airborne was (since as a child she had few legal rights). See Solovay, *Tipping the Scales of Justice*, 229-232.

35. Elizabeth Fisher's story can be found at http://www.ifisher.com/.

36. SeaFATtle's website is http://www.seafattle.org/. Their memorial to Carolyn, the woman who died in a car accident because her seat belt did not fit, is in author's possession.

37. In *The Forbidden Body: Why Being Fat Is Not a Sin*, Shelley Bovey includes the voices of numerous women who recount explicit and insulting encounters with prospective employers who told them that unless they lost weight they would not be hired. The comments ranged from euphemistic references to the "image the company has to maintain" to explicit suggestions for diets and weight loss clubs. Sondra Solovay analyzed at length the 1992 study that demonstrated that employers are reluctant to hire a person they find "unattractive." Fatness leads the list of unattractive traits and, moreover, is seen as one for which the person is responsible, unlike, say, scarring or deformed features. Solovay further points to the studies that demonstrate explicit penalties fat people pay for being fat. Fat men, a *New York Times* study found, make one hundred dollars less per year *per pound* they are overweight. A *New England Journal of Medicine* study found that fat women make $6,710 less in income per year than do thin women. As Solovay poignantly concludes, "Women do not become fat because they are poor, they become poor because they are fat." Rothblum, "The Relationship Between Obesity, Employment Discrimination, and Employment-Related Victimization"; Kolata, "Burden of Being Overweight"; Gortmaker, "Social and Economic Consequences of Overweight"; Solovay, *Tipping the Scales of Justice*, 106.

38. Fernandez, "Teacher Says Fat, Fitness Can Mix."

39. "Dance Instructor Wins Weight Discrimination Battle!"

40. Solovay, *Tipping the Scales of Justice*, 64; Avocado, "Anamarie Regino-Martinez."

41. Belkin, "Watching Her Weight."

42. Ibid., 33.

43. Ibid.

44. Avocado, "Anamarie Regino-Martinez."

45. Ibid.

46. Ibid.; Solovay, *Tipping the Scales of Justice*, 76.

47. Deborah Harper, personal interview, Washington DC, June 30, 2003.

48. For a variety of perspectives on the stigma faced by fat gay men, see Pyle and Loewy, "Double Stigma"; Mosher, "Setting Free the Bears"; Bunzi, "Chasers."

49. NAAFA, "Weight Loss Surgery."

50. Gawande, "The Man Who Couldn't Stop Eating," 75.

51. Mason, "My Fat History."

52. Manheim, *Wake Up, I'm Fat!* 120.

53. "A Conversation with Camryn Manheim," a multipage advertisement for heart-health products appeared in issues of *Newsweek* in 2008.

54. From NAAFA's "Fat Activism P's and Q's," in author's possession. The current NAAFA website is http://www.naafaonline.com/.

55. For more on this organization, see http://www.cswd.org/. The work of the Council on Size and Weight Discrimination is emblematic of much of the activism currently being done within the fat acceptance movement. Such activist work focuses on what members see as the fallacies propagated within the medical profession regarding the dangers of fat, the dishonest and dangerous practices of the diet industry, and the myriad ways that fat people are discriminated against within employment, education, access to public facilities, parental rights, and medicine.

56. NoLose, "NoLose Manifesta."

NOTES TO THE CONCLUSION

1. Conrad, *Heart of Darkness*, 178.

2. Moore, *Fat Girl*, 53.

3. Ibid., 23.

4. Landau, "College's Too-Fat-to-Graduate Rule Under Fire"; Inside Higher Education, "Lincoln University Ends Obesity Rule."

5. Anspaugh, *Fat Like Us*, 239.

6. For a study on the prevalence of fat stigma within media, see Himes and Thompson, "Fat Stigmatization in Television Shows and Movies."

7. Miley, "New Year, New Round of Diet Programs."

Bibliography

Adler, Jerry. "The Great Sorority Purge: When a Group of 'Sisters' Were Kicked Out of Their Chapter House, Many Blamed Hair Color and Dress Size." *Newsweek*, March 12, 2007, 47.

Allison, David B., and the TOS Obesity as a Disease Writing Group. "Obesity as a Disease: A White Paper on Evidence and Arguments Commissioned by the Council of the Obesity Society." *Obesity* 16 (June 2008): 1161–1177.

American Medical Association. *Nostrums and Quackery*. Chicago: Press of American Medical Association, 1912.

American Obesity Association. "Obesity Surgery." n.d., http://www.obesity.org/education/advisor.html. Accessed April 1, 2005. In author's possession.

American Society for Metabolic and Bariatric Surgery. "Bariatric Surgical Society Takes on New Name, New Mission, and New Surgery." August 22, 2007, http://www.asmbs.org/. Accessed October 5, 2008. In author's possession.

Andolsen, Barbara Hilkert. *Daughters of Jefferson, Daughters of Bootblacks*. Macon: Mercer University Press, 1986.

Angel, J. Lawrence. "Constitution in Female Obesity." *American Journal of Physical Anthropology* 7 (September 1949): 433–471.

Anspaugh, Jean Renfro. *Fat Like Us*. Durham, NC: Generation Books, 2001.

Aquilante, Dan. "Britney a Bust." *New York Post*, September 10, 2007.

Avocado, Laurie. "Anamarie Regino-Martinez." n.d., http://www.geocities.com/laurie-avocado/Anamarie.html. Accessed July 25, 2005. In author's possession.

Bacon, L., J. Stern, M. Van Loan, and N. Keim. "Size Acceptance and Intuitive Eating Improve Health for Obese, Female, Chronic Dieters." *Journal of the American Dietetic Association* 105, no. 6 (2005): 929–936.

Bacon, Linda. *Health at Every Size*. Dallas: BenBella Books, 2008.

Baker, Jean. *Sisters: The Lives of America's Suffragists*. New York: Hill and Wang, 2005.

Bancroft, Hubert Howe. *The Book of the Fair: An Historical and Descriptive Presentation Viewed Through the Columbian Exposition at Chicago in 1893*. New York: Bounty Books, 1894.

Banting, William. *Letter on Corpulence*. London: Harrison and Sons, 1863.

Becker, Anne. *Body, Self, and Society: The View from Fiji*. Philadelphia: University of Pennsylvania Press, 1995.

Bedard, Paul, Liz Halloran, Suzi Parker, and Kevin Whitelaw. "Washington Whispers." *U.S. News and World Report*, February 11, 2008, 8.

Bederman, Gail. *Manliness and Civilization: A Cultural History of Gender and Race in the United States, 1880–1917*. Chicago: University of Chicago Press, 1995.

Belasco, Warren. *Appetite for Change: How the Counterculture Took on the Food Industry, 1966–1988*. New York: Pantheon Books, 1989.

Belkin, Lisa. "Watching Her Weight." *New York Times Magazine*, July 8, 2001, 30–33.

Biddle, Frederic M. "Drugs, Net Lead to Lean Times at Jenny Craig." *Wall Street Journal*, July 12, 1999.

Bloom, John. *To Show What an Indian Can Do: Sports at Native American Boarding Schools*. Minneapolis: University of Minnesota Press, 2001.

Bordo, Susan. *Unbearable Weight: Feminism, Western Culture, and the Body*. Berkeley and Los Angeles: University of California Press, 1993.

Boston Women's Health Book Collective. *The New Our Bodies, Ourselves*. New York: Simon and Schuster, 1984.

———. *Our Bodies, Ourselves*. New York: Simon and Schuster, 1973.

———. *Our Bodies, Ourselves: A New Edition for a New Era*. New York: Touchstone, 2005.

Bovey, Shelley. *The Forbidden Body: Why Being Fat Is Not a Sin*. London: Pandora, 1989.

Bradshaw, Watson. *On Corpulence*. London: Philip and Son, 1864.

Braziel, Jana Evans, and Kathleen LeBesco, eds. *Bodies Out of Bounds: Fatness and Transgression*. Berkeley and Los Angeles: University of California Press, 2001.

Brillat-Savarin, Jean Anthelme. *The Physiology of Taste: Or, Meditations on Transcendental Gastronomy*. Translated by M. F. K. Fisher. Washington, DC: Counterpoint, 1949.

"Britney Spears Unveils Bikini Body as She Shows Off 'New Man.'" *London Daily Mail*, May 21, 2009.

Brumberg, Joan Jacobs. *The Body Project: An Intimate History of American Girls*. New York: Vintage Books, 1998.

———. *Fasting Girls: The History of Anorexia Nervosa*. New York: Plume, 1988.

Bunzi, Matti. "Chasers." In *Fat: The Anthropology of an Obsession*, edited by Don Kulick and Anne Meneley, 199–210. New York: Penguin, 2005.

Burros, Marian. "In Her Own Fun-Poking Words, Mrs. Obama on the First Family's Household." *New York Times*, March 21, 2009.

Campos, Paul. "Fat Judges Need Not Apply." *The Daily Beast*, May 4, 2009, http://www.thedailybeast.com/blogs-and-stories/2009-05-04/fat-judges-need-not-apply/. Accessed May 5, 2009.

———. *The Obesity Myth: Why America's Obsession with Weight Is Hazardous to Your Health*. New York: Gotham Books, 2004.

Centers for Disease Control and Prevention. "CDC's National Leadership Role in Addressing Obesity." June 14, 2005, http://www.cdc.gov/media/pressrel/r050615.htm. Accessed August 11, 2010.

———. "Telebriefing Transcript: Overweight and Obesity: Clearing the Confusion." June 2, 2005, http://www.cdc.gov/od/oc/media/transcripts/t050602.html. Accessed July 25, 2005. In author's possession.

Chambers, Robert, ed. *The Book of Days: A Miscellany of Popular Antiquities, in Connection with the Calendar*. London and Edinburgh, 1863.

Chesser, Eustace. *Slimming for the Million: The New Treatment of Obesity*. London: Rich and Cowan, 1939.

Ciola, Tom. *Moses Wasn't Fat: A Bible Guide to Health and Fitness*. Orlando: Axion Publishers, 2001.

Clarke, Michael Tavel. *These Days of Large Things: The Culture of Size in America, 1865–1930.* Ann Arbor: University of Michigan Press, 2007.

Clinton Foundation. "Alliance for a Healthier Generation." n.d., http://www.clintonfoundation.org/what-we-do/alliance-for-a-healthier-generation/. Accessed August 11, 2010.

Cogan, Jeanine, and Paul Ernsberger. "Dying to Be Thin in the Name of Health: Shifting the Paradigm." *Journal of Social Issues* 55 (Summer 1999): 187–205.

Collens, William S. *Collens System of Diet Writing, Including Diet Calculator, Obesity Chart, 100 Menu Prescription Forms.* New York: Form Publishing Company, 1933.

Collier-Thomas, Bettye. "Frances Ellen Watkins Harper: Abolitionist and Feminist Reformer, 1825–1911." In *African American Women and the Vote, 1837–1965,* edited by Ann D. Gordon, 41–65. Amherst: University of Massachusetts Press, 1997.

Collins, Patricia Hill. *Black Feminist Thought: Knowledge, Consciousness, and the Politics of Empowerment.* New York: Routledge, 1991.

Cooper, Charlotte. *Fat and Proud: The Politics of Size.* London: Women's Press, 1998.

Conrad, Joseph. *The Heart of Darkness, and Other Tales.* Edited by Cedric Thomas Watts. New York: Oxford University Press, 2002.

Cosmetic Surgery Directory. "Buttock Augmentation with Implants vs. Fat Injections." n.d., http://www.the-cosmetic-surgery-directory.com/article_buttock.html. Accessed January 22, 2009.

Cott, Nancy. *The Grounding of Modern Feminism.* New Haven: Yale University Press, 1987.

Cramp, Arthur. *Nostrums and Quackery.* Chicago: American Medical Association, 1911.

Critser, Greg. *Fat Land: How Americans Became the Fattest People in the World.* Boston: Houghton Mifflin, 2003.

Cuvier, Georges. "Extrait d'observations faites sur le cadavre d'une femme connue à Paris et à Londres sous le nom de Vénus Hottentotte." *Mémoires du Muséum d'Histoire naturelle* 3 (1817): 259–274.

"Dance Instructor Wins Weight Discrimination Battle!" *ISAA News,* May 7, 2002.

Daughters of Bilitis. "Purpose of the Daughters of Bilitis." *The Ladder* 3, no. 12 (1959): 2.

Deford, Frank. "Commentary: America's Struggle with Obesity in Children an Epidemic." National Public Radio, March 12, 2003.

Deford, Frank, with George Dohrmann. "The Secret Life of Kirby Puckett: The Rise and Fall of a Sports Idol." *Sports Illustrated,* March 17, 2003, 58–69.

Delta Zeta Sorority. "Delta Zeta Files Federal Lawsuit Against DePauw University." March 28, 2007, http://www.deltazeta.org/. Accessed May 22, 2007. In author's possession.

Densmore, Helen. *How to Reduce Fat: The Curative Action of Regimen.* New York, 1896.

Depauw University. "Delta Zeta Sorority Files Lawsuit." April 18, 2007, http://www.depauw.edu/student/greek/deltazetanews.asp. Accessed May 22, 2007.

Dillon, Sam. "DePauw Cuts Ties with Controversial Sorority." *New York Times,* March 12, 2007.

———. "Evictions at Sorority Raise Issue of Bias." *New York Times,* February 25, 2007.

Dlamini, Ndaba. "Fat Black Women Sing It Like It Is." February 17, 2009, http://www.joburg.org.za/content/view/3477/266/. Accessed June 5, 2009.

Dovidio, John F., Brenda Major, and Jennifer Crocker. "Stigma: Introduction and Overview." In *The Social Psychology of Stigma,* edited by Todd Heatherton, Robert Kleck, Michelle Hebl, and Jay Hull, 1–30. New York: Guildford Press, 2000.

Dowd, Maureen. "Should Michelle Cover Up?" *New York Times*, March 8, 2009.

Edut, Ophira. *Body Outlaws: Rewriting the Rules of Beauty and Body Image*. New York: Seal Press, 2003.

Eisenhower, Dwight D. "Farewell Radio and Television Address to the American People," January 17, 1961. In *Public Papers of the President*, 1035–1040. Ann Arbor: University of Michigan Press, 2005.

Enke, Ann. *Finding the Movement: Sexuality, Contested Space, and Feminist Activism*. Durham: Duke University Press, 2007.

Enstad, Nan. *Ladies of Labor, Girls of Adventure: Working Women, Popular Culture, and Labor Politics at the Turn of the Twentieth Century*. New York: Columbia University Press, 1999.

Ezzell, Carol. "Fat Chances." *Scientific American*, August 1998, 94.

Fabrey, Bill. "All Set to Fight Discrimination." *Radiance*, Spring 1989.

Fallon, Patricia, Melanie A. Katzman, and Susan C. Wooley, eds. *Feminist Perspectives on Eating Disorders*. New York: Guilford Press, 1994.

Faludi, Susan. *Backlash: The Undeclared War Against American Women*. New York: Crown, 1991.

Fernandez, Elizabeth. "Teacher Says Fat, Fitness Can Mix." *San Francisco Chronicle*, February 24, 2002.

Finck, Henry T. *Girth Control: For Womanly Beauty, Manly Strength, Health, and a Long Life for Everybody*. New York: Harper and Brothers, 1923.

Finnegan, Margaret. *Selling Suffrage: Consumer Culture and Votes for Women*. New York: Columbia University Press, 1999.

Fishman, Sara Golda Bracha. "Life in the Fat Underground." *Radiance*, Winter 1998, http://www.radiancemagazine.com/issues/1998/winter_98/fat_underground.html. Accessed August 10, 2010..

Flexner, Eleanor. *Century of Struggle: The Woman's Rights Movement in the United States*. Cambridge: Harvard University Press, 1996.

Fox, Ben. "Marine Shed Weight to Fight, Dies in Iraq." *Patriot News* (Harrisburg, PA), July 11, 2004.

Fraser, Laura. *Losing It: False Hopes and Fat Profits in the Diet Industry*. New York: Plume, 1998.

Freedman, Rory, and Kim Barnouin. *Skinny Bitch*. Philadelphia: Running Press, 2005.

———. *Skinny Bitch: Bun in the Oven*. Philadelphia: Running Press, 2008.

———. *Skinny Bitch in the Kitch*. Philadelphia: Running Press, 2007.

Freespirit, Judy, and Aldebaran. "Fat Liberation Manifesto, November 1973." In *The Fat Studies Reader*, edited by Esther Rothblum and Sondra Solovay, 341–42. New York: New York University Press, 2009.

Fry, Michael, and T. Lewis. "Over the Hedge." United Feature Syndicate, July 11, 2006, http://comics.com/over_the_hedge/2006-07-11. Accessed August 10, 2008.

Gaesser, Glenn. *Big Fat Lies: The Truth About Your Weight and Your Health*. New York: Fawcett Columbine, 1996.

Gard, Michael, and Jan Wright. *The Obesity Epidemic: Science, Morality, and Ideology*. New York: Routledge, 2005

Gawande, Atul. "The Man Who Couldn't Stop Eating." *New Yorker*, July 9, 2001, 66–75.

Gilman, Charlotte Perkins. "The Yellow Wallpaper." In *Herland, and Selected Stories*, edited by Barbara H. Solomon, 165–180. New York: Signet, 1992.

Gilman, Sander. *Diets and Dieting*. New York: Routledge, 2008.

Gilmore, Stephanie, ed. *Feminist Coalitions: Historical Perspectives on Second-Wave Feminism in the United States*. Urbana: University of Illinois Press, 2008.

Goffman, Erving. *Stigma: Notes on the Management of Spoiled Identity*. New York: Simon and Schuster, 1963.

Gorn, Elliot, and Warren Goldstein. *A Brief History of American Sports*. New York: Hill and Wang, 1993.

Gortmaker, Steven L. "Social and Economic Consequences of Overweight in Adolescence and Young Adulthood." *New England Journal of Medicine* 399, no. 14 (1993): 1008–1012.

Gregory, Deborah. "Heavy Judgment: A Sister Talks About the Pain of 'Living Large.'" In *The American Body in Context*, edited by Jessica R. Johnston, 311–318. Wilmington, DE: Scholarly Resources, 2001.

Griffith, Ruth Marie. *Born Again Bodies: Flesh and Spirit in American Christianity*. Berkeley and Los Angeles: University of California Press, 2004.

Hall, Stuart. "The Spectacle of the Other." In *Representation: Cultural Representations and Signifying Practices*, edited by Hall, 223–279. London: Sage Publications, 1997.

Hallam, Elizabeth, and Brian Street. *Cultural Encounters: Representing Otherness*. New York: Routledge, 2000.

Hannah, Sharon Bas. "Naomi Cohen Choked on the Culture." *Sister*, September 1974, 1.

Harter, Pascale. "Mauritania's 'Wife-Fattening' Farm." *BBC News*, January 26, 2004.

Harvey, John. *Corpulence, Its Diminution and Cure, Etc.* London, 1864.

Henig, Robin Marantz. "Losing the Weight Stigma." *New York Times Magazine*, October 5, 2008, 24.

Hesse-Biber, Sharlene. *Am I Thin Enough Yet? The Cult of Thinness and the Commercialization of Identity*. New York: Oxford University Press, 1996.

Hewitt, Bill. "Kicked Out!" *People*, March 12, 2007, 197–198.

Hickey, Mary C., and Kate Lawler. "A Conversation with the Obamas." *Parents*, November 2008, 144–45, 230.

Himes, Susan M., and J. Kevin Thompson. "Fat Stigmatization in Television Shows and Movies: A Content Analysis." *Obesity* 15 (March 2007): 712–718.

Hobson, Janell. *Venus in the Dark: Blackness and Beauty in Popular Culture*. New York: Routledge, 2005.

Holmes, Rachel. *African Queen*. New York: Random House, 2007.

House, Margaret. "Fat Is a Feminist Issue: Another View." *off our backs*, April 30, 1979, 18.

Johnson, Cecil Webb. *Why Be Fat?* London: Mills and Boon, 1923.

Jones, Karen. "Fat Women and Feminism." *Connecticut NOW Newsletter*, October–November 1974. Fat Liberation Archives, http://www.eskimo.com/~largesse/Archives/CTNOW.html. Accessed August 13, 2010.

Kantor, Jodi. "Where the Votes Are, So, Unfortunately, Are All Those Calories." *New York Times*, November 23, 2007.

Kingsolver, Barbara, with Steven L. Hopp and Camille Kingsolver. *Animal, Vegetable, Miracle: A Year of Food Life*. New York: HarperCollins, 2007.

Kipling, Rudyard. "The White Man's Burden." *McClure's Magazine*, February 1899, 290–291.

Klein, Richard. *Eat Fat*. New York: Pantheon, 1996.

Kolata, Gina. "The Burden of Being Overweight: Mistreatment and Misconceptions." *New York Times*, November 22, 1992.

Koop, C. Everett. "In Spite of Diet Drug Withdrawal, the War on Obesity Must Continue Says Dr. C. Everett Koop, Shape Up America!" September 19, 1997, http://www.shapeup.org/about/arch_pr/091997.php. Accessed August 11, 2010.

Kulick, Don, and Anne Meneley, eds. *Fat: The Anthropology of an Obsession*, New York: Penguin, 2005.

LaBute, Neil. *Fat Pig*. New York: Faber and Faber, 2004.

Landau, Elizabeth. "College's Too-Fat-to-Graduate Rule Under Fire." *CNN Health*, November 30, 2009, http://www.cnn.com/2009/HEALTH/11/30/lincoln.fitness.overweight/index.html. Accessed November 30, 2009.

Lappé, Frances Moore. *Diet for a Small Planet*. New York: Ballantine Books, 1971.

LeBesco, Kathleen. "Quest for a Cause: The Fat Gene, the Gay Gene, and the New Eugenics." In *The Fat Studies Reader*, edited by Esther Rothblum and Sondra Solovay, 65–74. New York: New York University Press, 2009.

———. *Revolting Bodies? The Struggle to Redefine Fat Identity*. Amherst: University of Massachusetts Press, 2004.

"Lincoln University Ends Obesity Rule." *Inside Higher Ed*, December 7, 2009, http://www.insidehighered.com/news/2009/12/07/lincoln. Accessed December 18, 2009.

Lombroso, Cesare, and Guglielmo Ferrero. *Criminal Woman, the Prostitute, and the Normal Woman*. Edited and translated by Nicole Hahn Rafter and Mary Gibson. Durham: Duke University Press, 2004.

Long, Thomas. *AIDS and American Apocalypticism: The Cultural Semiotics of an Epidemic*. Albany: SUNY Press, 2005.

Lovart, Luke. *Too Fat: A Domestic Difficulty*. Bristol, UK: J. W. Arrowsmith, 1885.

Lowe, Margaret A. *Looking Good: College Women and Body Image, 1875–1930*. Baltimore: Johns Hopkins University Press, 2003.

Manheim, Camryn. *Wake Up, I'm Fat!* New York: Broadway Books, 1999.

Mark, David H. "Deaths Attributable to Obesity." *Journal of the American Medical Association* 293 (April 2005): 1918–1919.

Marshall, Andrew. "No One's Getting Fat Except Mama Cass." *Guardian Unlimited*, July 26, 1999, http://www.guardian.co.uk/world/1999/jul/26/gender.uk1. Accessed July 5, 2010.

Marshall, Susan E. *Splintered Sisterhood: Gender and Class in the Campaign Against Woman Suffrage*. Madison: University of Wisconsin Press, 1997.

Mason, Susan. "My Fat History." n.d., http://www.eskimo.com/~leiba/history.html. Accessed August 13, 2010.

McBride, Angela Barron. "Fat Survivors in Thin Society." *Women's Review of Book* 1, no. 6 (1984): 9–10.

Miley, Marissa. "New Year, New Round of Diet Programs." *Advertising Age*, January 12, 2009, 6.

Military City. "Marine Lance Corporal Justin T. Hunt." n.d., http://www.militarytimes.com/valor/marine-lance-cpl-justin-t-hunt/268641/. Accessed August 13, 2010.

Mitchell, S. Weir. *Fat and Blood: And How to Make Them*. Philadelphia: J. B. Lippincott, 1877.

Moore, Judith. *Fat Girl: A True Story*. New York: Plume, 2005.

Moore, Peter. "The Challenger." *Men's Health*, November 2008, 176–181.

Morgan, Lewis Henry. *Ancient Society*. London: Macmillan, 1877.

Morrison, Toni. *The Bluest Eye*. New York: Plume, 1994.

Mosher, Jerry. "Setting Free the Bears: Refiguring Fat Men on Television." In *Bodies Out of Bounds: Fatness and Transgression*, edited by Jana Evans Braziel and Kathleen LeBesco, 166–193. Berkeley and Los Angeles: University of California Press, 2001.

Moskin, Julia. "Still Skinny, but Now They Can Cook." *New York Times*, January 2, 2008.

National Association to Advance Fat Acceptance. "All Set to Fight Discrimination." *Radiance*, Spring 1989.

———. "Weight Loss Surgery." n.d., http://www.naafaonline.com/dev2/about/Policies/WEIGHTLOSSSURGERY.pdf. Accessed July 28, 2010.

National Institutes of Health. "Prevalence Statistics Related to Overweight and Obesity." n.d., http://win.niddk.nih.gov/statistics/index.htm. Accessed December 17, 2009.

"National Short Takes—Indiana." *Ms.*, Spring 2007, 20.

Neergaard, Lauran. "Child Obesity Taken Too Lightly, Experts Say." *Patriot News* (Harrisburg, PA), September 14, 2006.

Nichols, Grace. *The Fat Black Woman's Poems*. London: Virago, 1984.

Nichter, Mimi. *Fat Talk: What Girls and Their Parents Say About Dieting*. Cambridge: Harvard University Press, 2000.

NoLose. "The NoLose Manifesta." n.d., http://nolose.org/activism/manifesta.php. Accessed June 4, 2009.

Noveck, Jocelyn. "Harshest Words Saved for Britney's Body." *USA Today*, September 11, 2007.

O'Leary, Kevin. "Anatomy of a Breakdown." *Us Weekly*, September 24, 2007, 76–80.

Oliver, J. Eric. *Fat Politics: The Real Story Behind America's Obesity Epidemic*. New York: Oxford University Press, 2006.

Open NY. "The Measure of a Man." *New York Times*, October 6, 2008.

"Oprah's Weight Loss Confession." January 5, 2009, http://www.oprah.com/health/Oprahs-Weight-Loss-Confession. Accessed May 11, 2009.

Orbach, Susie. *Fat Is a Feminist Issue: A Self-Help Guide for Compulsive Eaters*. New York: Paddington Press, 1978

———. *Fat Is a Feminist Issue II: A Program to Conquer Compulsive Eating*. New York: Berkley Books, 1982.

Parton, James. *From Eminent Women of the Age: Being Narratives of the Lives and Deeds of the Most Prominent Women of the Present Generation*. Hartford: S. M. Betts, 1868.

Pollack, Ruth. *One Woman, One Vote*. PBS Home Video, 2005.

Pollan, Michael. *The Omnivore's Dilemma: A Natural History of Four Meals*. New York: Penguin Books, 2006.

Preble, William E. "Obesity and Malnutrition." *Boston Medical and Surgical Journal* 172, no. 20 (1915): 741.

Pyle, Nathaniel C., and Michael I. Loewy. "Double Stigma: Fat Men and Their Male Admirers." In *The Fat Studies Reader*, edited by Esther Rothblum and Sondra Solovay, 143–150. New York: New York University Press, 2009.

Qureshi, Sadiah. "Displaying Sara Baartman, the 'Hottentot Venus.'" *History of Science* 42 (2004): 233–257.

Rafter, Nicole Hahn, and Mary Gibson. "Introduction." In Cesare Lombroso and Guglielmo Ferrero, *Criminal Woman, the Prostitute, and the Normal Woman*, edited and translated by Rafter and Gibson, 3–33. Durham: Duke University Press, 2004.

Razza, Connie. "Running With Her Head Down: Oprah Winfrey and Middle-Class Black Women's Discourses of Fitness." In *Sports Matters: Race, Recreation, and Culture*, edited by John Bloom and Michael Nevin Willard, 264–278. New York: New York University Press, 2002.

Rothblum, Esther. "'I'll Die for the Revolution but Don't Ask Me Not to Diet': Feminism and the Continuing Stigmatization of Obesity." In *Feminist Perspectives on Eating Disorders*, edited by Patricia Fallon, Melanie A. Katzman, and Susan C. Wooley, 53–76. New York: Guilford Press, 1994.

———. "The Relationship Between Obesity, Employment Discrimination, and Employment-Related Victimization." *Journal of Vocational Behavior* 37 (December 1990): 251–66.

Rothblum, Esther, and Sondra Solovay, eds. *The Fat Studies Reader*. New York: New York University Press, 2009.

Samuels, Allison. "What Michelle Means to Us." *Newsweek*, December 1, 2008, 28–32.

Saukko, Paula. "Fat Boys and Goody Girls: Hilde Bruch's Work on Eating Disorders and the American Anxiety About Democracy, 1930–1960." In *Weighty Issues: Fatness and Thinness as Social Problems*, edited by Jeffery Sobal and Donna Maurer, 31–52. New York: Aldine de Gruyter, 1999.

"Scandal Hurts Jenny Craig Ad Campaign." *Detroit Free Press*, January 6, 2000.

Scharff, Virginia. *Taking the Wheel: Women and the Coming of the Motor Age*. New York: Free Press, 1991.

Schiebinger, Londa. *Nature's Body: Gender in the Making of Modern Science*. New Brunswick: Rutgers University Press, 1993.

Schlosser, Eric. *Fast Food Nation: The Dark Side of the All-American Meal*. Boston: Houghton Mifflin, 2001.

Schoenfielder, Lisa, and Barb Wieser, eds. *Shadow on a Tightrope: Writings by Women on Fat Oppression*. Iowa City: Aunt Lute Press, 1983.

Schwartz, Hillel. *Never Satisfied: A Cultural History of Diets, Fantasies, and Fat*. New York: Doubleday, 1986.

Seiler, Cotten. *Republic of Drivers: A Cultural History of Automobility in America*. Chicago: University of Chicago Press, 2008.

Seitler, Dana. "Unnatural Selection: Mothers, Eugenic Feminism, and Charlotte Perkins Gilman's Regeneration Narratives." *American Quarterly* 55, no. 1 (2003): 61–88.

Shaffer, Marguerite. *See America First: Tourism and National Identity, 1880–1940*. Washington, DC: Smithsonian Institution Press, 2001.

Shanewood, B. "An Interview with Medical Rights Champion Lynn McAfee." *Radiance*, Winter 1999, http://radiancemagazine.com/issues/1999/winter_99/truth.html. Accessed August 13, 2010.

Shaw, Andrea Elizabeth. *The Embodiment of Disobedience: Fat Black Women's Unruly Political Bodies*. New York: Lexington Books, 2006.

Sheffield, Shirley, and Trish Bailey. "Spotlight on the Padded Lillies." *Without Measure*. n.d., http://www.size-acceptance.org/without_measure/wom_archive/wom_04_2001/wom0401_page3.html. Accessed July 25, 2010.

Sheppard, Alice. *Cartooning for Suffrage*. Albuquerque: University of New Mexico Press, 1994.

Sinclair, Upton. *The Jungle*. New York: Doubleday Books, 1906.

Singer, Natasha, and Duff Wilson. "Medical Editors Push for Ghostwriting Crackdown." *New York Times*, September 18, 2009.

Smith, Edward. *How to Get Fat: Or, the Means of Preserving the Medium Between Leanness and Obesity*. London, 1865.

Smith, Kyle. "Disney's 'WALL-E': A $170 Million Art Film." June 26, 2008, http://kyle-smithonline.com/?p=1319. Accessed July 1, 2008.

Sobal, Jeffery, and Donna Maurer, eds. *Weighty Issues: Fatness and Thinness as Social Problems*. New York: Aldine de Gruyter, 1999.

Solovay, Sondra. *Tipping the Scales of Justice: Fighting Weight-Based Discrimination*. Amherst, NY: Prometheus Books, 2000.

"Some Jenny Craigs Reject Lewinsky Ads." *Detroit News*, January 6, 2000.

Sontag, Susan. *Illness as Metaphor; and, AIDS and Its Metaphors*. New York: Anchor Books, 1988.

Stanley, Alessandra. "Plus-Size Sideshow." *New York Times*, August 24, 2008.

Stanton, Elizabeth Cady. *Eighty Years and More (1815–1897): Reminiscences of Elizabeth Cady Stanton*. London: T. Fisher Unwin, 1898.

———. *Elizabeth Cady Stanton as Revealed in Her Letters, Diary, and Reminiscences*. Edited by Theodore Stanton and Harriot Stanton Blatch. Vol. 1. New York: Harper and Brothers, 1922.

Stanton, Elizabeth Cady, and Susan B. Anthony. *The Selected Papers of Elizabeth Cady Stanton and Susan B. Anthony*. Vol. 1, *In the School of Anti-Slavery*. Edited by Ann D. Gordon. New Brunswick: Rutgers University Press, 1997.

Stearns, Peter N. *Fat History: Bodies and Beauty in the Modern West*. New York: New York University Press, 1997.

Stimson, Karen. "Fat Feminist Herstory, 1969–1993: A Personal Memoir." n.d., Fat Liberation Archives, http://largesse.net/Archives/herstory.html.

Stinson, Kandi. *Women and Dieting Culture: Inside a Commercial Weight Loss Group*. New Brunswick: Rutgers University Press, 2001.

Stinson, Susan. *Belly Songs: In Celebration of Fat Women*. Northampton, MA: Commonwealth Printing Company, 1993.

Tabor, Martha. "Fat Is a Feminist Issue: One View." *off our backs*, April 30, 1979, 18.

Tauber, Michelle, and Mark Dagostino. "100 and Counting." *People*, November 18, 2002, 104–110.

Thompson, Becky W. *A Hunger So Wide and So Deep: American Women Speak Out on Eating Problems*. Minneapolis: University of Minnesota Press, 1994.

Thompson, Charlie, and Jan Murphy. "No Pay Raise: About 2,000 Shouting 'Oink' Denounce Hike." *Patriot News* (Harrisburg, PA), September 27, 2005.

Thompson, Vance. *Eat and Grow Thin: The Mahdah Menus*. New York: E. P. Dutton, 1914.

Tickner, Lisa. *The Spectacle of Women*. Chicago: University of Chicago Press, 1988.

Tillmon, Johnnie. "Welfare as a Woman's Issue." *Ms.*, Spring 1972, 111–116.

Tomrley, Corinna, and Ann Kaloski-Naylor, eds. *Fat Studies in the UK*. York, UK: Raw Nerve Books, 2009.

Tuchman, Gay. "The Symbolic Annihilation of Women by the Mass Media." In *Hearth and Home: Images of Women in the Mass Media*, edited by Gaye Tuchman, Arlene Kaplan Daniels, and James Benet, 3–38. New York: Oxford University Press, 1978.

Wann, Marilyn. *FAT!SO? Because You Don't Have to Apologize for Your Size*. Berkeley, CA: Ten Speed Press, 1998.

Williams, Leonard Llewellyn Bulkeley. *Obesity*. London: Humphrey Milford, 1926.

Williams, Lillian Serece, and Randolph Boehm. *Records of the National Association of Colored Women's Clubs, 1895–1992*. Bethesda, MD: University Publications of America, 1993–94.

Wilson, Duff, and Natasha Singer. "Ghostwriting Is Called Rife in Medical Journals." *New York Times*, September 11, 2009.

Wilson, Jane. "Fat Underground Throws Weight Into Obesity War." *Los Angeles Times*, January 8, 1976.

Winfrey, Oprah, with Bob Greene. *Make the Connection: Ten Steps to a Better Body—and a Better Life*. New York: Hyperion Books, 1996.

———. *Make the Connection . . . It's About Changing Your Life*. Burbank, CA: Buena Vista Home Video, 1997.

Wolf, Naomi. *The Beauty Myth: How Images of Beauty Are Used Against Women*. New York: William and Morrow, 1991.

Wyatt, Edward. "Tolstoy's Translators Experience Oprah Effect." *New York Times*, June 7, 2004.

Index

About the Author

Photo by Caroline Elizabeth Savage

AMY ERDMAN FARRELL is John and Ann Curley Faculty Chair in Liberal Arts and Professor of American Studies and Women's and Gender Studies at Dickinson College in Carlisle, Pennsylvania. She is the author of *Yours in Sisterhood: Ms. Magazine and the Promise of Popular Feminism.*

CPSIA information can be obtained at www.ICGtesting.com
Printed in the USA
BVOW04s0328140816

458739BV00001B/2/P